THE ORIGINS OF PROTESTANT AESTHETICS
IN EARLY MODERN EUROPE

The aesthetics of everyday life, as reflected in art museums and galleries throughout the Western world, is the result of a profound shift in aesthetic perception that occurred during the Renaissance and Reformation. In this book, William Dyrness examines intellectual developments in late medieval Europe, which turned attention away from a narrow range of liturgical art and practices and toward a celebration of God's presence in creation and in history. Though threatened by the human tendency to self-assertion, he shows how a new focus on God's creative and recreative action in the world gave time and history a new seriousness and engendered a broad spectrum of aesthetic potential. Focusing in particular on the writings of Luther and Calvin, Dyrness demonstrates how the Reformers' conceptual and theological frameworks pertaining to the role of the arts influenced the rise of realistic theater, lyric poetry, landscape painting, and architecture in the sixteenth and seventeenth centuries.

William A. Dyrness is Senior Professor of Theology and Culture at Fuller Theological Seminary, California. A scholar of the art and religion of Reformation Europe, he is the author of *Reformed Theology and Visual Culture: The Protestant Imagination from Calvin to Edwards* and more recently, *Poetic Theology, God, and the Poetics of Everyday Life*.

THE ORIGINS OF PROTESTANT AESTHETICS IN EARLY MODERN EUROPE

Calvin's Reformation Poetics

WILLIAM A. DYRNESS

Fuller Theological Seminary

CAMBRIDGE
UNIVERSITY PRESS

CAMBRIDGE
UNIVERSITY PRESS

University Printing House, Cambridge CB2 8BS, United Kingdom

One Liberty Plaza, 20th Floor, New York, NY 10006, USA

477 Williamstown Road, Port Melbourne, VIC 3207, Australia

314-321, 3rd Floor, Plot 3, Splendor Forum, Jasola District Centre, New Delhi - 110025, India

103 Penang Road, #05-06/07, Visioncrest Commercial, Singapore 238467

Cambridge University Press is part of the University of Cambridge.

It furthers the University's mission by disseminating knowledge in the pursuit of
education, learning and research at the highest international levels of excellence.

www.cambridge.org
Information on this title: www.cambridge.org/9781108717823
DOI: 10.1017/9781108593311

© Cambridge University Press 2019

First published 2019
First paperback edition 2022

A catalogue record for this publication is available from the British Library

Library of Congress Cataloging in Publication data
NAMES: Dyrness, William A., author.
TITLE: The origins of Protestant aesthetics in early modern Europe : Calvin's Reformation
poetics / William A. Dyrness, Fuller Theological Seminary, California.
DESCRIPTION: I [edition]. | New York : Cambridge University Press, 2019. |
Includes bibliographical references and index.
IDENTIFIERS: LCCN 2018058441 | ISBN 9781108493352 (hardback : alk. paper) |
ISBN 9781108717823 (pbk. : alk. paper)
SUBJECTS: LCSH: Christianity and art–Reformed Church–History–16th century. |
Christianity and art–Europe–History–16th century. | Aesthetics–Religious
aspects–Reformed Church–History–16th century | Calvin, Jean, 1509-1564.
CLASSIFICATION: LCC BX9423.A77 D968 2019 | DDC 261.5/7094–dc23
LC record available at https://lccn.loc.gov/2018058441

ISBN 978-1-108-49335-2 Hardback
ISBN 978-1-108-71782-3 Paperback

CONTENTS

List of Illustrations   *page* vi
Preface   ix

1   Introduction: The Medieval Context of the Reformation   1
2   Presence and Likeness in Holbein, Luther, and Cranach   19
3   Calvin: Creation, Drama, and Time   53
4   Calvin, Language, and Literary Culture   84
5   Portraits and Dramatic Culture in Sixteenth-Century England   113
6   The Emerging Aesthetic of Early Modern England:
    A New World with Echoes of the Past   138
7   The New Visual Culture of Reformed Holland and France   166
8   Epilogue: The Cultural Afterlife of Protestant Aesthetics   199

Bibliography   213
Index   227

ILLUSTRATIONS

1 Workshop of Leonardo da Vinci, *Portrait of a Woman,*
   the Belle Ferronière, 1490–1495   *page* 18
2 Hans Holbein the Younger, *The Ambassadors,* 1533   23
3 Hans Holbein the Younger, *The Dead Christ in the Tomb,*
   1521–1522   29
4 Lucas Cranach the Elder, *Law and Gospel,* 1529 (Gotha version)   32
5 Lucas Cranach the Elder, *Law and Gospel,* 1529 (Prague version)   33
6 Lucas Cranach, *Adam,* 1530   36
7 Lucas Cranach, *Eve,* 1530   36
8 Lucas Cranach, *Wittenberg Altarpiece,* 1547   46
9 Hans Holbein the Younger, *An Allegory of Old and New Testament,*
   early 1530s   51
10 Giotto di Bordone, *Francis Receiving the Stigmata,* c. 1300   76
11 Initial "C" (for Constantine) from John Foxe, *Acts and*
   Monuments, 1563   120
12 Jores Hoefnage, *Queen Elizabeth and the Three Goddesses/*
   The Judgement of Paris, 1569   121
13 Nicholas Hilliard, *Elizabeth I: Pelican Portrait,* c. 1573–1575   122
14 Attributed to Frederigo Zuccaro, *Elizabeth I: Darnley Portrait,*
   c. 1575   122
15 Engraving by J. Case, *Sphaera Civitatis,* 1588, frontispiece of Magistro
   Johanne Caso Oxoniensi, *Sphaera Civitatis*   124
16 Engraving by F. Delaram, after Hilliard (1617–1619), frontispiece of
   William Camden, *Historie of the Most Renowned and Victorious Princesse*
   Elizabeth, Late Queen of England (1630)   125
17 Attributed to George Gower, *Elizabeth I: Armada Portrait,* 1588   126
18 Marcus Gheeraerts the Younger, *Elizabeth I: Ditchley Portrait,* 1592 127
19 Anonymous woodcut of William Farel, from Theodore Beza,
   Icones id est verae imagines virorum doctrina simul et
   pietate illstrium (1580)   136

20   Johannes van Doetecum the Elder, after Pieter Bruegel, *Soldiers at Rest*,
     from the large landscape series, c. 1555–1556   181
21   Jacob van Ruisdael, *Three Great Trees in a Mountainous
     Landscape*, 1667   184
22   Rembrandt van Rijn, *Bathsheba at Her Toilet*, 1643   187
23   Anonymous, *Last Supper Scripture*, c. 1581, Haarlem, Great
     or St. Bavo Church   190
24   Tuileries gardens and palace, 1567, designed by Philiberto
     Delorme, grotto by Bernard Palissy   196

PREFACE

This book attends to the emergence of particular aesthetic attitudes that can reasonably be described as Protestant, especially in Geneva, England, and Holland, and that developed between 1500 and 1650. It may be thought anachronistic in this early modern period to describe a developing aesthetics – since the word, in its modern sense, was not used before Alexander Gottlieb Baumgarten wrote his famous *Aesthetica* in 1750. In that work the philosopher sought to place aesthetics – what he termed *scientia cognitionis sensitivae*, or the science of sensuous knowing – along with logic, as a source of theoretical knowledge. His goal was to describe the perfection of sense knowledge as beauty itself, which he believed represented the perfected attainment of knowledge through the senses.[1]

Baumarten's formulation, however influential, was not entirely original. In fact one can argue that he is reprising conversations that were prominent in the medieval period. Thomas Aquinas, for example, describes beauty in closely related terms: "Beauty . . . has to do with knowledge, and we call a thing beautiful when it pleases the eye of the beholder. This is why beauty is a matter of right proportion, for senses delight in rightly proportioned things as similar to themselves, the sense-faculty being a sort of proportion itself like all other knowing faculties. Now since knowing proceeds by imaging, and images have to do with form, beauty properly involves the notion of form."[2] Clearly the human affective response to beauty of form and sound is perennial; it did not await the Enlightenment to be noted and appreciated, even if its significance and place in the order of things has changed and developed.

---

[1] See Gesa Elsbeth Thiessen, ed., *Theological Aesthetics: A Reader* (Grand Rapids, MI: Eerdmans, 2004), p. 156.

[2] *Summa Theologiae*, vol. 2: *Existence and Nature of God* (Ia. 2-11), trans. Timothy McDermott (London: Blackfriars, 1964), pp. 71, 73.

Still we must avoid reading modern and Enlightenment categories back into those earlier conversations. Because beauty was central in many medieval conversations, modern readers, thoroughly schooled in discussions spawned by Baumgarten, are tempted to understand those experiences in modern terms.[3]

This danger arises from the fact that, arguably, aesthetic experience has come to play a more central role in the twenty-first century than it did in any previous century. Robert Wuthnow has documented the fact that, in America at least, each generation during the last one hundred years has been progressively more interested and invested in the arts and aesthetic experience.[4] And it is precisely this expansion of aesthetic interest that serves as the starting point of my reflections on the early modern period. As I will point out in Chapter 1, this wide-ranging interest in the arts – and the particular institutions that have arisen to support this – stands in marked contrast to the medieval situation. And, I will argue, the events consequent to the Protestant Reformation have played a considerable role in laying groundwork for the expansion of interest and attention to the arts that modern people have come to take for granted.

Though it may be anachronistic to speak of Reformation aesthetics, as Clark Hulse notes, it is a potentially useful anachronism.[5] He goes on to argue that the more familiar term in the sixteenth century would have been "poetics," which designated language characterized by *mimesis*, or imitation, both of classical forms, as in rhetoric that sought to persuade and order, and of nature, which in its development often reflected its Reformation context. Both forms of imitation, I argue, were famously developed in Calvin's work, and both became characteristics that defined the emerging category of "literature." Aesthetics then can be used as a broader term under which poetics, dealing specifically with language, may be understood, and as indicative of other aspects of the emerging system of the arts familiar to a modern person. My argument is that though rhetoric and literature were central to the emerging Protestant aesthetic, it is mistaken to see the Reformation as involving a simple replacement of image with the word, or even more

[3] Something even the classic treatment of Umberto Eco does not always avoid. See *Art and Beauty in the Middle Ages*, trans. Hugh Bredin (New Haven, CT: Yale University Press, 1986).
[4] Wuthnow, *All N'Sync: How Music and Art Are Revitalizing American Religion* (Berkeley: University of California Press, 2003), p. 66. See William Dyrness, *Poetic Theology: God and the Poetics of Everyday Life* (Grand Rapids, MI: Eerdmans, 2011), pp. 11–13.
[5] Hulse, "Tudor Aesthetics," in Arthur F. Kinney, ed., *Cambridge Companion to English Literature: 1500–1600* (Cambridge: Cambridge University Press, 2000), p. 33. For what follows, see pp. 34–38, though the connection with Calvin is my observation.

reductively, seeing with hearing. Rather, their more comprehensive vision of society and its accountability to God provided space for other forms of art to appear – specifically, realistic theater, landscape painting, and neo-classical architecture, in addition to literature.

The danger persists in any historical reflection to read back into earlier periods attitudes and practices that developed only later. For this reason Chapter I makes an attempt to understand the medieval situation on its own terms, in order to contrast that world with the world born during the Renaissance and Reformation. As I will seek to show, contrary to what is sometimes assumed, the Reformation represented a development of medieval attitudes rather than simply a radical break with the past, even if eventually it would form a world that would look and feel very different from that past. The relatively long period under investigation allows us to see ways in which the Reformation only gradually brought about changes in experiences and practices, and allowed, with respect to the arts, a modern world to emerge that modern people will recognize.[6]

Written by a theologian of culture rather than a historian, this work seeks to provide a fresh angle of vision on this endlessly fascinating period of history, and especially on some of its central figures – Martin Luther and, in more detail, John Calvin. My argument is that their novel interpretation of the human religious situation had the additional result of expanding the attention given to the *theatrum mundi*, with long-term significance for aesthetics no less than for other areas of human investigation. While this broader attention to the world is often thought of as an incipient secularization, in the minds of the Reformers it was nothing of the kind. Rather, Luther and Calvin sought to extend, albeit in different ways, the accountability one owed to God more broadly to their life in the world. This enlarged sense of responsibility and the attention it sparked, I will argue, led both directly and indirectly to development in the arts.

Parts of the argument of this book include material previously published in articles that have been revised for this work, and I want to express my appreciation for permission to use this material. "The Perception of Spirituality: Hans Holbein's 'The French Ambassadors'" appeared in *Art as Spiritual Perception: Essays in Honor of E. John Walford*, ed. James Romaine (Wheaton: Crossways Books, 2012); "God's Play: Calvin, Theatre and the Rise of the

---

[6] This reflects and learns from more recent scholarship on the Reformation that takes a longer-term view of the changes and fractures that occurred during this period. See the critical discussions developing this perspective in Nicholas Tyacke, ed., *England's Long Reformation: 1500–1800* (New York: Routledge, 1998).

Book" formed a chapter of *Calvin and the Book: The Evolution of the Printed Word in Reformed Protestantism*, ed. Karen Spierling (Göttingen: Vandenhoeck & Ruprecht, 2015); "God, Language, and the Use of the Senses: The Emergence of a Protestant Aesthetic in the Early Modern Period" will appear in *Protestantism and Aesthetics*, ed. Sarah Covington and Kathryn Reklis (New York: Routledge, forthcoming); "Text and Media: Portraits and Representation in Elizabethan England" was published in *Arts, Portraits and Representation in the Reformation Era*, ed. Herman Selderhuis (Göttingen: Vandenhoeck & Ruprecht, 2018); and "Hiding in Plain Sight: Theology and Visual Culture in Early Modern Calvinism" will be a chapter of *The Handbook of Calvinism*, ed. Bruce Gordon and Carl Trueman (Oxford University Press, forthcoming). All Scripture references are to the *New Revised Standard Version* unless otherwise noted.

I owe large debts of gratitude to people who know far more than this writer about the subjects of the following chapters, especially John Lee Thompson, John Witvliet, Matthew Rosebrock, Randall Working, Sarah Covington, Kathryn Reklis, Jérôme Cottin, Cornelius Van der Kooi and Mia Mochizuki. And I have profited much from conversations with Robert Johnston, Patrick Coleman, Martin Shannon, Joseph Prabhu, Henry Luttikhuizen, and Timothy Verdon. I want to express special gratitude to the management and staff of the Henry E. Huntington Library, which has offered a particularly congenial environment for the research and writing of this book, and in particular for the support of Christopher Adde and Nathan Pendlebury. And I am grateful for the encouragement and support of Beatrice Rehl, and the assistance of Ayyappan Sindhujaa, Stephanie Sakson, and the always competent staff of Cambridge University Press.

I

INTRODUCTION
The Medieval Context of the Reformation

I
T IS HAZARDOUS TO GENERALIZE ABOUT THE CONTEMPORARY
art scene – that sprawling reality called the "art world." But even casual
visitors to modern art museums and art fairs would come away with one
overriding impression: no object in the world, nor any sector of human
experience, is considered out of bounds or banned from possible aesthetic
attention – even if no one is quite sure what is "aesthetic" about the work in
question. Apart from the proliferation of media, one is struck with the
endless vistas, materials, and experiences that "art" has come to embrace.
One result of this promiscuous artistic attention is the equivocal status of
images – what Harold Rosenberg has called the anxious object.[1] Increasingly, artists, even visual artist, are paying less attention to the objects they
seek to portray or designate, and are seeking to draw viewers into the
complex ecosystems in which these may (or may not) be glimpsed. But
here too the very notion of art object or image is reconstituted and deployed
in ever expanding aesthetic situations – whether in video, installations,
performance art, or virtual reality. This dramatic expansion of aesthetic
projects is taken for granted to such an extent that it is often overlooked.

But things have not always been this way. During the medieval period, for
example, artisans who made what we call art objects were mostly restricted
to particular motifs that served special religious purposes. Panel painters
working in the thirteenth century would be amazed at the range of materials – and purposes – that today's paintings display, to say nothing of other
kinds of objects – found and made – that are subject to artistic treatment and
attention. Things began gradually to change in the fifteenth century, when
motifs from the natural world found their way into paintings or manuscript

---

[1] Rosenberg, *The Anxious Object: Art Today and Its Audience* (New York: Horizon Press, 1964).

illuminations, and beautiful objects were crafted to serve non-religious purposes. But it was during the sixteenth century, in what we call the Renaissance and Reformation, when the world was opened up for scientific and artistic investigation. The transformation I have in mind is related but not identical to the change from image to art that Hans Belting pointed to a generation ago. He was concerned to trace the change from images treated as "persons" that were "worshipped, despised or carried" to their treatment as "art" that came to serve the very different purposes of aesthetic contemplation.[2] I am more concerned with the conditions that made such developments possible.

The focus of this book is not so much on the artistic object, though this cannot be ignored, as on the changing aesthetic situation in which artifacts were made and received. That change of aesthetic consideration in the emerging modern world leads one to ask: How did it come about that makers of artwork, including drama, music, and literature, turned their attention away from a rather narrow range of subject matter and began to examine the broader range of human experience? That surely changed the way we think about art, as Belting has argued, but more importantly it reflected a change in the way we have come to explore, investigate, and appreciate the details of the natural order. One result was that art was being liberated to explore the full breadth of the human and natural world.

This is my argument: during the 150 years from about 1530 to the late 1600s, the Protestant Reformation, and the Calvinist Reform in particular, encouraged the move to direct aesthetic attention, not toward the rituals and sacred objects of worship, but outward toward the life of what was already called the *theatrum mundi*. This expansion is closely related to the larger movement, sparked by the humanism of the Renaissance, to investigate and attend to all the details of the expanding world. To be clear I will not argue that the magisterial Reformers brought about the changes I will describe; rather, they reflect a process that went back to the thirteenth century, as I will show. But the Reformers, and Calvin in particular, definitively promoted these changes in such a way that they became normative for modern ways of conceiving art and aesthetics. It is this promotion and the resulting changes that I describe in what follows.

---

[2] *Likeness and Presence: A History of the Image before the Era of Art,* trans. Edmund Jephcott (Chicago: University of Chicago Press, 1994), p. xxi. He regrets the decision of art historians to declare all specially shaped objects "art," "thereby effacing the very differences that might have thrown light on our subject" (p. 9). These differences will move to the center of attention in this book.

One of the achievements of Belting's important book is to alert students to the hazards of reading back into the early modern period ideas about art and aesthetics that are the product of succeeding centuries, and that even now are highly contested.[3] So it is important for me to detail the notion of aesthetics that I have in mind in formulating my argument. I have been especially helped by the attempts of Frank Burch Brown to move toward a more capacious notion of aesthetics – one that I would argue better suits the transformation of the aesthetic situation I have in mind and, as he shows, that is deeply related to human religious practices. He proposes we think about aesthetics as "All those things employing a medium in such a way that its perceptible form and 'felt' qualities become essential to what is appreciative and meaningful."[4] All those things employing a medium certainly makes possible the unlimited aesthetic and artistic potential to which I am calling attention, but it does something else: it highlights the attraction – the shock or delight – that this broad range of human experiences can spark. And while Brown's broadened definition has in view the manifold aesthetic objects and experiences on offer today, it suggests a particularly helpful way of framing the changes that led from a narrow focus on sacred objects and practices to a wider aesthetic attention to the whole world that I will describe. Calvin and his followers would certainly not have framed their project in the aesthetic terms I will use – though I will argue their language and impulse was aesthetic in terms they understood. Still their neglect of certain practices and their adoption of others opened the way for an understanding of aesthetics – occasions of delight and awe – that would later come to be described in this broadened way.

While attending to the world of art and artifact studied by art historians, the initial concern of this work is with changes in religious worship practices. This is important for a firm grasp of this period, not only because, during the sixteenth century, religious observance and attendance was required of everyone – at least in Geneva and England where this study concentrates, but also because it was in the experience of corporate worship that the emerging patterns of observation and interaction with the larger world were formed and developed. In these corporate practices – the hearing of sermons,

[3] The resistance I have in mind is best reflected in Nicholas Wolterstorff's recent book *Art Rethought* (New York: Oxford University Press, 2016), where, contrary to modern notions of aesthetics as disinterested contemplation, he argues that art has always involved a wide range of social practices, which ought properly to be recognized and assessed.

[4] Brown, *Religious Aesthetics: A Theological Study of Making and Meaning* (Princeton, NJ: Princeton University Press, 1989), p. 22. Though he does not comment on this, Brown may reflect here his own Protestant heritage.

learning the catechism, corporate singing of hymns – were birthed the habits
of thought and practice that eventuated in new ways of relating to the
world. This angle of vision, I will argue, illumines subsequent artistic
developments in ways that are often overlooked in traditional discussions
of art history.

The focus on worship practices further highlights an important theological emphasis that motivates this study. Modern descriptions of
sixteenth-century changes often frame moves that appear to direct attention
away from God and worship and toward the larger world – in a Protestant
focus, for example, on portraits and landscapes – as secular in intent. For
example, in a contemporary exhibition of British paintings, Malcolm
Warner explains the emerging choice of subject matter in this way:
"Since the sixteenth century when the Protestant Reformation in Britain
swept away religious images that were the mainstay of art in the Middle
Ages, British art has been dominated by the secular genres of portraiture and
landscape."[5] The argument I will make undercuts this tendency by pointing
out the theological motivation for this enlarged aesthetic attention. It was
the conviction of the major Reformers that God's presence was not limited
to specific religious practices, but was evident in all the details of the natural
order and, indeed, potentially in all that humans made of that created order.
This is true even if, as I have noted, the Reformers did not single-handedly
bring about this larger conception of the works and world of God. As Jeffrey
Hamburger has noted, and as will be explored later, already in the thirteenth
and fourteenth centuries artists had rejected the notion that God's presence
was limited to particular kinds of (sanctified and canonical) images as in the
Eastern church. Art objects even then were becoming free to do multiple
things and encourage multiple affective responses – even if these were still
largely connected to devotional practices.[6] A similar expansion of possible
responses can be shown in the period of my study.

While this period saw major cultural and political changes, I want to
question the usual assumption that the Reformation caused a drastic cultural
disruption. The received narrative goes something like this: whereas medieval worship involved participation in sacred practices and, in particular, a
devotional gaze at sacred images, the Reformation focus on preaching and

[5] "Anglophilia into Art," in M. Warner and Robyn Aselson, eds., *Great British Paintings from American Collections: Holbein to Hockney* (New Haven, CT: Yale University Press, 2001), p. 2.
[6] "The Place of Theology in Medieval Art History," in J. Hamburger and Anne Marie Bouché, eds., *The Mind's Eye: Art as Theological Argument in the Middle Ages* (Princeton, NJ: Princeton University Press, 2006), p. 17.

teaching led to a cognitive and confessional focus that was hostile to the imagination and the arts. This is not to say, at least at first glance, that there is no support for such views: Doesn't the Reformation represent a reduction of sacramentals, of places where believers can encounter God – no more altarpieces, saints' plays, devotional images, or pilgrimages – and therefore a consonant reduction of sites for spiritual seeing? Wasn't the focus now on preaching and teaching specific doctrines? Wouldn't this necessarily result in reduced attention to art and a growing cognitive focus?

But this book suggests the story may be told another way. While the images and artifacts of medieval worship were often abandoned, this was not true in all places touched by the Reformation, and in some cases the changes were not permanent. Moreover, even in places where they were discarded, they were soon replaced by other liturgical practices and associated artifacts – preaching, singing, communal prayers, and prayer books – reflecting an emerging Protestant view of God's relation to the world that carried deep implications for the role of sight and the senses.

The challenge I intend to mount suggests three qualifications to the received narrative. First, as will become clear, I do not intend to reinforce the common assumption that the Reformation simply replaced images with words, changing from a focus on what is seen to what is heard.[7] While language became increasingly central to the Reformation project, as I will show, this directed a new and broadened attention to what was both seen and heard. As a result, I will challenge Robert Scribner's claim that the Reformation replaced the medieval sacramental seeing with what he calls the "cold gaze"; a seeing that involved participation in the object was replaced by a cognitive seeing as understanding.[8] As I will argue in a later chapter, the new importance Luther and Calvin gave to language reflected broader cultural changes that these theologians made use of but did not initiate. Moreover, their attention to language and its aesthetic

---

[7] This assumption dates to an earlier generation of Reformation studies and can perhaps be traced to Walter Ong. See, for example, Ong, *The Presence of the Word: Some Prolegomena for Cultural and Religious History* (New Haven, CT: Yale University Press, 1967). Even Belting is guilty of promoting this oversimplification when he reports that, at the Reformation, the word was assimilated by hearing and not by seeing. *Likeness and Presence*, p. 15. I have attempted, along with many others, to broaden the understanding of what was going on in Dyrness, *Reformed Theology and Visual Culture: The Protestant Imagination from Calvin to Edwards* (Cambridge: Cambridge University Press, 2004).

[8] This conception of clarity of sight, Scribner thinks, illustrates contemporaneous developments in optics: sight was coming to be understood as seeing through a lens that made everything clear. "Popular Piety and Modes of Visual Perception," in *Religion and Culture in Germany 1400–1800* (Leiden: Brill, 2001), pp. 120–125.

(and rhetorical) uses did not predetermine how images and other cultural artifacts would be produced and evaluated.[9] My argument insists that the charge of Reformation logocentrism obscures the rhetorical situation that Calvin in particular intended to create and the change of dramatic focus that this implied, and indeed the enhanced role sight and senses came to play in this change. This will be argued in detail in Chapters 3 and 4.

Second, I do not claim that the changes I describe simply reflect a parallel transformation of the focus from what is external – images, novenas, and pilgrimages – to what is inward – a faithful adherence to God's promises. This common view reflects the assumption that since the Reformers denied that God was accessible by way of these outward sacramental practices, believers turned inward to encounter the presence of God.[10] To insist on a growing inward orientation during the Reformation is not wrong, but it oversimplifies a complex reality. First, as I will show later in this chapter, the Reformation inherited a long-standing movement encouraging the inner life of prayer and meditation. Second, the inward focus of spirituality that became visible later, for example, in the stark inner orientation of John Donne's poetry or in the later Pietist movements, represented developments that *succeeded* the period of the Reformation even as they fed off the mystical traditions that preceded it. Thus it is important to carefully assess the role of the major Reformers in these developments. While Luther was deeply influenced by Rhenish mystics and his own monastic heritage,[11] Calvin had never been a monk. Though the struggle with the consciousness of sin was important for him, Calvin was famously hesitant to make use of the rich medieval mystical tradition, and he did not encourage the introspective obsession with evidences of election that came later to characterize this tradition.[12]

Third, I want to resist the common tendency to see iconoclasm as the guiding metaphor for the Reformers' understanding of cultural objects and

---

[9] On this subject, see Jérôme Cottin, *Le regard et la Parole: Une théologie protestante de l'image* (Geneva: Labor et Fides, 1994), especially chapters 11 and 12.

[10] An important exponent of this view is Edward Muir, who famously argued that during the medieval period, worshipers used their whole bodies in worship; during the Reformation this was restricted to the part above the neck. *Ritual in Early Modern England* (Cambridge: Cambridge University Press, 1997), p. 184. In my earlier work I was guilty of encouraging this simplified view that I have come to feel is mistaken. *Reformed Theology*, p. 304.

[11] See Rémi Valléjo, "Les visions de quelques mystiques rhénans: formes, functions, sens," lecture at the University of Strasbourg, Colloquium on the Reformation and the Arts, May 19, 2017.

[12] See Bruce Gordon, *John Calvin's "Institutes of the Christian Religion": A Biography* (Princeton, NJ: Princeton University Press, 2016), p. 27. Cf. François Wandel, *Calvin: The Origin and Development of His Religious Thought*, trans. Philip Mairet (London: Collins, 1965), pp. 244, 277.

practice. The tendency, for example, to contrast the richly furnished medieval cathedrals with bare whitewashed walls of Protestant worship spaces misreads the complexity of the cultural tensions and cross-currents. It is true that there was a deep-seated iconoclastic impulse behind the work of the major Reformers, but this did not focus directly on images, or even on art more generally, but rather on the entire medieval imaginative framework as they understood it. In fact, both Luther and Calvin, though for different reasons, were opposed to the destruction of images in the churches. And the most notorious episodes of iconoclasm mostly preceded the period of the Reformation, which is the center of my attention – beginning in 1530.[13] And for Calvin in particular the focus on what was lost, though not inconsequential, sometimes obscures the challenge he faced in forging new cultural initiatives. When he arrived in Geneva in 1536, as we will see, the Mass had already been abolished, images removed from churches, and so on; his challenge was not how to dismantle that world, but how to determine what should replace it.

These qualifications indicate our growing awareness of the political and cultural complexity that characterized this period and its early modern setting. This complexity suggests caution in making pronouncements about the fate of "art" during this period. While the major Reformers did focus their efforts on preaching, teaching, and writing (and printing) the Word of God, in Calvin's case this did not exclude a growing appreciation of the visible spectacle of the worship service and, indeed, the visible glory of the splendors of the created order. In the case of Luther, though stressing the importance of the external word, he gradually came to have a positive view of visual images as important vehicles for the address of God mediated in worship. Moreover, to understand these changes it is important to place them in the context of long-standing developments leading up the Reformation, which will be the focus in what follows in this chapter.

Medieval Context of Images and Sight

In resisting the easy assumption that the Protestant Reformation represents a sea change in views of art and culture, I want to show ways the Reformation

---

[13] Much iconoclastic practice predated the Reformation. Henri Naef, *Les Origines de la Réforme à Genève* (Genève: Librairie Droz, 1968), vol. I, p. 276; and Mia Mochizuki has pointed to iconoclastic practices such as whitewashing church walls, long before the Reformation. Mia M. Mochizuki, *The Netherlandish Image after Iconoclasm: 1566–1672: Material Religion in the Dutch Golden Age* (Aldershot: Ashgate, 2008), pp. 1–3.

in some cases opposed medieval notions, in others developed them in characteristic ways. To prepare for making this case, in the remainder of this chapter, I will focus specifically on the evolving role that visual elements played in medieval devotion, and the gradually expanding range of objects this encompassed. I will begin with the famous instruction of Gregory the Great, and then reflect on the later practice of praying before icons in the Orthodox tradition, especially as this came to influence the use of images in medieval Europe, and, eventually, the developing liturgical notions in Protestant worship. I argue that, though the objects of aesthetic attention were in the process of drastic evolution, Protestant ideas of sight and seeing were as much a *development* of this Western tradition as a departure from it. Moreover, I believe, recalling ideas of prayer and worship involving icons and images provides a lens with which, mutatis mutandis, later Protestant practices can be more fruitfully understood and evaluated. Though the media of attention were altered – and broadened – the religious (and aesthetic) experience elicited was often comparable.

Images and Icons as a Way to God

It is customary to begin with Pope Gregory the Great's letter to Bishop Serenus of Marseilles in 600. Word had come to him that Serenus had destroyed pagan images in the ancient sanctuaries, and he felt this was mistaken:

> We commend you indeed for your zeal against anything made with hands being an object of adoration; but we signify to you that you ought not to have broken these images. For pictorial representation is made use of in Churches for this reason; that such as are ignorant of letters may at least read by looking at the walls what they cannot read in books. Your Fraternity therefore should have both preserved the images and prohibited the people from adoration of them, to the end that both those who are ignorant of letters might have wherewith to gather a knowledge of the history, and that the people might by no means sin by adoration of a pictorial representation.[14]

What is significant in Gregory's instruction is that "reading" the images, so far from promoting superstition as Calvin would later charge, provided the means of avoiding "sin by adoration of a pictorial representation" – that is, one *uses* images to understand and appropriate the history that is portrayed

---

[14] *Nicene and Post-Nicene Fathers*, series 2, trans. Philip Schaff and Henry Wace (New York: Scribners, 1900), vol. XII, p. 53, ii/xiii.

there and respond in suitable ways. Gregory's pastoral concern motivated him to open the way for the many who could not read to appropriately reflect on the pathway to God. Gregory here provides an early template for the role that images (and relics) would play in moving one from physical sight to the contemplation of God. As Herbert Kessler notes of this period, "as a first step, by engaging physical sight, art might at least attract attention away from the mundane world and call attention to more elevated things."[15] That is, the image was to initiate a process, Kessler says, of linking and replacing one thing – the physical – with something better – the spiritual. Of course the physical image itself could lead believers astray, as Bishop Serenus feared, so it was itself involved in the spiritual struggle of medieval believers. But in their minds, there was no way of escaping the need for the mediation that images provided.

In the East, the focus of this mediation came to rest on the icon, especially the icon portrait, which provided the privileged means of lifting the mind. But in reflecting on Eastern conceptions of sight and seeing, it is important to remember that images were not meant to provide a mystical way to God that belittled the physical world or human sight. St. John of Damascus was emphatic that "the eloquent Gregory says that the mind which is determined to ignore corporeal things will find itself weakened and frustrated. Since the creation of the world the invisible things of God are clearly seen by means of images."[16] When we make an image of the God incarnate in Christ who converses with us, the Damascene believed, we are making an image of what can be seen, and, in so doing, he insists, we honor matter: "I salute all remaining matter with reverence, because God has filled it with his grace and power."[17] In this way physical seeing was not despised but enhanced, as the Damascene says, "leading us through matter to the invisible God."

The correspondence of the image to its prototype moreover involved an important likeness. This was not a physical likeness, of course, but a theological one, which Orthodox theologians insist could be traced back to the time of Christ's apostles. Each of the icons then provided a veridical window into the heavenly reality, indeed into the very reality of salvation as this was accomplished by the Incarnation and embodied in the liturgy.[18] In this

---

[15] "Turning a Blind Eye," in Hamburger and Bouché, eds., *The Mind's Eye*, p. 415. And for what follows, see p. 417.

[16] *On the Divine Images*, trans. David Anderson (New York: St. Vladimir's Press, 2002), p. 11.

[17] *On the Divine Images*, p. 20. Following quote is at p. 67.

[18] Leonid Ouspensky and Vladimir Lossky. *The Meaning of Icons*, ed. Urs Graf-Verlag, trans. G. E. H. Palmer and E. Kabloubovsky (Crestwood, NY: St. Vladimir's Press, 1982), pp. 27, 28. Icon painting corresponds "to what the Gospels preach and relate" (p. 30).

process believers were lifted up beyond the physical, indeed, beyond time itself. As a modern scholar notes, the process of *lectio, meditation,* and *oratio* (reading, meditation, and prayer) before an icon, which lifts the soul to God, involves a suspension of time.[19]

Icons then represented a particular notion of "symbol" that is important to my argument. The images – of Christ Pantokrator or the Theotokos (Mary as God-bearer) – embody the "presence" of what is symbolized; the icons *stand in* for this presence. The seeing that was elicited was not merely didactic; it appealed, Paul Evdokimov claims, "to the contemplative faculty of the mind, to the real imagination, both evocative and invocative."[20] This surely would have included an aesthetic response to the beauty of the icon, but one that was deeply integrated with its spiritual purposes. This symbolism, and the incarnational theology that funded it, implied a broader conception of aesthetic and spiritual possibilities, even though this was undeveloped at the time.[21] The tradition was aware of the dangers of idolatry and carefully distinguished appropriate veneration from idolatrous adoration. As Ouspensky and Lossky note: "The icon is not a representation of the Deity, but an indication of the participation of a given person in the divine life." The goal of praying with these figures, they argue, is that worshippers become themselves an "icon" capable by word and deed of creating external icons, embodying this divine life in the world.[22] These portrait icons made the reality of the divine life present; they were the extension of the invisible "in the world of sight."[23]

Notice that though physical sight and material reality are not despised they are intentionally integrated into an ascetic and spiritual process. That is, one appropriates these media of the divine life in the process of linking and replacement involved in the journey toward God.

The Medieval Appropriation of Icons

As is well known, Byzantine portrait icons were foundational to the development of Western panel painting. As Italian painters took over these images

---

[19] Gregory Collins, *The Glenstal Book of Icons* (New York: Liturgical Press, 2002), p. 7.

[20] Paul Evdokimov, *The Art of the Icon: A Theology of Beauty,* trans. Steven Bigham (Redondo Beach, CA: Oakwood Publications, 1990), p. 167.

[21] Cf. Gregory Collins: "Iconography is a contemplative art. It opens up the possibility of a Christian aesthetic, a redeemed way of seeing and depicting the world." *The Glenstal Book,* p. 19.

[22] *The Meaning of Icons,* p. 36.

[23] Sixten Ringbom, *Icon to Narrative: The Rise of the Dramatic Close-Up in Fifteenth-Century Devotional Painting* (Abo: Akademi ABO, 1965), p. 40.

in the 1200s, however, they gradually began to emphasize the realistic and emotional elements. As Victor Lazareff describes this: "It was the thirteenth-century Italian artists, who, seeking a more adequate medium of expressing religious concepts, took over the most productive elements of Byzantine art and prepared the ground for the new realism which found its brilliant culmination in Giotto."[24] Both the growing emotional expression and the increasing realism are important to my argument and they call for attention here.

In the thirteenth-century treatise "The Mind's Journey to God" (*Itinerarium mentis in Deum*, 1259),[25] the Franciscan philosopher Bonaventure lays out the steps of the spiritual life, what was called the ladder of the medieval mystical journey to God, and which would provide the subtext of Dante's famous pilgrimage a generation later. Bonaventure describes the steps that the mind (or soul)[26] takes as it "arranges itself to climb thoroughly [*conscendendum*] into God" (1.4), steps that are "implanted in us by nature" (1.6). In chapter 2, Bonaventure makes clear that one cannot ascend to God other than via the natural world, which offers *vestiges* of God that enter the mind through the gates of the five senses – what Bonaventure, following Augustine, calls the lower light of our external sight. Through a process of abstraction and purification, as we are attracted by the qualities of beauty and delight, these *vestiges* enter our soul. "All these things are imprints through which we can look upon [*speculari*] our God" (2.6). From this external sight one turns inward to the spiritual sight that enables us to see the image of God, in which we are made, and by which we climb to God.[27]

That this external appropriation of *vestiges* specifically relates to the practices of art (*ars*), Bonaventure makes clear in another treatise, "Retracing the Arts to Theology" (*De Reductione Artium ad Theologiam*), written sometime earlier.[28] Art of course in this period refers to the full

---

[24] "Studies in the Iconography of the Virgin," *Art Bulletin*, 20 (1938): 26–65, at p. 65.

[25] *Itinerarium mentis in Deum,* http://faculty.uml.edu/rinnis/45.304%20God%20and%20Philosophy/ ITINERARIUM.pdf.

[26] The soul was considered, following Aristotle, the form of the body made up of matter and form. Sister Emma Healy, *St. Bonaventure's De Reductione Artium ad Theologiam* (St. Bonaventure, NY: St. Bonaventure College, 1939), p. 97.

[27] In this movement God leads us, Bonaventure says, "by hand even unto this, to re-enter ourselves, that is our mind, in which the Divine image glitters." *Itinerarium mentis in Deum*, ch. 3.1, p. 17. Caroline Bynum notes that theologians were never quite sure how exactly these *vestiges* related to God; often they resorted to Augustine's theory of signs laid out in *De Doctrina Christiana*. *Christian Materiality* (New York: Zone Books, 2011), p. 154.

[28] Emma Healy suggests it was written between 1348 and 1357 in Paris, *St. Bonaventure's De Reductione Artium*, p. 30. Pages in the text refer to Healy's translation of Bonaventure's text.

range of mechanical skills including hunting, farming, weaving, and tool making. But of these arts Bonaventure singles out dramatic art (which embraces every form of entertainment – music, drama, or pantomime) as that whose aim is "consolation and amusement" – and it is clear that this includes the specially made artifacts made for enjoyment, what later would be called art (41). "The first light, since it enlightens the mind for an appreciation of the arts and crafts [*figuras artificiales*], which are as it were exterior to man and intended to supply the needs of the body, is called the light of mechanical skill [*artis mechanicae*]" (39). Though this level of perception represents the first (and lowest) light, mechanical knowledge includes, even here, the glimpse of God in *vestiges* refracted from the higher lights of intellectual and saving knowledge (the latter obtained through sacred Scripture). One can see operative even in this lower sphere the fundamental spiritual pattern of human life (*vivendi ordinem*) – represented by the eternal generation of Christ, by which all things are made, and which becomes the dynamic template drawing all things toward union with God. In the wisdom represented by the mechanical arts are to be found already a parable in which the spiritual sense can "see . . . the union of the soul with God" (51). As artificers incarnate their vision in the material, they enact the Divine Wisdom that Bonaventure calls the "pattern of human life."

It is on this level that the soul experiences the delight of longing for God – what has been described as the center of medieval aesthetics.[29] As Bonaventure notes, if we consider delight (*oblectamentum*), "we see therein the union of the soul with God." So, he continues, "our spiritual senses must seek longingly, find joyfully, and seek again without ceasing the beautiful, the harmonious, the fragrant, the sweet, or the delightful to the touch" (51), because these serve as steps to lift the soul. Bonaventure rhapsodizes: "Behold how the Divine Wisdom lies hidden in sense perception and how wonderful is the contemplation of the five spiritual senses" (51), for the very same process of divine reasoning by which God brought salvation through the incarnation of Christ is to be "found in the illumination of the mechanical arts" (53). Desire, awakened even by natural or art objects, for Bonaventure exemplifies the movement of the soul toward God.

---

[29] Cf. Umberto Eco. "We have merely to cast our eye upon the visible beauty of the earth to be reminded of an immense theophanic harmony, of primordial causes, or the Divine Persons." *Art and Beauty in the Middle Ages*, trans. Hugh Bredin (New Haven, CT: Yale University Press, 1986), p. 57.

For Bonaventure the connection between the observer and the object – understood in a physical way as each of the five senses responds to the natural world[30] – is clearly described in emotional and aesthetic terms, and these terms are inscribed in the artifact. Notice the whole of the sensible world, remade as artifice, has taken on symbolic quality and potential – expanding the expressive possibilities previously assigned to icons. In the medieval West, of course, the spiritual ladder was laid out in its most explicit form in the medieval Mass, which was the central enactment of the eternal generation of Christ. But Bonaventure is beginning the process of expanding this focus. Through their emotional and aesthetic attraction anything made could (potentially) stimulate the spiritual journey, even if in actual practice artisans produced specific objects with this goal in mind. Clearly the process Bonaventure laid out expanded both the emotional and aesthetic possibilities of making things.[31] But it also, at the same time, made possible a new role for the viewer observing what is being made.

Under the influence of the Franciscan movement, and teachers like Bonaventure, painters such as Giotto gradually began to focus more on the emotional identification of the viewer with the subject. To the theological and didactic purposes of art that had been constant from the Early Church, and were emphasized by Gregory the Great, gradually a third "empathic" purpose was added. Sixten Ringbon notes that after Nicea II it was increasingly common to have a "deeply emotional experience" before religious images, designed to foster their emotional identification with the holy personages they contemplate. But, he notes, only later in the medieval period does the individual reaction before images begin to attract attention – as in the process described by Bonaventure. Ringbom believes even Gregory suggested the need for emotional response in one of his letters, but this becomes something commonly expected only in later medieval devotional images.[32] But notice, because of these new emphases, the idea of *presence* is undergoing a subtle shift – one that will continue in the Reformation. Presence here does not invoke the divine presence in the painting, which in the West had always aroused suspicion; that presence has been relegated in

---

[30] As Bonaventure describes this: "The sensitive life of the body partakes of the nature of light for which reason it thrives in the nerves which are naturally unobstructed and capable of transmitting impressions, in these five senses it possesses more or less vigor according to the greater or less soundness of the nerves." *De Reductione Artium*, p. 43.

[31] That process of course needed the social context of the emerging guilds and workshops in which these possibilities could be realized. These artisans surely would have found inspiration in texts like this – though their precise influence is hard to assess.

[32] *Icon to Narrative* (Åbo: Åbo Akedemi, 1965), pp. 12–15.

Bonaventure to a parable of the soul's union with God. Now the emphasis is shifting to the presence of the viewer and the experience the image was meant to solicit.

In arguably the most influential theological text of the late thirteenth century, the illustrated *Meditations on the Life of Christ*, by an anonymous Franciscan monk, the pious reader is encouraged to ponder the images of Christ's life reproduced and described. This text might be said to represent the pastoral application of Bonaventure's teaching on images (and was earlier thought to be written by Bonaventure himself). Readers are to exercise their spiritual senses by discerning the basic pattern of human life and its journey to God by way of the images provided – both in the narrative stories and in images of these stories. In such reflection, he says, "through frequent and continued meditation on his life the soul attains so much familiarity, confidence and love that it will disdain and disregard other things and be exercised and trained as to what to do and what to avoid."[33] For example, the author encourages the reader to reflect on the visit of the Magi at Christ's birth, or the flight to Egypt, recounted in Matthew's "imagined representations": "Be present at this event," he says, "and be attentive to everything, for, as I have said before, herein lies the whole strength of these contemplations." Here the writer of the text and the artisan who composed the images are following Bonaventure's direction by making explicit the pattern of human life as this was exemplified in the life of Christ. Viewers were invited to become eyewitnesses to the events described in great visual detail, to join themselves emotionally to the holy persons they are looking upon.

This call to identify with the elaborated life of Christ had multiple counterparts in the popular culture of this period. And this had great implications for medieval notions of "seeing" – including early experiments in optics.[34] While initially the dramatic and emotional focus of sight was limited to the Mass, and located within the space of the church, as early as the tenth century, representational plays began to break away from this, and cycles of saints' plays and later mystery plays were developed out of this

---

[33] *Meditations on the Life of Christ: An Illustrated Manuscript of the Fourteenth Century*, trans. and ed. Isa Ragusa and Rosalie B. Green (Princeton, NJ: Princeton University Press, 1961), p. 2. Later quote is at p. 50.

[34] Roger Bacon's treatises on optics written in the thirteenth century at Oxford and Paris developed notions of *perspectiva* that would prove critical to developing notions of seeing. This should caution us from seeing developments in optics as lying behind the Reformation's "cold gaze," as Robert Scribner claims. Those developments were under way two centuries before the Reformation! See Katherine H. Tachau, "Seeing as Action and Passion in the Thirteenth and Fourteenth Centuries," in Hamburger and Bouché, eds., *The Mind's Eye*, pp. 336–359.

liturgy – as in the "Mystere d'Adam," and "Resurrecion." Significantly, the Eucharistic drama was now spilling out from the space of the church, out into the streets of the city, where spectators were becoming participants in the drama.

As with the *Meditations*, the object of these saints' plays, as of the Mass, was to call observers to participate in the timeless drama of redemption as this was described in Scripture and presented in the Mass.[35] Medieval images literally incarnate the idea that creation constitutes a ladder of light that connects the visible world to the invisible one. Moreover, this world is illuminated by a spiritual light that infuses divine things and eventually illumines human intellectual understanding. As Katherine Tachau notes, this light was understood in physical terms – it was not metaphor that explains how we know things. Thus images played a central role in both the metaphysical and spiritual framework of the medieval world.[36] This focus reflected the medieval understanding of the world as hierarchical and timeless, and sight as the privileged means of accessing this reality. Tachau quotes Roger Bacon insisting that "nothing is completely intelligible to us unless it is displayed in figures before our eyes."[37] Indeed the notion of ascent is itself an ocular image; it is expressive of a particular metaphysic grounded in Platonic idealism. These metaphysical assumptions about matter, light, and time, along with the physical connection that human sight involved, provided the basis for the admonition in the *Meditations on the Life of Christ* to imagine that we are physically present to the persons and events depicted.

It was the Franciscan focus on emotional identification that moved the viewer to participate – to be present – in the dramatic action performed. While images no longer necessarily carried the same theological content of icons, they still carried spiritual weight and increasingly called for subjective response, even participation. As we noted earlier, Jeffrey Hamburger argues it was in part because images did not need to be "the embodiment of

---

[35] This is not to say medieval people had no sense of chronology (they knew God's creation was in the beginning and the Last Judgment at the end), but their sense of time was "layered"; that is, they lived simultaneously in multiple (hierarchical) temporalities. But what Jacques Le Goff has called "church time" can reasonably be called "timeless" in that it did not fit easily into single linear history as we understand this. However, this was changing with the rise of Le Goff's notion of "merchant time," a change that eventuates in the situation I will describe in the Reformation. See the discussion in Stephanie Trigg, "Medievalism and Theories of Temporality," in Louise D'Arcens, ed., *Cambridge Companion to Medievalism* (Cambridge: Cambridge University Press, 2016), and the literature cited there.

[36] As Caroline Bynum insists, these conveyed power as physical and visual objects. *Christian Materiality*, pp. 21–22.

[37] Roger Bacon, *Opus Maius*, 4, quoted in Katerine Tachau, "Seeing as Action," p. 355.

Truth," as in the Orthodox East, that they were able to serve multiple spiritual goals. He writes: "Paradoxically it was ... because less importance was attributed to images in the Latin tradition that they so successfully escaped most attempts to control them."[38]

Ever since Johann Huizinga's classical study *The Waning of the Middle Ages*, it has often been assumed the late Middle Ages represents a wearing-out of forms and a lassitude of piety.[39] Carlos Eire argued more recently that the increasing "externalization of piety" was a critical contributing cause of the Reformation.[40] But Margaret Aston, in a discussion of Huizinga's influence, contests this assumption by pointing out that the growing complexity of devotion might suggest exuberance and growth, not decay.[41] One need not discount the abuses represented by the offer of indulgences[42] to recognize the multiple movements toward reform that were taking place and the growing proliferation of social and spiritual purposes that art objects were being made to play.[43] And one reason these objects and practices were allowed to serve these multiple purposes lay in the increasing participation being called for on the part of the viewer, which was itself an important harbinger of the Reformation.

The proliferation of roles images came to play – in processions, novenas, prayer books, as well as the mystery plays, encouraged then the late medieval process of what scholars have called subjectification, a seeing that conferred agency on the viewer, who could become an initiator of action rather than a passive observer.[44] Clearly the increasing realism of the images, as

---

[38] Jeffrey Hamburger, "The Place of Theology in Medieval Art History," in Hamburger and Bouché, eds., *The Mind's Eye*, p. 17. Hamburger thinks this is an important reason why the West never developed a consistent theory of art, thus giving it greater potential power as idea and thing (p. 23). See the complaint of Evdokimov that the West always limited images to ornamental purposes, which he thinks poisoned art at its source, thus accounting for the dead ends of contemporary art. *The Art of the Icon*, p. 167.

[39] *The Waning of the Middle Ages: A Study of the Forms of Life, Thought and Art in France and the Netherlands in the Fourteenth and Fifteenth Centuries* (London: Edward Arnold, 1927).

[40] Carlos Eire, *War against Idols: The Reformation Worship from Erasmus to Calvin* (Cambridge: Cambridge University Press, 1986), p. 16.

[41] *Faith and Fire: Popular and Unpopular Religion 1350–1600* (London: Hambledon Press, 1993), pp. 146–152.

[42] Eire makes his judgment quoted earlier after noting that the commissioning of ecclesiastical art increased a hundred-fold in Zurich between 1500 and 1518. *War against Idols*, p. 13.

[43] Cf. Bynum: "There were in the later middle ages, many crafted and beautiful objects that were neither cult objects nor in any sense religious objects." *Christian Materiality*, p. 323n106.

[44] See Viviana Comensoli et al., "Subjectivity, Theory and Early Modern Drama," *Early Theatre*, 7/2 (2004): 89. The key influence on this was the work of Louis Montrose. James H. Forse shows that development of saints' plays was associated with efforts to reform the church. "Religious Drama and Ecclesiastical Reform in the Tenth Century," *Early Theatre*, 5/2 (2002): 47–70. And see the

elaborated, for example, in narrative images (*sacra conversione*), provided growing purchase for this enhanced subjectification, preparing the way for the central themes in Thomas à Kempis's *Imitatio Christi* and the educational program of the Brethren of the Common Life. In the increasingly common *sacra conversione* of this century viewers were being invited to consider themselves a part of this community of saints, a participation that was to be both aesthetic and spiritual.

We earlier noted that with icons the likeness was theological rather than physical – the question of actual resemblance to some person was secondary. But this was changing dramatically by the fifteenth century. There one finds a markedly different emphasis. We have called attention to the realism represented by Giotto and that was implied in the elaborate imagery of the *Meditations on the Life of Christ*. Over time the impulse to realism was increasing, and this impulse is best seen in canons of portraiture. As Alasdair MacIntyre notes, in the fifteenth century, portraits began to portray actual people: "the heavy eye-lids, the coifed hair, the lines around the mouth, undeniably represent some particular woman, either actual or envisaged"[45] (see Figure 1). But the question we want to address is: How properly to assess this changing focus on what we see? Is it the case, as MacIntyre suggests, that "resemblance has usurped the iconic relationship"? Does it represent the triumph of the didactic, as Orthodox critics argue? Is it simply a matter of featuring, as Evdokimov charges, "more and more the representation of a human model, made solely by the hand of man" that eclipses the ability to enter this sacred space?[46]

These charges reflect what has been the default view of late medieval iconography: the sacred images were losing their power, as a growing realism made secular interpretations increasingly plausible. But I would suggest this movement toward realism reflects a changing conception of the world, one that was already under way in the thirteenth century, and that was having increasing impact on the making and viewing of artifacts. The aesthetic and spiritual focus of viewers was changing from the earlier

---

classic article by David Aers, "Reflections on the Current Histories of the Subject," *Literature and History*, Second Series, 2.2 (1991): 20–34. He rejects the post-Cartesian "invention" of the contrast between the inner and outer, and calls attention to "the widespread preoccupation with subjectivity in late medieval writing, secular and sacred" (p. 23).

[45] *After Virtue: A Study in Moral Theory* (Notre Dame, IN: Notre Dame University Press, 1981), pp. 176–177. One might locate the origin of Scribner's cold gaze here, rather than at the Reformation.

[46] *The Art of the Icon*, p. 170. His reference to the "hand of man" is meant to contrast with the Holy Face that is made by God's own hand.

1 Workshop of Leonardo da Vinci, *Portrait of a Woman, the Belle Ferronière*, 1490–1495. Musée du Louvre. Paris.

attention to the drama of the liturgy and soul's journey to God, to a broader understanding of God's presence and appeal. Driving these changes were efforts we have noted: the Franciscan call to literally become little Christs and Thomas à Kempis's appeal to imitate Christ were already movements toward reform, making way for a new way of understanding God's presence and activity. This evolving notion of presence would become the central focus of the major Reformers, which, I claim, would make possible new ways of "seeing" and responding to the breadth and depth of the natural order.

And to understand how this anticipates developments during the period of the Reformation we turn to developments in portraiture at a critical moment, 1530, which could be said to reflect the definitive transformation from spiritual icon to secular human portrait but, I argue, might also be understood as the movement toward new spiritual forms that made possible a distinctively different aesthetic situation.

2

PRESENCE AND LIKENESS IN HOLBEIN, LUTHER, AND CRANACH

The Reformation reshaped what the visual image is.[1]

W E BEGIN OUR CLOSER LOOK AT THE EMERGING AESTHETIC situation by examining two important artists working – on diverging paths – in the 1530s, Hans Holbein the Younger (1497–1543) and Lucas Cranach the Elder (1472–1553). That decade was critical to Reformation developments for many reasons. As the decade opens Martin Luther had experienced the disappointment of the Marburg Colloquy (1529) where he had broken with Zwingli over the Mass. That same year the Speyer Protestation, which gave Protestants their name, asked the Emperor to settle matters "on the basis of Scripture," and threatened for the first time the unity of the Empire. The Lutheran Augsburg Confession, published in June 1530, did nothing to repair that unity;[2] the following year Luther delivered his critical lectures on *Galatians* (published in 1535). The decade was critical for John Calvin as well. In May 1536, the General Council of Geneva voted to abolish the Mass and live by the principles of the Gospel; two months later Calvin arrived, having already that year published the first edition of his *Institutes of the Christian Religion*, and took up his work as a pastor. In England in the early 1530s the fate of the Reformation seemed to rest on Henry VIII's decision to replace the Catholic Catherine of Aragon with the Evangelical-leaning Anne Boleyn. In this chapter, to understand the subtle changes taking place in notions of likeness and presence and explore their larger

---

[1] Joseph Leo Koerner, *The Reformation of the Image* (Chicago: University of Chicago Press, 2004), p. 246.

[2] Though the attempt at achieving a unified voice was sincere, as Peter Wilson comments, written creeds did not provide sufficient grounds for unity: "fixing arguments in writing simply made the disagreements more obvious." *The Heart of Europe: A History of the Holy Roman Empire* (Cambridge, MA: Belknap/Harvard University Press, 2016), p. 109.

significance for aesthetics, we focus on the work of Holbein and Cranach, in particular the double portrait, *The Ambassadors*, which Holbein painted in 1533, and Cranach's *Law and Gospel* painted in 1529.

Hans Holbein, designated "the younger" to distinguish him from his artist father, was born in the imperial city of Augsburg in 1497.[3] Though we know much about this period, Holbein himself remains something of a mystery: unlike his contemporary, Albrecht Dürer, he did not keep notebooks or diaries. By 1515 he had moved with his brother Ambrosius to Basel where he soon distinguished himself by his fine portraits and drawings – including illustrations (at age seventeen or eighteen) of *In Praise of Folly* by Erasmus, who was to become a close friend and patron. Unusually for a painter, Holbein studied with the humanist scholar Beatus Rhenanus, who taught him Latin and the classics. In addition to his portraits, during his time in Basel he no doubt painted religious subjects, some of which, it is believed, were destroyed during subsequent episodes of iconoclasm. By 1522 Basel had become a Lutheran city and was under the influence of the Reformer Johannus Oecolampadius. Holbein surely sat under his preaching and he provided illustrations for Luther's German translation of the New Testament when it was published in Basel in 1522, though as late as 1530 he wavered, unable to either join or reject the Reform.[4]

Holbein inherited the growing focus on realism and empathy that we traced in the last chapter, especially as these influenced emerging notions of Renaissance portraiture. Portraits at the time, called *contrefeit*, or *contrafactum*, were the focus of intense interest and discussion. On the one hand, portraiture mirrored the growing interest in portraying the true representation of objects of nature. Richly illustrated surveys of natural history had sparked a growing fascination with the closely observed description of the world. But Renaissance portraits also aspired to produce the illusion in the viewer of seeing the objects presented as though they were alive.[5] Accordingly, Renaissance portraits were to be painted *ad vivum*, from life, in a way that underlined the visceral connection

---

[3] A good introduction to his life is Derek Wilson, *Hans Holbein: Portrait of an Unknown Man* (London: Weidenfeld and Nicolson, 1996).

[4] Wilson, *Hans Holbein*, p. 90. Erasmus complained in 1524 that "Oecolampadius is reigning here," and left the city soon afterward (p. 96). See Oskar Bätschmann and Pascal Griener, *Hans Holbein* (Princeton, NJ: Princeton University Press, 1997), pp. 221–222n100, where they quote a town record from 1530 describing Holbein's uncertainty.

[5] See the discussion of "The Portrait, Time and Death," in Bätschmann and Griener, *Hans Holbein*, p. 149 and the extensive literature cited there. For what follows, see pp. 150, 151.

between the viewer and the image.[6] At the same time the portrait was a *contrefeit*, which can literally mean a forgery; that is, it stood in place of the living person offering a kind of mask that would be worn in the theater of the world even as it marked a moment in time that moved inexorably toward death. Holbein, standing at the cusp of Reformation developments, mesmerizes (and puzzles) viewers with his virtuoso treatment of this tension; Cranach, by contrast, I will argue, offers the viewer the consolation provided by Luther's spiritual hermeneutics.

Holbein and the Renaissance Icon

From 1521 until he left for London in 1526, his most productive period, Holbein continued to wrestle with issues of representation as he honed his skills in portraiture. As he engraved his prints and framed the inscriptions on his portraits he frequently registered his connection with Apelles, called by Pliny the Elder the greatest painter of the classical period who won the competition to draw the finest line.[7] The humanist tradition in general sought to recover the wisdom and virtue that lay behind the medieval world; the classical world hovered as an ideal and guide, like Virgil who leads Dante through the inferno and purgatory. Through his boast of being a contemporary Apelles, one has the sense that Holbein – like many of his humanist friends – was seeking to recover a lost (and lamented) past; they drew the future with the colors of this ideal past. One episode of that struggle is important to our narrative. In 1526 the contemporary competitor for the title of Apelles, Albrecht Dürer, engraved a portrait of Erasmus, with an inscription that read (in Greek): "His writing will present a better picture of him," pointing to the inevitable gulf between the literary and the visual – the one uncovering the inner (and higher) world, the other merely recording the external one. In an engraving portrait of Philipp Melanchthon, Luther's close colleague, done the same year, Dürer elaborated on this gulf: "Dürer could paint the external and vivid features of Philipp, but the learned hand could not paint the mind." Despite the advances in observing and recording the external world, that world was still subordinated to the inner world of the mind. As Bonaventure and the mystics had specified, it was in the latter world where one ascends to God. And it was precisely in the

---

[6] The notion of "living images" was central to the cultural tensions of the day and will become critical in our discussion of Calvin.

[7] Bätschmann and Griener, *Hans Holbein*, pp. 13–15. And see pp. 30, 31 for what follows.

portrait that this troubling dichotomy was most pronounced. What was its proper role in the emerging spirituality?

In his own portrait of Melanchthon, from 1532, Holbein appears to reject Dürer's limitation, insisting on the potential of (his own) creative power. His 1532 inscription reads: "You contemplate the facial features of Melanchthon, as if they were almost alive: Holbein has worked them out with incredible skill." Though he painted religious subjects during this time, most notably *The Body of the Dead Christ in the Tomb* (1521–1522), which I discuss later, and *The Solothurn Madonna* (1522), and *The Darmstadt Madonna* (1526–1529), sparkling portraits of Basel's leading figures were his main work in this period. In these portraits Holbein's figures emerge from their often dark and barren backgrounds as living figures; the role and prospect of the viewer remains unclear.[8]

In 1526 Holbein returned to London, with a recommendation from Erasmus, where he was warmly received by the humanists there, including Sir Thomas More, whose portrait he soon painted. He was probably motivated to leave Basel by the iconoclastic episodes that were increasing, assuming, rightly as it turned out, that there would be no market for his religious painting there. In England, More was influential in obtaining multiple commissions for Holbein whose portraits were admired in the royal court. From 1529 to 1532 he was back in Basel where the Reformer Oecolampadius was desperately seeking to manage radical elements intent on throwing down images in city churches. Holbein struggled to avoid taking sides during this time and quietly worked on portraits and murals. Though no records remain of his movements during this period, it is widely believed he visited Italy or at least was exposed to Italian work by his travels in France. By 1532 he was back in London where his reputation easily attracted patrons. As we explore further in Chapter 5, England had no native tradition of portraiture and Holbein brought a widely admired Renaissance style to the country.

Early in 1533 Jean of Dinterville, the French Ambassador to England, contacted Holbein to do a portrait of himself and a visiting friend, Bishop Georges de Selve. The large-scale portrait (207 × 209 cm; see Figure 2) entitled *The Ambassadors*, was finished by mid-year in time for Dinterville to take back with him when he returned in November to his home in Polisy, in the south of France. This magnificent portrait, the largest Holbein painted and one of the most impressive double portraits of the period, captures well

---

[8] This uncertainty is reflected in Bätschmann and Griener's comment that scholars have been puzzled by the function and purposes of his religious subjects: *Hans Holbein*, p. 104.

2 Hans Holbein the Younger, *The Ambassadors*, 1533.
Courtesy of the National Gallery Picture Library, London.

the struggle – spiritual and aesthetic – that was troubling Europe during this period. Like Holbein himself, Dinterville and de Selve find themselves caught between forces they could neither support nor resist. Viewers – then and now – also find it hard to resist either the attraction of lively figures and details or the pathos of the signs of discord and death it offers, leading them to wonder: Does it suggest the potential of Renaissance ambitions or their limitations?

Perhaps this is uniquely modern query. Though the painting has long been admired, many of the details, even the identity of the subjects of this famous double portrait, were lost to historians until 1900, when Mary Hervey published a scrupulously researched study of the painting and of the two figures.[9] She brought to light many details of the portrait and its subjects. Jean de Dinterville, to the left, was the twenty-nine-year-old ambassador of Francis I to the court of Henry VIII. His friend Bishop Georges de Selve, aged twenty-five, was serving as an ambassador to the Emperor Charles V. De Selve was in England visiting Dinterville, whom he had known for years. The two friends shared concerns over the religious divisions in Europe and the violence that threatened, turmoil that de Selve had occasion to witness firsthand, and they no doubt communicated this concern to Holbein.

Dinterville had special reasons to be worried. A liberal Catholic, he had had significant interaction with Reformers in France. In fact, earlier Francis I had placed his youngest son, Prince Charles, under Dinterville's personal care. And Francis, no doubt influenced by Dinterville, called on the famous Reformer Lefèvre d'Étaples to educate his son.[10] Up to this point, however, Dinterville had been able to keep himself above the battles that were brewing. When this picture was being made this was becoming increasingly difficult.

Dinterville had returned to England in February 1533 for his second assignment as ambassador. By all accounts he had proven himself a highly successful diplomat. But now in early 1533 things were not going well between Francis and Henry, and Dinterville struggled to smooth things over or at least delay a breach.[11] England at the time reflected Holbein's own double-mindedness about the Reform. The rising fortunes of Anne Boleyn and her family suggested England might fully embrace the Reform; though 1530–1532 also saw the first martyrdom of Evangelicals.[12] On the night Dinteville returned, February 4, he was welcomed by Henry with a great banquet. Henry, who had secretly married an already pregnant Anne Boleyn in January, was anxiously awaiting news about his proposed divorce from Katherine of Aragon, which he expected Dinterville had brought with him. It was around this time that Dinterville approached Holbein to paint a portrait of himself and his friend, Georges de Selve.

---

[9] Mary F. S. Hervey, *Holbein's "Ambassadors": The Picture and the Men* (London: George Bell and Sons, 1900).

[10] *Holbein's "Ambassadors,"* pp. 40–43. Hervey comments, "At no time, perhaps, were the prospects of the Reformation brighter at the court of France than in these years" (p. 45).

[11] *Holbein's "Ambassadors,"* p. 96. See account of Dinterville's arrival, pp. 70–77.

[12] For an authoritative account of the English Reformation during these years, see Pater Marshall, *Heretics and Believers: A History of the English Reformation* (New Haven, CT: Yale University Press, 2017), pp. 185–202. On Anne's pregnancy, see p. 205.

Portrait and Presence

Surely the painter intends to represent something beyond a simple reminder of a friendship and a visit to England. The display of rich drapery and robes typically located the sitters in their social and economic situation and gives some indication of their interests and vocation. The floor patterning (copied from the floor of the Westminster Abbey) picked up a central Renaissance trope symbolizing humanity as a microcosm in the macrocosm. The two men lean on a sideboard, or whatnot, with an upper level containing objects for exploring the heavens, the lower with references to life on the earth.[13] Of particular interest on the lower shelf, along with a book of mathematics, are a lute with one broken string (a sign of a lost harmony?) and a German Lutheran hymnbook. While the hymnbook may have been familiar to Holbein from Basel, since both his sitters were Catholics, it is not likely that he would have included this without their consent – probably that of Bishop de Selve in particular, since the book is at his side. Perhaps the hymn "Veni Sanctus Spiritus" – "Come Holy Spirit" (from the eleventh century), which is clearly visible, is meant as an appeal to the whole of Christendom to pray for the unity that the Bishop sought, but that only the Spirit could bring.

From this richly furnished space the two figures stare out dispassionately at the viewer, Dinteville dressed in ermine and wearing the Order of St. Michael, de Selves dressed in a clerical fur-lined robe and collar. All this is characteristic of Renaissance portraits of this time. But as Erika Michael says, Holbein was known for his "augmentation of the formal and pictorial language of the Renaissance."[14] That is, Holbein is taking that language further than any previous painter had been able to do. Indeed, it is to the interrogatory presence and gaze that the viewer is drawn in looking at the picture. While the objects display a world and time out of joint, the human figures stand out sharply from this background story. They look back at our looking. There is evidence of Italian influence on this work, and the attention to detail recalls the Netherlandish painters. But as scholars point out: "It is difficult to decide whether Holbein was following Netherlandish or German models, or if he drew

---

[13] A good description of the objects and their meaning is found in Susan Foister, Ashok Roy, and Martin Wyld, *Making and Meaning: Holbein's Ambassadors* (Washington, DC, and New Haven, CT: National Gallery and Yale University Press, 1997), pp. 30–43.

[14] "The Legacy of Holbein's *Gedankenreichtum*," in Mark Roskill and John Oliver Hand, eds., *Hans Holbein: Painting, Prints and Reception* (Washington, DC, and New Haven, CT: National Gallery and Yale University Press, 2001), p. 227.

rather on Italian patterns."[15] In the event he was able to draw on all these influences to forge an illusion of individual presence that has captivated viewers and artists ever since. Though, according to the usual custom, the elements were chosen jointly by the patron and the artist, there is little doubt that the overall feel of the picture is the result of Holbein's intentions. In fact, Erika Michael goes so far as to say the image represents the "self-fashioning of Holbein."[16]

But the significance of this work is more than personal; it represents a historical crossroads that is relevant to the changing aesthetic situation. Keith Moxey has argued that the magnitude of this portrait lies in Holbein's place at the seam of a cataclysm over representation that was taking place at this time.[17] These portraits radiate a presence, Moxey believes, because Holbein "exploit[s] verisimilitude for anthropological purposes that are much older and deeper, and which are associated with the kind of power attributed to images in [medieval] spiritual practice."[18] The struggles reflected in the portrait were not only religious and political, but also deeply metaphysical. In the picture Holbein has managed to integrate the dichotomy between the inner and outer, with the medieval hierarchical division between heaven and earth, and the ideal of perfect representation inherited from the classical world in a single image. But there is another dichotomy that lies behind and reflects the upper and lower shelves of the sideboard. And this calls for special attention from the viewer. In the lower center of the picture an anamorphotic skull appears, that, to be seen properly, forces the viewer to bend down and look from the left below. The skull as a vanitas symbol of death and mortality was a common medieval trope. Interestingly, however, Holbein's portraits seemed ordinarily uninterested in mortality.[19] Moxey sees in the anamorphotic skull a clue to Holbein's struggle with representation. The fact that the shadow of this image falls in the opposite direction to others in the picture suggests to Moxey that Holbein intends more than a subtle reference to mortality. While it may underline Dinteville's melancholy at his fruitless diplomacy and de Selve's despair over the religious conflicts, it surely does more than this: the skull tears at the fabric of the picture surface, suggesting Holbein intends it as a metaphor for the

---

[15] Bätschmann and Griener, *Hans Holbein*, p. 102. Though they are speaking of his paintings of the Virgin, this comment applies as well to this portrait.
[16] "The Legacy of Holbein's *Gedankenreichtum*," p. 228.
[17] "Mimesis and Iconoclasm," *Art History*, 32/1 (2009): 59–73.
[18] "Mimesis and Iconoclasm," p. 59.
[19] Susan Foister, *Making and Meaning: Holbein's Ambassador*, p. 46.

iconoclasm of the period – a trace of the cataclysm that challenged the medieval representation of reality.[20]

In a picture diffused with melancholy and even depression, Holbein presents the dilemma of Renaissance advances. On the one hand, the objects on the whatnot speak of the growing mastery and understanding of the natural world, which can now be seen and measured with great precision. Accordingly, Holbein's figures emerge from their space and confront the viewer as though they are alive. On the other hand, looked at from another system of perspective, these figures dwell in a world characterized by violence and death. The skull that tears at the fabric of the picture speaks of the growing struggles that threaten the future of Europe. As Bätschmann and Griener comment, the space of the *theatrum mundi* seen in the light of the scientific wisdom signified on the shelves "is denounced as a pale illusion soon destined to be ravaged by death."[21]

To fully understand this struggle, it is necessary to remind ourselves of the context of this painting, which we briefly described in Chapter 1. The religious longings of the time had issued in what might be called a crisis of representation. This involved two related questions: How does one represent God, and the transcendent world? Second, how can that reality be appropriated? The Eastern tradition had sought to limit the means available to the icon and its role in the liturgy – these provided windows to the sacred reality; the medieval images expanded on this possibility. As we saw in Chapter 1, the medieval image had its origin in the tradition of the icon, but the medieval church sought to enlarge the options for portraying spiritual truth and, in the process, developed a wider range of rituals and artifacts with sacramental potential.[22] This movement, as we have seen, included an impulse toward realism and an increasing solicitation of emotional identification of the viewer and led to an increasing breadth of practices and objects endowed with spiritual and aesthetic meaning.

And since the physical image was a necessary medium to the participation that was invoked, the eye had been privileged. The exchange that took place between what one sees and the eye that sees was understood to be an actual physical exchange. For this reason, while images told stories of the saints and biblical personages, they did more than instruct readers; they solicited their emotional participation. In 1492, a generation before Holbein, a Dominican preacher, Fra Michele da Carcano, described the levels on which medieval

---

[20] "Mimesis and Iconoclasm," pp. 67, 73.   [21] *Hans Holbein*, p. 188.

[22] On the significance of this sacramentality, see James F. White, *The Sacrament in Protestant Practice and Faith* (Nashville, TN: Abingdon, 1999), pp. 13–30.

images were understood to work that carried forward these long-standing assumptions. Images were important, he said, for three reasons:

> First, on account of the ignorance of simple people, so that those who are not able to read the scriptures can yet learn by seeing the sacraments of our salvation and faith in pictures ... Second, images were introduced on account of our emotional sluggishness; so that men who are not aroused to devotion when they hear about the histories of the Saints may at last be moved when they see them, *as if actually present*, in pictures. Third they were introduced on account of our unreliable memories ... Images were introduced because many people cannot retain in their memories what they hear, but they do remember if they see images.[23]

To the didactic function dating to Gregory the Great, Carcano adds the empathic connection, as though the viewers themselves were present in the picture. The visual likeness awakens the emotional sluggishness, because, for him, the eye was more effective than the ear for holding something in the mind – memory with its visual imaginative habits being such an important component of what Mary Carruthers calls the medieval craft of thought.[24]

The Reformation and the ensuing political struggles served to call these assumptions into question, even as inherited expectations about the power of images survived. As Joseph Koerner observes: amid suspicion and banishment of religious imagery, sacred imagery never goes away; it only "promises that in some better new world it will disappear."[25] Koerner's comment illumines Keith Moxey's argument. The portrait at this period, Moxey observes, is "still haunted by its role in religious practice."[26] Holbein draws on this role only to undermine it; Cranach, I argue, will transform it even as he destabilizes its aesthetic power.

Something of the haunted power of Holbein's images is illustrated by the experience of viewers of an earlier work, *The Dead Christ in the Tomb* (1521–1522; see Figure 3). The long horizontal image of a decaying body, recalling a predella of a medieval altarpiece, has powerfully affected many viewers, but none more deeply than the writer Fyodor Dostoyevsky.[27]

---

[23] Quoted in Michael Baxandall, *Painting and Experience in Fifteenth-Century Italy*, 2nd edition (Oxford: Oxford University Press, 1988), p. 41. Emphasis added. Baxandall describes these as "readily accessible stimuli to meditation on the Bible and lives of Saints."

[24] Mary Carruthers, *The Craft of Thought 400–1200* (New York: Cambridge University Press, 1998).

[25] *The Reformation of the Image*, p. 440. We will have occasion to dispute some of the major conclusions of Koerner in what follows.

[26] "Mimesis and Iconoclasm," p. 61.

[27] The story has been told by Anna, his wife, in her *Reminiscences*. See Erika Michael, "The Legacy of Holbein's *Gedankenreichum*," in *Hans Holbein: Paintings, Prints and Reception*, p. 202.

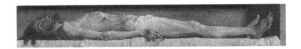

3 Hans Holbein the Younger, *The Dead Christ in the Tomb*, 1521–1522.
Image courtesy of Kunstmuseum Basel.

Perhaps it was his Orthodox practice of praying before an icon that motivated him in 1876 to stand transfixed before this image, while visiting Basel in
1876. His wife described the experience:

> [Dostoyevsky] stood for twenty minutes before the picture without
> moving. On his face there was the frightened expression I have often
> noticed during the first moments of his epileptic fits. He had no fit at the
> time, but he could never forget the sensation he had experienced . . .: the
> figure of Christ taken down from the cross, his body already showing signs
> of decomposition, haunted him like a horrible nightmare.[28]

For Dostoyevsky the image told the story of Christ taken down from the
cross ready for burial, but it did more: it moved him to devotion by showing
the body *as if it were actually present* – the long, thin legs; swollen feet; spindly
fingers reaching out beyond the picture plane; and gaping mouth of a man
who is God capture a power that can only be described as spiritual in its
impact. In the words that Swiss writer Jules Baillods put in Holbein's mouth:
"I, Hans Holbein, do not lie! There is your God. He is dead. You cannot
doubt it, can you? Look at him . . . behold those eyes of a cadaver – are you
weeping? – the eyes turned up, turned toward somewhere else in limitless
desperation, in total defeat, absolute surrender. Look at your God."[29]
Baillods here captures not only the energy of this image but also something
of the habits of seeing that allow that power to be seen and felt.

What can be said of the aesthetic situation that Holbein has created for the
viewer? There is certainly an expansion of attention to the details of human
life and experience, both religious and secular. They are all laid out before
the viewer as emblems of human meaning, placed in order like objects on
the shelves. Almost as an afterthought, in the small space behind the curtain
at the upper left corner behind the curtain of *The Ambassadors* there appears a
small crucifix. But what is its meaning? It is well known the crucifix could

---

[28] From the preface to the *Idiot*, quoted in John de Gruchy, *Christianity, Art and Transformation*
(Cambridge: Cambridge University Press, 2001), p. 99. This experience almost certainly influenced Dostoyevsky's portrayal of Prince Myshkin in that novel.

[29] From his essay "Le Christ Mort," 1942, quoted in Michael, "The Legacy," pp. 231, 232.

serve as a prophylactic to ward off illness and disease, even the death signaled by the skull. Like the objects on the shelves, each of these has its individual meaning, but the ensemble is unfocused, assembled piecemeal in the same way that Holbein – in practice – put together his images. The aesthetic range is broadened, the viewer is entranced, but there is no unified narrative that draws the viewer, no single dramatic focus that attracts attention. Though the crucifix recalls the medieval faith, one has to ask: Where is God in the struggle tearing families and communities apart?

Cranach and the Spiritual Interpretation

By way of comparison and contrast, I suggest we examine an artist working on the other side of the seam introduced by the Reformation, Lucas Cranach the Elder (1472–1553), who became a close friend and colleague of Martin Luther in Wittenberg. Though born in Cranach (now Kronach, Germany), and trained there by his father, also a painter, he spent his early years working in Vienna acquiring an international reputation (and becoming, under the influence of Dürer, an important figure in what became known as the Danube School). In 1505 he was called to Wittenberg as the court painter of the Elector, Frederick the Wise, who later became the protector of Luther.

Recently, Steven Ozment has argued that during this time Cranach, before any direct influence of Luther, was undergoing his own struggles over the Renaissance style he had inherited. As Holbein demonstrates, the Renaissance style had embodied its own contradictions; Ozment observes that in 1520 art's major challenge was the Renaissance itself: "High Renaissance art threatened to become monolithic art." Cranach during this period responded constructively to this challenge, Ozment thinks, "by integrating expressive, non-conforming elements of Gothic art into his own well absorbed Danube and developing Wittenberg style."[30] Ozment argues that Cranach, before significant contact with Luther, was already developing motifs that paralleled, and perhaps influenced, Luther's later formulations. He even suggests that two early paintings (in 1516 and 1518) could have been sources for Luther's formulation *simul iustus et peccator* (that believers are at the same time justified and sinner).[31]

---

[30] *The Serpent and the Lamb: Cranach, Luther, and the Making of the Reformation* (New Haven, CT: Yale University Press, 2011), pp. 26, 27. This suggested to some "the end of art," Ozment opines.

[31] *The Serpent and the Lamb*, pp. 52, 83, 84. Ozment's proposal that the influence between Cranach and Luther may have been as much from the painter to the theologian, as the reverse, is contested and will spark further conversation.

After Luther was assigned to teach at the University of Wittenberg in 1510 and in 1517 initiated the Reform, at the urging of the Elector Frederick, Cranach and Luther became close friends.[32] The artist's work was widely distributed in engravings and woodcuts – often illustrating Luther's tracts and Bible translations – and his portraits of the major figures and altarpieces constitute a visual history and record of the German Reform. Ozment argues that Luther and Cranach, working together, responded to the cultural and spiritual shaking of the foundations by creating a unique Wittenberg style that allowed viewers "to see through the image to the didactic charge." The use of images and words in the ways Luther and Cranach framed them allowed the experience of seeing and hearing to be "taken to heart," promoting maximum effect without the entrancement solicited by medieval images.[33]

I begin with Ozment's suggestions, because they offer an alternative perspective for understanding Cranach that is critical to my argument. Art historians have often praised the work of the thirty-year-old Cranach in Vienna, while disparaging his later work as, in Neil MacGregor's words, "the word made paint … art as argument."[34] In the 1530s Max Friedlander declared: "Had Cranach died in 1505, he would have lived in our memory as an artist charged with dynamite. But he did not die until 1553, and instead of watching his powers explode, we see them fizzle out."[35] On his account, the encounter of the painter and Reformer resulted in a demotion of imagery to illustrating the Reformer's theology, a narrative that Ozment and others want to challenge.[36] A major focus of Friedlander's lament would certainly be the famous *Law and Gospel* paintings of 1529, which became emblematic both of Luther's theological innovations and of the pedagogical, theological, and even aesthetic use of imagery in the Lutheran Reformation.

In one, the so-called Gotha version (Figure 4) (named for its present location), the picture is divided into two halves – like two pages of an open

---

[32] Ozment notes that Cranach, at this stage, worried about the iconoclastic impulses of the reform, a worry that Luther would later come to share. *The Serpent and the Lamb*, p. 134.

[33] *The Serpent and the Lamb*, p. 134.

[34] Neil MacGregor, with Erika Langmuir, *Seeing Salvation: Images of Christ in Art* (London: National Gallery, 2000), p. 202. See on this point the excellent article by Dieter Koepplin, "Cranach's Paintings of Charity in the Theological and Humanist Spirit of Luther and Melanchthon," in Bodo Brinkmann, ed., *Cranach* (London: Royal Academy of Arts, 2008), pp. 63–79.

[35] "Introduction," in Max Friedlander and Jakob Rosenberg, *The Paintings of Lucas Cranach*, revised edition (Ithaca, NY: Cornell University Press, 1978), p. 16. Friedlander claims that at this period there was no artistic tradition in Germany and that all artists came from elsewhere (p. 17).

[36] See the discussion in Jérôme Cottin, "Loi et Evangile chez Luther et Cranach," *Revue d'Histoire et de Philosophie Religieuses*, 76/3 (1996): 293–314.

4 Lucas Cranach the Elder, *Law and Gospel*, 1529.
Staatliches Museum, Gotha, courtesy of Art Resource, New York.

book – separated by a large tree in the middle, dead on the left and green on
the right. On the left half, the law side, a man flees a skeletal figure in the
lower portion, while Christ the judge sits in heaven and Adam and Even eat
the apple in Eden below; on the right half, a man (the same or another?) is
directed toward the cross, standing before an empty tomb, while, above, a
resurrected Christ holds up a hand in blessing. A second version, called the
Prague version (Figure 5), has a single man seated under the tree that divides
the sections, turned toward a man lying in a tomb below the scene in
the garden and Israel in the wilderness, but being directed by a prophet
and John the Baptist toward the crucified Christ on the right. As Jérôme
Cottin points out, the antithesis of Old and New Testament, of death and
judgment on the left, eternal life on the right, are not innovations in art.
What is new, especially in the Prague version, is their juxtaposition into a
single synthetic image.[37] Here a complex theological narrative, a dialectic of
judgment and grace, and the double consciousness of human life, is
embodied in a simplified but integrated image that all can read and

---

[37] "Loi et Evangile," p. 298. He also finds the precedent for the single seated man in a previous
portrayal of Hercules sitting at the crossroads, choosing between the way of virtue and vice
represented by two women one clothed another nude (p. 304).

5 Lucas Cranach the Elder, *Law and Gospel*, 1529.
Prague National Gallery, courtesy of the Prague National Gallery.

understand. The implications of this bear closer scrutiny. To properly judge Cranach's achievement, we must pay attention to the pastoral setting but also the to the developing role of art objects and the implications of this for new aesthetic possibilities.

As we have seen, art historians have not been impressed with Cranach's reformation imagery. Joseph Koerner has more recently joined those critical of Cranach's later work, describing it as a visual transcription of Luther's theology that lays bare the impoverishment of art in the service of pedagogy.[38] While in his earlier work, Koerner believes, Cranach continued the medieval pattern of doing what he could to make his viewers feel they are physically present at the scene, later he falls under the influence of Luther, and his work becomes, Koerner thinks, a step by step guide through the Protestant theology of justification by faith – where "coherence is sought

[38] *The Reformation of the Image*, pp. 36, 37. Here he shows his indebtedness to Hegel.

not in the scene's *appearance*, but in its *meaning*."[39] The result, Koerner thinks, is that Cranach marks the end of medieval art, "for its inward religion brought that epic to a close," producing images before what Hans Belting calls the era of art.[40]

In Chapter 1, I have challenged the assumption Koerner makes that the Reformation is responsible for making religion primarily a matter of the inner response, arguing that the medieval period was already embracing the inner journey to God. But the larger challenge of Koerner and others must not be simply dismissed. In the first place, in ways many art historians overlook, Koerner recognizes the deep entanglement between Luther's words and Cranach's images. This is an important recognition even if one would reject Koerner's oversimplified charge that this has "linguistified" Cranach's work: "transformed [it] from an object in the world to a reference of words."[41] It is true that in these paintings Cranach's objects in the world are interpreted in terms of Luther's words, but it is also the case that both the images and the words make a fresh and, for many, convincing interpretation of the larger world and, more importantly, of the viewer's place in that world. This is something Koerner seems unable to recognize. In a few places Koerner hints at the significance of the interaction between the world laid out in Cranach's narratives and the world of the viewer, but he does not follow up these hints. In one place, for example, he observes that Luther invented "religion as an interpretive act: in the word, believers grasp the content that saves them."[42] In another place he reiterates this claim by noting that *Law and Gospel*, having lost the experiential immediacy of a work by a painter like Holbein, calls rather for the viewer's "interpretive attention."[43] It is precisely the interpretive demand being placed on the viewer that lies at the center of what I argue is innovative, and not without aesthetic significance, in Cranach's work. That demand, it is true, calls for a religious response on the part of the viewer, but this does not in itself diminish the visual and aesthetic response called for; in fact, it potentially enhances that response. Here, I suggest, Koerner overlooks the way Cranach and Luther were responding to the changing political and cultural circumstances by allowing for an enhanced experience of the viewer, one that involved both seeing and hearing. Further, I argue, this expanded

---

[39] *The Moment of Self-Portraiture in German Renaissance Art* (Chicago: University of Chicago Press, 1993), pp. 375–379, quote at p. 375. Emphasis in original. This also marks the end of the self-image of the Renaissance artist, Koerner believes.

[40] *The Reformation of the Image*, p. 35.   [41] *The Reformation of the Image*, p. 204.

[42] *The Reformation of the Image*, p. 36.   [43] *The Moment of Self-Portraiture*, p. 375.

involvement of the viewer created a new aesthetic situation with a greater potential for affective response. The larger question Koerner raises, remains: In what way does Cranach's images facilitate (or not) this enhanced response?

Though I am calling special attention to his famous – and maligned *Law and Gospel* paintings (done in 1529), I begin with brief comments on an important *Adam* and *Eve* paintings from 1530 (see Figures 6 and 7). But to prepare for viewing these works appropriately I follow Koerner's lead and pay close attention to what Luther actually calls for in attending to images of this kind. It is well known that Luther's attitude toward art and imagery went through an important evolution from seeing these as matters of indifference in the early 1520s to coming to a mature view in the 1530s that saw an important role for images as an alternative means of communicating Christian truth.[44] If visual imagery can be part of what Luther termed the external word, it is important to understand how Luther intended the readers of Scripture and the viewers of Cranach's work to respond to this external word. What exactly is the "interpretive attention" that Koerner thinks Luther asks of the viewer?

In a recent dissertation, Matthew Rosebrock, following Oswald Bayer and John Kleinig, has argued that the key to understanding this interpretive process lies in the spiritual hermeneutic Luther was developing during this period. This process, Rosebrock argues, came to be formulated in the steps represented by prayer, meditation, and testing (*oratio, meditatio, tentatio*).[45] Here Luther is developing and transforming the monastic process of *lectio divina*, which specified the steps monks were to follow in their spiritual exercises. The very Latin words that Luther uses reference his own monastic heritage – which stood over against the scholastic tradition the Reformer belittled. But notice that Luther is making significant changes in the received order of these monastic practices. In the well-known *Ladder of Monks*, for example, Guigo II (1140–1188), a Carthusian monk, lays out the goal of the

---

[44] Jérôme Cottin reviews the evolution in Luther's attitude toward images in *Le Regard et la Parole: Une Théologie Protestante de l'Image* (Geneva: Labor et Fides, 1994), pp. 265–268.

[45] For the following I am dependent on the PhD dissertation by Matthew Rosebrock, "The Highest Art: Martin Luther's Visual Theology in Oratio, Meditatio, and Tentatio" (Fuller Theological Seminary, 2017). Rosebrock sees these steps being developed in Luther's important "Lectures on Galatians" given in 1531 (and published in 1535), though he acknowledges that the spiritual hermeneutical method was not published in definitive form until 1539. See also Bayer, "Hermeneutical Theology," trans. Dr. Gwen Griffith-Dickson, *Scottish Journal of Theology* 56/2 (2003): 131–147; and John Kleinig, "*Oratio, Meditatio, Tentatio*: What Makes a Theologian?," *Concordia Theological Quarterly*, 66 (2002): 255–267.

6 Lucas Cranach, *Adam*, 1530.
Norton Simon Museum, courtesy of the Norton Simon Art Foundation, Pasadena, California. M.1971.1.P.

7 Lucas Cranach, *Eve*, 1530.
Norton Simon Museum, courtesy of the Norton Simon Art Foundation, Pasadena, California. M. 1991.1.P.

spiritual life that became normative for the medieval mystical tradition.
He writes: "One day while I was busy working with my hands I began to
think about our spiritual work, and all at once four stages in spiritual exercise
came into my mind: reading (*lectio*), meditation (*meditatio*), prayer (*oratio*),

and contemplation (*contemplatio*). These make up a ladder for monks by which they are lifted up from earth to heaven."[46]

In the medieval tradition, then, one begins with *lectio*, the careful reading of a Scriptural text – "concentrating all one's powers on it" – then proceeding to *meditatio*, prolonged meditation – "the busy application of the mind to seek … hidden truth," digging within Scripture for its treasure. Since it is not in meditation's power alone to seize this treasure, the monk is led to *oratio* – "the heart's devoted turning to God" – in which the monk recognizes their dependence on God. This leads in turn over time to *contemplatio* – "when the mind is in some sort lifted up to God, and held above itself, so that it tastes the joys of everlasting sweetness," facilitating union with God as the goal of the spiritual life, the final step of the ladder the monks climb.[47]

This journey was spiritual but also aesthetic. When Guigo specifies the mind is "lifted up to God" so that "it tastes the joys of everlasting sweetness," he is laying out the fundamental principles of medieval aesthetics. As Herbert Kessler says of these developments, art's first role is to engage physical sight as a way of attracting "attention away from the mundane world and call[ing] attention to more elevated things."[48] While this spiritual path was laid out for what the medieval world called the "religious," that is those having taken vows and living in community ("the cloistered"), Luther repurposes this journey as a path that all Christians are invited to take: they may all be lifted up in this way to enjoy the sweetness of God's grace. But Luther makes two significant changes in this medieval practice that brings into focus the re-formation of the aesthetic situation that I am describing. First, he begins the journey with dependence on God represented by *oratio*, which stands at the beginning and conditions the process. This is similar to Calvin's proposal that the vision of God is the beginning and not the end of the Christian life. No one will make progress in the Christian life, Luther insisted, apart from this sense of complete dependence on God and the mercy God has made available in Christ. Only in such a situation can one properly read and meditate on Scripture, as Luther proposes in the following step, *meditatio*. Second, and tellingly, Luther replaces the final step, *contemplatio*, with *tentatio* (or German *Anfechtung*). This represents Luther's famous "Theology of the

---

[46] Guigo II, *The Ladder of Monks: A Letter on the Contemplative Life*, trans. Edmond Colledge and James Walsh (Kalamazoo, MI: Cistercian Publications, 1981), pp. 67–68.

[47] Guigo II, *Ladder of Monks*. Quotes at p. 68. See also the recapitulation on p. 79.

[48] "Turning a Blind Eye," in Hamburger and Bouché, eds., *The Mind's Eye*, p. 415. And for what follows, see p. 417.

Cross," which stands over against a "Theology of Glory" or an overrealized eschatology, in which one seeks to escape the trials of this life and, apart from God's external promises, reach a place of union with God in this world. But this change signals something else: it places at the center of the believers' spiritual life their everyday life in the world, with its inevitable suffering and testing. I argue this move anticipates Calvin's move to frame the believer's life in the world as the ultimate drama of the Christian life. In placing the believer's *Anfechtung* as the culmination of a spiritual process, Luther has opened the potential for discovering in that worldly life a more comprehensive aesthetic situation – a larger canvas on which to paint the delights and stresses of human experience. The question I explore is how, and to what extent, Luther and Cranach were able to develop this potential.

This method of interpretation Luther applied primarily to Scripture as the primary sourcebook for the salvation God has made available in Christ, but since Luther came in the 1530s to believe images can contribute to proclaiming the external word, Rosebrock argues, this process finds a clear parallel in how one should "interpret" the images of Lucas Cranach's work. To make this case Rosebrock offers three lines of evidence. First, it is not a coincidence that Luther's growing appreciation of the role of art occurred at just the time that Cranach was painting his *Law and Gospel* images. They were close friends, standing beside one another at their marriages and serving as godfathers of each other's children. So, it is not hard to believe that Luther in fact was being prompted by his older and respected colleague (Cranach was eleven years Luther's senior) – who Luther frequently refers to as Master Cranach, even as Cranach's images were also influenced by Luther's teaching. Rosebrock asserts, developing a point made by Ozment, "A connection can be made between Luther's increasingly positive promotion of the visual arts, and Cranach's first dogmatically oriented painting of 'Law and Gospel (1529).'"[49] Second, Rosebrock examines closely the text of Luther's Galatian lectures and not only finds evidence of his growing appreciation of the visual word, but also notices direct references to images of Christ and the need to direct one's eyes to the image of Christ crucified as in Cranach's painting.[50] In his lectures Luther recognizes that God's word is delivered through human discourse, what Luther called the external word, which the Reformer came to believe could include images. Luther goes on to insist

---

[49] Rosebrock, *The Highest Art*, p. 36. As Jérôme Cottin puts this collaboration between Cranach and Luther: "Le peintre a exécuté les motifs, mais c'est le théologian qui les a pensés." (The painter has executed the motifs, but the theologian thought them.) "Loi et Evangile," p. 293.

[50] Rosebrock, *The Highest Art*, pp. 119–142.

that believers are called on to respond to this word by fixing their eyes on images of Christ, through the process of prayer and meditation (*oratio, meditatio*) in order to prepare to face the many trials of life (*tentatio*).[51] In commenting on Gal. 3:1, Luther suggests Paul's words are as though some painter portrayed Christ as crucified "before their eyes." In this passage, Luther, following Paul, stresses the fact of Christ crucified placed *before our eyes*. This can be done, he acknowledges, by a variety of means, by "hearing or reading or writing or drawing [*pingendo*]."[52] Still, for Luther, the word of preaching is privileged, as he writes: "No painter can depict Christ as accurately to you with his colors, as I have depicted him with my preaching. And yet you persist in your bewitchment."[53]

Throughout these lectures, Luther points out that Paul returns time and again to the need to see a true image of Christ. In his comments on Gal. 2:20, Luther insists in words that recall Cranach's images:

> Therefore Christ is not Moses, not a taskmaster or a lawgiver; He is the Dispenser of grace, the Savior, and the Pitier. In other words, He is nothing but sheer, infinite mercy, which gives and is given. Then you will depict (*pinxeris*) Christ correctly. If you let Him be depicted (*depingi*) to you any other way, you will soon be overthrown in the hour of temptation (*tentationis*). The highest art among Christians (*summa ars Christianorum*) is to be able to define Christ this way; it is also the most difficult of arts.[54]

Note the spiritual hermeneutics that Luther describes in this passage: hearers are urged to apprehend, take hold of the Christ thus portrayed before their eyes. As Mark Mattes describes this process, "the portrait of Christ is received through the ear and thereby implanted in the heart. That oral portrait of Christ is made available for faith which then grasps Christ, clings to him and thus sees or knows Christ."[55]

In urging believers to see God not as a judge but as merciful savior, it is not unreasonable to imagine that, even as the painter was making use of Luther's teaching, Cranach's *Law and Gospel* was serving as a visual resource for Luther's reflection on Galatians. Throughout the lectures he labored to

---

[51] At the very beginning of his lectures Luther admonishes readers "to exercise yourselves by study, by reading, by meditation and by prayer, so that in temptation you will be to instruct consciences." *Lectures on Galatians. Gal 3:1. Luther's Works*, ed. J. Pelikan (St. Louis, MO: Concordia, 1963 [1535]), vol. 26, p. 10. Hereafter *LW*. Cf. *The Highest Art*, p. 114.

[52] *Lectures on Galatians LW 26*, p. 62.

[53] *Lectures on Galatians. Gal 3:1. LW 26*, p. 199.

[54] *Lectures on Galatians LW 26*, p. 178.

[55] Mark C. Mattes, *Martin Luther's Theology of Beauty: A Reappraisal* (Grand Rapids, MI: Baker Academic, 2017), p. 150. Mattes stresses that for Luther there is no imageless word (p. 137).

make Paul's Gospel vividly available to the reader, who is called on repeatedly to come before the Lord in prayer, to meditate constantly on the text of Scripture, and to be ready to face the trials of life in the world with new hope. Rosebrock notes that references to prayer, meditation, and testing occur specifically in connection with the need to look at Christ.[56] The third line of evidence Rosebrock proposes involves a close examination of Cranach's images with this interpretive process in mind to see the obvious influence on Cranach's own work, not simply in providing the subject matter but in offering an interpretive program in which those images come alive – something we will attempt in what follows. Rosebrock concludes that Cranach "ushered in a new Reformation aesthetic that carried the theology of Luther before their eyes."[57]

While Cranach had earlier painted allegorical scenes, frequently with classical allusions common in the Renaissance period, during the 1520s as his friendship Martin Luther and his associate Philip Melanchthon developed, Cranach began to paint biblical scenes and later important altarpieces. But what changes as the painter and Reformer mutually influence each other is not primarily the subject matter, I would argue, but the process the believer is called on to enact before the images. The "presence" being highlighted in this artistic style is not, as in the medieval period, the spiritual power of images, but the presence and response the viewer is called on to embody.[58] Consider *Adam* and *Eve*, painted in 1530. This version of the double painting reflects many earlier renderings going back to the first decade of the century (there were probably as many as fifty examples in all). But during this period Luther's teachings change the way the viewer appropriates the image.[59] In his commentary on Genesis Luther stresses the dependence of believers on the work of God, and the need to approach these images with prayer. In commenting, for example, on Gen. 2:23 when Adam acknowledges Eve as "bone of my bone, flesh of my flesh," Luther notes that it is as though Adam were saying, "I have seen all the animals ... but they are of no concern to me. But at last is flesh of my flesh and bone of my bones. I desire to live with her and to accede to God's will by procreating descendants," showing his overwhelmingly

---

[56] *The Highest Art*, p. 114.   [57] Rosebrock, *The Highest Art*, p. 182.

[58] However, as we saw in Chapter 1, this subtle change in notions of presence was already beginning in the earlier period.

[59] Friedlander notes that shortly after 1520 Cranach became more intensely interested in the naked human form initially in the "secular" spirit of the Renaissance, though he makes no connection with the possible interaction of this with Luther's spiritual hermeneutic. "Introduction," p. 23.

passionate love.[60] They were naked and not ashamed, Luther notes, "to show how much evil this nature has acquired through original sin." Then it was commendable to be naked; "we have lost the glory of our bodies, so that it is a matter of utmost disgrace to be seen naked." Now our flesh is kindled with a passion that is satisfied in secret. Before lust was not aroused; as Adam looked at Eve he acknowledged God's goodness. After Adam's sin, we can no longer look at the images in this way. For us, Luther writes, these images recall this impasse between what we could have been and the violence and death associated with what we have become. Cranach's work repays reflection on Luther's words; it embodies and challenges both a renaissance ideal of feminine beauty and its erotic potential. Ozment argues that Cranach's "alluring images of women drove home the awesome power of divine blessing of human sexuality in the which life is created."[61] Neither Cranach or Luther hesitated to explore the seductive power of such images. But as Huston Diehl observes, as Cranach explores this seductive power of female beauty, he "destabilizes the implied male gaze by linking the eroticized female body to violence and death."[62]

The interpretive attention Luther's commentary provides offers a deeper insight into the theological context of Cranach's images. The question scholars debate is what the images themselves contribute to the interpretive process. For Cranach, it would seem, provides a version of the first of Carcano's prescriptions about images: viewers can learn of the "sacraments of our salvation and faith in pictures," but what about the other two – especially the emotional force of these figures being actually present, actually looking back at us? What is to be held in mind for Luther is not these images the eye sees, but the narrative that one must use to interpret them. Even if Luther presses the optical metaphor – seeing Christ on the cross – we are meant to feel our failure before the law. Joseph Koerner dismisses these images as "confessional portraits" and contrasts them with the visceral sense of presence of Holbein's portraits.[63]

---

[60] *Lectures on Genesis*, LW (1958), vol. 1, Gen. 2:23 in loc. For what follows, see 3:1–7 in loc. Though these lectures were given in 1535, they surely reflect teaching that Luther had given earlier in other contexts.

[61] Ozment even calls them "incomparable couriers of history and the gospel." *The Serpent and the Lamb*, p. 250. He describes Luther's frequent reference, often in explicit language, to the delights of human sexuality.

[62] *Staging Reform, Reforming the Stage: Protestantism and Popular Theatre in Early Modern England* (Ithaca, NY: Cornell University, 1997), p. 59.

[63] Koerner, "Confessional Portraits," in Roskill and Hand, eds., *Hans Holbein*, p. 125. His altarpieces, Koerner thinks, are the visual equivalent of confessional texts. In Cranach's work, he claims, one sees in part the emergence of the confessional church (p. 130).

Cranach's project, he thinks, is a mirror of disenchantment – explaining why perhaps so many commentators see Cranach's work as almost modern in its impact. Here is Koerner's summary: "Lucas Cranach represents persons in order to demand what persons ought to do. They give orders and establish order, positioning bodies in a field of force." Whereas, by contrast, behind Holbein's portraits, Koerner says, "supported only by substances whose earthy names have been revived, stand presences singular, local and real."

Jérôme Cottin, however, provides a richer interpretation that allows for a theological reference that Koerner's description lacks. The images become signs, Cottin believes, rather than symbols (Luther used the term *Merckbild*). They are not a sign of God's presence in the world – one is to read these not as an icon but as a sign of the Word of God in the world. That is, the image is carried within the word and becomes useful because of God's mercy – the image, Cottin avers, is an indirect theology of the Word.[64] The use that God makes of images in teaching, recalling, and filling out what is heard and reflected on in the word, Cottin argues, allows Luther to escape the simple charge of literalism. As Rosebrock notes, it is in the practice of prayer, meditation, and testing, which he refers to as "serious play," that the transformation happens and the visual language is properly appropriated.[65] Similarly, Mark Mattes argues that for Luther imaging is at the core of the way the proclaimed word portrays Christ as gift. He notes: "Imaging is not only a central category for theological anthropology but also is the means by which the gospel is conveyed, precisely as it pictures Jesus Christ as benefit for sinners." In this way Luther's images are meant to govern and reorient the Christian imagination.[66]

Bonnie Noble offers a comparable assessment of Cranach's images. *Law and Gospel*, she thinks, provides a Lutheran image as a supplement to the written word: "It appropriates meanings of its own based on the properties of its own medium."[67] The significance of this, Noble proposes, lies in the way imagery here replicates Luther's rhetorical strategies of antithesis,

---

[64] Cottin, *Le Regard et la Parole*, pp. 279, 279.   [65] *The Highest Art*, pp. 206, 212.

[66] Mattes, *Martin Luther's Theology of Beauty*, pp. 133, 134. Quote at p. 133. However, he does not relate Luther's imagery specifically to Cranach's paintings.

[67] Noble, *Lucas Cranach the Elder: Art and Devotion of the German Reformation* (Lanham, MD: University Press of America, 2009), p. 29. For what follows, cf. pp. 33–47. Quotes that follow at pp. 33 and 46, respectively.

creating a field of meanings that allows for interpretive freedom. This field of meanings involves a reciprocity of Scriptural meaning and pictorial content, where the image becomes a "heuristic tool to aid the viewer in the correct understanding of the Bible." Central to Noble's discussion is the dependence of the power of this imagery on Luther's theological claims. Medieval imagery, for Luther, was embedded in a system of works righteousness. Cranach's imagery, by contrast, insists the viewer's ability is severely limited and is dependent on God's grace. *Law and Gospel* then "reconfigures [the self's] relationship to God by reducing its ability to secure salvation."

This interpretive process becomes clearer when we examine in more detail Cranach's *Law and Gospel* painting of 1529 (Figure 5). In the Prague version the date is recorded on the tree trunk [15]29 (though there are predecessors dating to 1525). A tree divides the picture, flourishing on the right and dried up on the left; the man is oriented to the left but his face is turned toward the right. As with the classical figure of Hercules, he is called on to choose the way of virtue. But the call to choose is framed in terms of a larger story that begins with Adam receiving the fruit from Eve on the left and Moses kneeling as he receives the tablets of the law. To the left a man lies in the tomb, though he is made to face toward the right side, his eyes are directed there. On the gospel (right) side Mary stands in the clouds, her hands out to receive the gift of the Christ child coming down to her – paralleling Moses' hands extended to receive the law on the left side. Below her is Christ on the cross, and below that, Christ emerges from his tomb. A lamb is positioned below the mountain where Mary appears. According to Bonnie Noble the painting originally contained inscriptions over the figures that were lost during a restoration, and below the image there were originally six inscriptions from Scripture.[68]

The imagery is mostly carried over from medieval sources, as I have noted, but it has now been reinterpreted in the light of Luther's theology. Mary, for example, is not a mediator to whom prayer is offered, but is the one who receives humbly the child and offers him to the world, echoing Moses' reception of the law on the left side. Consistent with Luther's focus on justification by faith, viewers are not encouraged to lift themselves by spiritual practices – to climb the ladder of ascent to God; rather, they are directed to receive the salvation God offers in Christ – "Immanuel" (God with us) was originally inscribed above the Christ child. This message is made clear in the six columns of Scriptures found at the bottom of the

---

[68] *Lucas Cranach the Elder*, p. 34.

original image of the Gotha panel: Hell and judgment of Christ, the devil and death with the spear, Moses and the prophets, the man of faith, John the Baptist, and Christ's death and resurrection as the Lamb of God.[69] Thus as Koerner has put it, we are led step by step through Luther's theology of justification by faith. But we are not led as passive observers, as that critic implies, but called to be active participants in the drama portrayed.

Koerner is reiterating Max Friedländer's earlier complaint about Cranach's late work. That historian had concluded: "An intense faith is fertile soil for pictorial creation, but theology is stony ground."[70] But I would argue that it is the theological framework that makes possible a faithful reading of the images and, by extension, of the world at large. What is promoted is not an abstract theology, but a personal appropriation of Scriptural promises. The images are brought to life by the faith of the viewer. As Jérôme Cottin notes, in Luther and Cranach's project the image is made available, in God's hands, as a gift of the word (*parole*) to be made useful, something that a merely literal reading could not allow. Koerner believes that its redundancy causes the imagery to dissolve into its surroundings; Bonnie Noble counters that Koerner misreads the picture as description rather than prescription – a call to respond.[71] We should remember that in this period to consider art useful would have been mostly assumed – rather than despised, the hierarchies of art we take for granted were only beginning to emerge. Indeed, in most cases, it was precisely a painting's utility that gave it value. This was taken for granted by both Holbein and Cranach.[72] Holbein pushed against this assumption; Cranach worked comfortably within it.

But there is more to be said about the aesthetic potential in Cranach's work, considered on its own merits. I would argue that Luther, in his openness to imagery, gestures toward an opening toward something more, a broader and deeper aesthetic, but one that neither he nor Cranach were able to fully appropriate. We have noted that Luther understood the human propensity to imagine; his "Against the Heavenly Prophets" written in 1525 admits that it is not possible for humans to read the biblical accounts without forming images – they can be used to testify, remind, and signify. This inescapable inclination, Cottin thinks, provides a potential "anthropological" argument for image making. Luther understood the embodied nature of persons, and affirmed the value of the material and the movement of faith does nothing

---

[69] Described in *The Highest Art*, pp. 191–193.   [70] "Introduction," p. 29.

[71] Noble, *Lucas Cranach the Elder*, p. 102.

[72] See Dyrness, *Reformed Theology*, pp. 103, 104. Derek Wilson tells us that Holbein most certainly shared the utilitarian attitudes toward art common in his time. *Hans Holbein*, p. 113.

to undermine this assessment. Cottin proposes insightfully that for Luther "a person has need of images not only to better understand what God has said, but also to understand himself before God (*pour se comprendre devant lui*)."[73] This represents – and expands – the necessity of images that had been constant in the medieval tradition. Note too that this references a real physical seeing and a specific human response to the images painted. Luther's contribution, Mattes has claimed, lies in his movement away from the medieval intellectualizing of beauty and toward a human experience of the senses.[74]

But what work did the images of Cranach, as images, do? Luther was clear, as Rosebrock says, that they were "for consolation of conscience, not for the dissemination of abstract ideas."[75] And there is every indication they did this work for believers. But I would argue they did something more: they gestured toward a broader aesthetic, where, to recall Frank Burch Brown's definition, it was the felt qualities of these images, nourished by practices of prayer and meditation, that made this visual culture appreciative and meaningful. Luther's images invoked sense experience that had affective impact as well as cognitive content.[76]

This impulse to enlarge the frame of reference of images, and see them as part of the larger project of Reformation spirituality, is further evident in the famous *Wittenberg Altarpiece*, finished in 1547 by Cranach (Figure 8). Much has changed since the 1530s. Luther had died the previous year; the imperial army under the Duke of Alba would defeat the (Protestant) Schmalkaldic League that year, dethroning the Elector John Frederick and sending Cranach into exile. Many aspects would be similar to medieval altarpieces. The triptych form is carried forward; the symbolism of the font and crucifix would have been familiar, but these objects are given a Lutheran interpretation. The central image features the Last Supper, where Luther is memorialized along with the twelve disciples. There the Evangelical emphasis on the Eucharist in both the bread and wine is emphasized. On the side panels the sacraments are featured: baptism and confession. On the left, Melanchthon prepares to baptize a child, while behind on the right an aging Cranach holds a towel ready to dry the baptized infant; on the right the beloved pastor Johannes Bugenhagen holds the keys that symbolize the Confession of sin, which unlocks the heavenly kingdom. But it is the predella that has sparked the most attention of this altarpiece. It was finished by Lucas Cranach the Younger, though the elder Cranach surely contributed to the

---

[73] *Le Regard et la Parole*, p. 270.   [74] *Martin Luther's Theology of Beauty*, pp. 4–5.
[75] *The Highest Art*, p. 215.
[76] Brown, *Religious Aesthetics*, p. 22; Mattes, *Martin Luther's Theology of Beauty*, p. 5.

8 Lucas Cranach, *Wittenberg Altarpiece*, 1547.
St. Mary's Church, Wittenberg, courtesy of Art Resource, New York.

design. In contrast to the dead Christ of Holbein, in this space Luther preaches Christ crucified, visually present, alive on the cross, placed between the preacher and the congregation – the Gospel emerges in the foreground; the law has shifted to the background. This arrangement recalls Luther's own claim: "There is no painter that with his colors can so lively set out Christ unto you, as I have depicted him by my preaching."[77] And it brings to mind the more than 3,000 sermons that Luther preached in that place. Bonnie Noble in her description of this piece emphasizes that this Evangelical altarpiece features not saints nor donors, but a community.[78] Those pictured on the predella and the side panels are recognizable members of the Witten-berg congregation, along with their leaders Melanchthon, Luther, Bugenha-gen, and Cranach himself, among others. As she notes, the viewers are called to "see themselves in the rituals performed before them." The altarpiece is a portrayal of a real community, praying, reading, and suffering; it "puts forth an ideal of practice and belief." Cranach's imagery offers a pictorial version of ideal faith and practice. There Luther preaches before an attentive audience, establishing a reflexive relationship as a paradigm for viewer response.[79]

---

[77] Gal 3:1, *Commentary on Galatians LW*, in loc. I am grateful to Matthew Rosebrock for helpful comments on this piece in private correspondence.

[78] "'Wittenberg Altarpiece' an Image of Identity," *Reformation*, 11 (2006): 91. Quotes that follow at pp. 108 and 88, respectively.

[79] *Lucas Cranach the Elder*, pp. 103, 114. Cranach portrays himself here, she notes, not as a donor but as "particularized saved sinner" (p. 153).

Joseph Koerner in his extensive interpretation of this altarpiece argues that the predella connotes absence not presence. The cross itself stands isolated, "in strict formality everything about it says it is absent. An image of the heart's image before an absent God ... circumscribed by a continuous outline from which all accidents have been ironed out."[80] But Ozment responds that, to the contrary, it is "positive and celebratory"; the cross stands as a biblical "catcher in the rye." What the viewers see, he thinks, is not dry and inert but "a full refreshing three-dimensional anchored life in eternity: redemption and salvation one could believe in."[81] Bonnie Noble assesses these differences in a more positive light. Joseph Koerner, she thinks, is right about the Apostolic sense of the Reformers and their insistence on the Scriptural mediation of image and community, but he is mistaken in his tendency to simply describe these things. What must be recognized, Noble argues, is not description but prescription: what is to go on in the church in its presence.[82] Both Cranach and Luther are clear about this. As Ozment notes: "In St. Mary's Church they listened to sermons and meditated on the new art, as the congregation made peace with God on the Sabbath."[83] The faithful auditor, he thinks, has now become the "frame" of the picture, "live antennae for the Word of God"; the "organs of the Christian mind," Ozment argues, "are the true image makers."[84] The point of the religious (and aesthetic) situation is that the drama of things now lay in the reception, and enactment, of the biblical story in Wittenberg, not in the performance of the liturgy alone.

But Koerner's larger challenge still awaits a full response: what carries this weight, what does this work, are not the images of Cranach, but the images placed in the context of Scriptural promises, the Word of God – both word and images together. The images of Cranach must be consistently submitted to this word, *ancilla theologiae*.[85] When looking at *Adam* and *Eve* or at *Law and Gospel*, one is not drawn to reflect on the images; they do not *in themselves* serve either a religious purpose or an aesthetic one, though they might contribute to both. Their religious purpose is bound up, for Luther, with the word. Still, at the end of the day, their aesthetic purpose was actually belittled by Luther's insistence that images are ontologically neutral – that they are mere signs, *Merckbilder*.[86] But here Luther must be judged deeply

[80] *The Reformation of the Image*, p. 237. Quotes at pp. 88 and 108, respectively.
[81] *The Serpent and the Lamb*, p. 269.   [82] "Wittenberg Altarpiece," pp. 87, 88.
[83] *The Serpent and the Lamb*, p. 156.   [84] *The Serpent and the Lamb*, p. 134.
[85] Cottin, *Le Regard et la Parole*, p. 265.
[86] Cottin argues that Luther accepted images while limiting their polysemy and expressive functions. *Le Regard et la Parole*, p. 283.

mistaken, led astray by his nominalist heritage. Images and the objects they reference are never ontologically neutral; they are always entwined in a deeper and bigger story that they embody or betray. Moreover, when they are well wrought, with imagination and skill, they always say more than the artist intends. This is true because they reflect, as Luther knew, the human situation of the person before the face of God and God's world. And because of this created situation images are always capable of coming alive. This weakness may go some way toward explaining why Luther's long-term influence was so much more substantial in music than in visual arts, an influence that provides important evidence for the emergence of new Protestant aesthetic sensitivities.[87]

Luther and Music

Music provides a particularly telling illustration of Luther's aesthetic expansion since this was deployed so effectively and so universally as a carrier of his devotional and pedagogical goals. Christopher Boyd Brown estimates there were 5.2 million hymnbooks, song sheets, and related materials, deriving from the Lutheran Reformation, distributed in sixteenth-century Germany.[88] Singing was a major part of the aesthetic culture the Reformers encouraged and it supported the ministry of preaching; hymns were often paired with Scripture readings in services, and even served as texts for sermons. Like Cranach's images, "the Lutheran hymns conveyed doctrine in a way intended to be not only understood by the laity, but also actively applied by them, and to impart not only information but comfort."[89]

As Boyd Brown notes, music was a central part of the larger oral and visual world the people inhabited.[90] And the way music functioned as an interpretive medium is instructive for our purposes. Music supported, and often substituted for, the preached word, and in this role, it helped believers to

---

[87] His influence on sacred music and J. S. Bach in particular are well known. See Christopher Boyd Brown, *Singing the Gospel: Lutheran Hymns and the Success of the Reformation* (Cambridge, MA: Harvard University Press, 2005), and Prof. Beat Föllmi, "La dimension kérygmatique et esthétique de l'hymnologie protestante," Colloquium on the Contribution of the Reformation to Theology and the Arts, University of Strasbourg, May 19, 2017. And more recently, Mark Mattes, *Martin Luther's Theology of Beauty*, pp. 113–132.

[88] *Singing the Gospel*, p. 4. For what follows, cf. pp. 9, 10.

[89] *Singing the Gospel*, p. 15. Brown comments that like Cranach's imagery, hymns could be learned and remembered even by the illiterate; they "passed into the homes of the laity where they served as the basis of family devotion and religious instruction" (p. 76).

[90] *Singing the Gospel*, p. 86. The quote that follows is at this page. The account of Cranach's altarpiece and Herman's hymn and quote is at p. 87.

reinterpret the inherited symbols of visual culture, even as it served to establish "a new theological and symbolic context for Lutheran believers." Boyd Brown recounts an example of this process in connection with an altarpiece of Cranach in the Spitalkirche in Joachimsthal. The altarpiece, *The Engagement of St. Catherine to the Christ Child*, was done in 1516, before the Reformation came to the town. But the Catholic imagery was left untouched and was later reinterpreted by the hymns that believers sang in that newly reformed space. The imagery remained the same, but its meaning, by means of the hymn sung in that space, was radically reframed. In the image the infant Christ seated on Mary's lap places a ring on Catherine's finger, signifying her "marriage" to Christ in the monastic vows she took. Later Nicolas Herman (1500–1561), the cantor in the Spitalkirche and Joachimsthal's Latin School and one of Luther's closest associates, wrote a hymn, "A Dialogue between Two Christian Maidens on the Power and Benefit of Holy Baptism," that addressed Cranach's image. Here the ring becomes a symbol of Evangelical baptism. Herman repurposes the imagery: "Q. What signifies the shining sapphire gem? A. The Holy Spirit given me by him, and next to it, a stone of ruby bright. For by his blood I am made holy quite." Subsequent stanzas continue to follow closely Cranach's imagery. Boyd Brown comments: "Herman's transposition of the image of St. Catherine's entrance into the monastic life to Baptism was a pointed rejection of Roman Catholic teaching." Though the imagery that had previously carried that teaching was untouched, Luther's theology provided a new interpretive lens.

The parallel with the later *Adam* and *Eve* and *Law and Gospel* paintings is striking; a received image was taken over and simply reinterpreted. What mattered was the interpretive situation the Gospel had introduced. As Jérôme Cottin points out, even when the interpretation did violence to the image, Luther helped himself "to the images that surrounded him and then interpreted them in ways that served his purposes." But the justification for this in every case was that this process took seriously the situation of the one hearing the word, and the response this called for.[91] This call of the gospel trumped and shaped all aesthetic considerations. And in singing the gospel, the congregation registered its own response to this liberating word.[92]

---

[91] *Le Regard et la Parole*, p. 281. Cottin refers to this helpfully as the kerygmatic function of the imagery.

[92] Mattes, *Martin Luther's Theology of Beauty*, p. 114.

Luther's influence in music no doubt sparked creative developments in ways that were not evident in the visual arts.[93] But despite what was left undeveloped in this aesthetic expansion, it is important to my argument that we understand positively what Cranach offers to the developing understanding of the aesthetic situation. In submitting imagery to Luther's spiritual interpretation, he does not, as is often thought, simply belittle the visual, but he submits it to a larger interpretive strategy. As Huston Diehl describes this move, Cranach's images are meant to be disruptive; they challenge the viewer to interrogate her own response to the image, to be involved in the story the image recounts.[94] As will become necessary for viewers of Elizabethan theater (to which Diehl relates her discussion of Cranach), those who attend to the images of Cranach are asked to turn the imagery against itself – to deconstruct its force in the service of the larger narrative that it elicits.

Holbein was much more successful than Cranach in giving his images a life of their own, but he was not as clear as to the ends this life was ordered. A work done certainly after his final return to England in 1532 (where he eventually died in 1543) may give some hint as to his final attitude toward the use to which painting should be put. It is entitled *Allegory of Old and New Testament*, dated sometime around 1535 (Figure 9). It certainly must have been done with *Law and Gospel* in one of its versions or engravings in mind. There is the tree in the middle, flourishing on the right, desiccated on the left, and a single naked man in the very center, labeled "*HOMO*"; Adam and Eve are on the left marked with the Latin "*PECCATUM*." Here the man is turned toward the left while Isaiah and John the Baptist point to the cross and the resurrected Christ. It is meant as an allegory, that is, another version of the human story, which Holbein suggests we might enter. But like Cranach's *Law and Gospel* the images are stolid. Insofar as they attract the emotional identification of the viewer, it is because the story strikes them, not the images. Koerner is clearly bothered by the way Cranach dismantles the notions of self and image the Renaissance artist came to cherish, making art into a pious effacement, with images that display their effacement.[95]

---

[93] This may have had to do with the fact that unlike Calvin, Luther retained affection for medieval Catholic music. *Singing the Gospel*, p. 60. Luther's influence was less evident in the visual arts. Whatever the cause, Erwin Panofsky notes a decline in North German visual art in the late 1600s and through the 1700s. "Comments on Art and Reformation," in *Symbols in Transformation: Iconographic Themes at the Time of the Reformation. An Exhibition in Memory of Erwin Panofsky* (Princeton, NJ: The Art Museum, Princeton University, March 15–April 13, 1969), p. 12.

[94] Diehl, *Staging Reform*, pp. 61–64.

[95] *The Moment of Self-Portraiture*, p. 366; *The Reformation of the Image*, p. 248.

9 Hans Holbein the Younger, *An Allegory of Old and New Testament*, early 1530s, oil on panel; 64.2 × 74.2 cm.
National Gallery of Scotland, by permission of the National Galleries of Scotland.

This troubles modern historians; it was mostly a matter of indifference to sixteenth-century viewers.[96] But, as Holbein's work hinted, this was soon going to change.

In our own generation important voices have been raised to dispute the notion that images can ever be completely without power – that they can ever be neutral. David Freedberg has argued that the whole attempt to suppress images is futile. Indeed, he thinks aniconism is a myth. Since Plato, he argues, people have tended to invest images with divine quality, "as if that were the only way to grasp it."[97] There is no way he thinks that we can

---

[96] However, there are recent indications that scholarly opinion on Cranach is changing. In addition to Ozment, see the essays in *Cranach: A Different Renaissance*, ed. Anna Coliva and Bernard Aikema (Rome: 24 ore Cultura, 2010).

[97] *The Power of Images: Studies in the History and Theory of Response* (Chicago: University of Chicago Press, 1989), pp. 54–77, quote at p. 66.

divorce ourselves from this history entirely. More recently, W. J. T. Mitchell has argued that "there is no way of getting beyond pictures ... [they] are our way of gaining access to whatever ... things are."[98] Rather than images losing their aura, as Walter Benjamin predicted, they have increasingly come alive.[99] Mitchell thinks an epithet for our times is "not the modernist slogan: 'things fall apart,' but an even more ominous slogan: 'things come alive.'" He proposes that we understand images as "'go-betweens' in social transactions, as a repertoire of screen images or templates that structure our encounters with other human beings." What we cannot do is eliminate either their ubiquity or their power.

But something has to do with the expectation that viewers bring to images – with the way viewers are asked to interrogate the imagery. When we suppose images merely illustrate, that is what they will do. And there was something in Luther's teaching that suggested this to viewers. But what if we imagined that they did more? What if, when we were not noticing, they *did* do more? What if we stood before them as though they did? Freedberg notes that it is what viewers expect that determines the value of an image: it is only when stared at, when prayed before, that figures come alive.[100] Luther understood this, perhaps better than Calvin. Cottin puts this nicely: Luther offers us "the image without the aesthetic."[101] But, apart from its participation in the preached word, whether or not the image itself could open up a larger world of human drama and delight was of less interest to him. For Calvin it mattered deeply. And how viewers are asked to explore their own response to the media available, something Calvin's rhetoric makes necessary, will be a large part of the contribution of Protestantism to a developing aesthetic.

---

[98] *What Do Pictures Want? The Lives and Loves of Images* (Chicago: University of Chicago Press, 2005), p. xiv. Subsequent quotes are at pp. 335 and 351.

[99] See W. Benjamin, "The Work of Art in the Age of Mechanical Reproduction" (1935), in many editions.

[100] *Power of Images*, p. 320.

[101] This is the title of his chapter 11 on Luther. *Le Regard et la Parole*, p. 259. The following chapter on Calvin is entitled: "Calvin: An Aesthetic without the Image."

3

CALVIN

Creation, Drama, and Time

LUTHER, THROUGH HIS TEACHING AND PREACHING OF SCRIPTURE in Wittenberg, came gradually to his conviction that salvation was received in faith as a gift. One does not climb a mystical ladder to contemplate God, he had concluded; God has descended to us in Christ. This gradual process may account for the fact that Luther, as a faithful Augustinian monk, did not set out to reform the Church; in the course of his biblical study and teaching, its reformation was thrust upon him. This may also explain the continuities that existed between Lutheran and medieval worship. By contrast, when John Calvin arrived in Geneva in the summer of 1536 one could argue the Reformation, unleashed by Luther's teachings, was already accomplished; the iconoclastic episodes were in the past, and the city council had earlier that year voted to abolish Mass. The challenge Calvin faced was not how to dismantle the medieval church, but what kind of world would replace this.

This constructive challenge shows the inadequacy of reading the Reformation through the lens of iconoclasm, as I noted in Chapter 1. Recent histories of the Reformation have stressed the complexity of the multiple worlds that existed in the early sixteenth century: dozens of understandings of Christianity were emerging, all evangelical; a dynamic and multiform early modern Catholic Church has been described. As Lee Palmer Wandel reflects on this: "Utterly different worlds have come to light."[1] And this diversity exemplified a complex relationship to its medieval heritage. True enough, as Eamon Duffy has noted, in a generation, for many (in England especially) the entire symbolic structure of medieval life was swept away. As he put this, the Reformation "dug a ditch, deep and dividing, between

---

[1] Wandel, *The Reformation: Towards a New History* (Cambridge: Cambridge University Press, 2012), p. 10.

people and their religious past."[2] New sensitivities were emerging that
challenged past practices, but this work was as often supported by reform-
minded Catholics as by Protestants. And, in many places, there was as
much continuity with medieval traditions as discontinuity. As I argued in
Chapter 1, the iconoclastic impulse of both Luther and Calvin centered
more on the medieval construal of the journey to God than on images or
art – both Luther and Calvin opposed iconoclasm.[3] The key to understanding this, I argue, is to be found in the way the Reformers reconfigured the
space and practices of the liturgy, and the emerging theological vision that
lay behind this rearrangement, as evidenced in Chapter 2 on Luther and
Cranach. I now turn my attention to the reformation in Geneva. I argue in
this chapter that Calvin reconfigured the ritual in ways that decisively
influenced contemporary notions of time and drama, even as he promoted
a long-standing movement that encouraged increasing participation, both
emotional and physical, in the practices of worship – something I will
explore in the following chapter.

Part of the problem in properly assessing what I am calling the emerging
aesthetic situation is the overemphasis on what in modern terms are understood as art objects – images and sculptures, and the related evaluation of an
object's significance entirely in terms of its aesthetic value (often understood
as disinterested contemplation). This not only severely limits what is considered aesthetically significant, but fails to take into account the actual
(and multifaceted) role that objects and practices played in the devotion of
reformed believers. Nor does the struggle over images, in itself, necessitate
an aesthetic retreat; the iconoclastic impulse itself drew inescapable attention
to the role of sight and indeed of the senses more generally. It also made clear
that an image's meaning and accompanying word – seeing and hearing –
were deeply entangled with one another, even as the dynamics of their
relationship was undergoing drastic reformulation. As Stuart Clark has
argued, this reformulation "did not mean the reformed religion was without
'images.' They lay rather, in God's works and his word."[4] And this situation,

[2] Duffy, *Saints, Sacrilege and Sedition: Religion and Conflict in the Tudor Reformations* (London: Bloomsbury, 2012), p. 33. See also Brad Gregory, *The Unintended Reformation: How a Religious Revolution Secularized Society* (Cambridge, MA: Belknap/Harvard University Press, 2013).
[3] On the state of the arts in Geneva, see Henri Naef, *Les Origines de la Réforme à Genève* (Genève: Librairie Droz, 1968), vol. I, p. 276, and on iconoclasm, see Mia Michuzuki, *The Netherlandish Image* (Ashgate, 2008), pp. 1–3. Calvin actually began his work in Geneva *after* the major iconoclastic episodes; Luther's response to the radical Reformers is well known.
[4] A point elaborated by Stuart Clark in *Vanities of the Eye: Vision in Early Modern European Culture* (Oxford: Oxford University Press, 2007), pp. 161–165. Quote at p. 165.

I argue, made possible the emergence of new ways of framing aesthetic experience. In this chapter and in Chapter 4, I propose that Calvin's special focus on language and time led to a visual and dramatic rhetoric with deep aesthetic implications and influence.

Time, Drama, and the Medieval Mass

As became evident in Chapter 2, Renaissance imagery inherited the classical ideals of timeless beauty, reflecting the aesthetic virtues of *firmitas* (steadfastness), *utilitas* (usefulness), and *venustas* (loveliness) – which would especially influence emerging ideas of architecture. This rebirth provided an essential aspect of the context in which the Reformation emerged. Though this was a recovery of ancient ideals, it was also embedded in inherited medieval hierarchical notions of time, especially as these were embodied in the ritual of the Mass – and its representation of the real presence of Christ – as the culminating sacrament of medieval worship. As Thomas Aquinas argued, the Eucharist is the greatest of all sacraments, "because it contains Christ Himself substantially," because "all other sacraments seem to be ordained to this one as to their end," and because all the sacraments terminate in the Eucharist.[5] The focus was on Christ's actual presence per accidens in the elements, what was known as trans-substantiation. Marilyn McCord Adams notes this transformation was based on Aristotle's understanding of the hylomorphism of matter – that corporeal entities consist of a combination of forms and primordial matter, which Thomas appropriated for the Eucharist as the only philosophically adequate explanation that saved the givens of faith.[6]

The participation in the Mass invited the worshiper into the sacrifice represented and the ultimate union with Christ this prefigured. But as Adams points out, the Eucharist is "perfected" not in its use but "in the real presence of the Body and Blood of Christ under the forms of bread and wine." As she notes: "Every Eucharistic consecration put Christ's Body and Blood on the altar where forms of bread and wine seem to be, whether or not anyone eats or drinks."[7] This "presence," Adams notes, is the way Christ keeps his promise to be present with his disciples until the end of the age.

---

[5] He cites Dionysius in support. *Summa Theologica*, trans. Fathers of the English Dominican Province (London: Burns Oates, 1935), III, Q. 65, Art. 3, Reply Obj. 4.

[6] Adams, *Some Later Theories of the Eucharist: Thomas Aquinas, Giles of Rome, Duns Scotus and William of Occam* (New York: Oxford University Press, 2010), p. 87. Aristotle's hylomorphism and its role is described at pp. 4–19.

[7] *Some Later Theories*, p. 259. Also for the succeeding comments.

Believers, for their part, were honored to sit in Christ's presence (and the tabernacle that housed this), as in the presence of royalty; they could even be edified by seeing the raised host (what was called ocular communion). To eat the host, Adams points out, was a further step in the moving the worshiper into intimacy with God, since eating signified the eventual union with God that is the goal of faith.

We noted earlier that progress in the Christian life was likened by Guigo II to climbing the steps of the ladder of spiritual practices toward union with God. Dante, following Bonaventure's lead, likens this progress to a journey that he undertakes through the levels of Inferno, and then via these same spiritual practices up the mountain of Purgatorio, where he is prepared for the final ascent toward contemplation of God in the Paradiso. But as Thomas implies, all such practices find their ultimate meaning in the sacrifice of Christ, by which all things have been redeemed, and as this is symbolized in the Eucharist. The dramatic movement represented, both in the ritual and, indeed, in the structure of the cathedral itself, was from the material world, upward toward the spiritual world.

Visually, then, the celebration of Mass centered on the dramatic elevation and transformation of the host on the part of the priest. The Mass was the symbolic and timeless representation of an elaborate drama of the redemption of all things through the life, death, and resurrection of Christ, constituting a single and timeless story.[8] As the gaze of worshipers is drawn toward the raised host at the moment of transformation, so the dramatic movement is upward – as the soul of the worshiper is drawn toward union with God.

As we noted briefly in Chapter 1, the drama of the Mass soon began to move outside the space of the churches in the medieval saints' and mystery plays, though these in their own way invited observers to participate in the recurring drama of redemption enacted in the Mass. The dramatic structure of the Mass and the saints' plays mirrored a view of history as a timeless pattern of generation and return. As we described in Bonaventure's project, the aim of both art (*artis*) and Scripture was to show "the eternal generation and Incarnation of the Word, the pattern of human life [*vivendi ordinem*] and the union of the soul with God."[9] Worshipers were called to participate in

---

[8] O. B. Hardison, *Christian Rite and Christian Drama: Essays in the Origin and Early History of Modern Drama* (Baltimore, MD: Johns Hopkins University Press, 1965), p. viii. Andrew Pettegree notes: "The medieval dramatic tradition was born and nurtured in the Church; the first dramatic representations formed an important part of the liturgical rounds." *Reformation and the Culture of Persuasion* (Cambridge: Cambridge University Press, 2005), p. 77.

[9] Bonaventure, *De Reductione Artium ad Theologiam*, ed. and trans. Sister Emma Therese Healy (St. Bonaventure, NY: St. Bonaventure College, 1939), section 11, p. 53.

this one story (*historia*); the mystical movement promoted in the liturgy was an ascent, what Bonaventure called the "Soul's Journey to God," toward a final mystical union with God.

Modern discussions of the transformation of Reformation notions of God's presence (or absence) in the Eucharist tend to focus on questions of metaphysics. While this is not wrong, it leaves a great deal out of account. As David Jeffrey points out, these controversies may have had as much to do with a rejection of the hierarchical notions of medieval time as with metaphysical assumptions.[10] Marilyn Adams hints at this difference when she observes in the conclusion of her study: "Letting the contemplative ideal dictate the prequel and the sequel has the effect of spiritualizing God's interest in creation"[11] – and, we might add, of spiritualizing God's activity in time and history. Clearly, metaphysical ideas of substance and accidents were intrinsically connected to the medieval idea of *historia*; Reformation ideas in turn reflected a new view of time and history as much as a refusal of that metaphysic. But how did such changes in the understanding of time emerge? To understand this more fully, I turn to an explanation of Calvin's notion of drama, and the resulting impact of this on developing ideas of time and history.

Calvin, Ritual, and Drama

Victor Turner has argued that every society has a primary aesthetic-dramatic "mirror" by which it understands (and judges) itself, involving a movement in time that is "dramatic."[12] In the medieval period the ritual of the Mass might well be said to capture the aesthetic dramatic mirror Turner has in mind. In Calvin's community, by contrast, this drama, I argue, was constituted by the social performances believers were summoned to act out in the world outside the space of the church.

[10] Jeffrey, "English Saints' Plays," in Neville Denny, ed., *Medieval Drama* (London: Edward Arnold, 1973), pp. 72, 73.

[11] *Some Later Theories*, p. 291.

[12] Turner, "Are There Universals of Performance in Myth, Ritual and Drama?," in Richard Schechner and Willa Apel, eds., *By Means of Performance: Intercultural Studies of Theatre and Ritual* (New York: Cambridge University Press, 1990), p. 8. In another place he stresses this is a "social drama" that produces and is a product of time. See also Victor Turner, "Social Dramas and Ritual Metaphors," in *Dramas, Fields, and Metaphors: Symbolic Action in Human Society* (Ithaca, NY: Cornell University Press, 1974), p. 23.

Calvin did not allow images of Christ and the Saints in the space of the church, but it does not follow that this space was empty.[13] It was soon filled with the regular preaching of the Word of God in Scripture (embodied in various oral and visual forms), with the learning of the catechism, with baptism and Eucharist and the congregational singing of psalms – all of which will be considered in detail in what follows. Calvin dismissed physical images of the Saints as "dead images," but these were to be replaced with what he called "living images" represented in the preaching of the Scriptural promises, and the associated objects and rituals.[14] For performing what Calvin called the "Lord's Supper" significant changes were made in the space of the church. The focus on the altar was replaced by celebration around a common table that was moved into the center of the nave. Believers were taught to think of this supper "not as a sacrifice to be offered to please God, but rather as a meal by which God nourished the faithful."[15]

Though these living images become the focus of visual and emotional attention in a way that recalls the medieval Eucharist, their goal is markedly different. During the celebration the minister would ask worshipers to "lift their hearts and spirits to things above" in ways that recall the medieval Eucharist and its attendant imagery. But in contrast to the medieval Eucharist, this ritual was "perfected" in its use, not in its performance. That is, it was intended to join believers in fellowship with Christ, by the Spirit, to the end that they might be strengthened to live out this out in love and service of their neighbor.[16] By contrast, the practice of filling the church with images, Calvin taught, was a stimulus to superstition. He goes on in words with distinct aesthetic import: "it seems to me unworthy of [the churches'] holiness for them to take on images other than those living and symbolical ones which the Lord has consecrated by his Word. I mean Baptism and the Lord's Supper, together with other rites by which our eyes must be too intensely gripped and too sharply affected to seek other images forged by human ingenuity."[17] In this way Calvin intended that the space of the church become a living, formational

---

[13] Mia Mochizuki has called this reigning assumption the "mythic vacuum" of Protestant churches. *The Netherlandish Image*, p. 3.

[14] On Calvin's "living images," see Randall Zachman, *Image and Word in the Theology of John Calvin* (Notre Dame, IN: Notre Dame University Press, 2007), pp. 7–9.

[15] John Witvliet and Nathan Bierma, "Liturgy," in Herman Selderhuis, *The Calvin Handbook* (Grand Rapids, MI: Eerdmans, 2009), pp. 407–418, quote at p. 414. For what follows, see p. 415.

[16] See Calvin's comments on I Cor. 11: 17: "The purpose of the mysteries is to give us practice in devotion and love." Trans. John Fraser. *Commentary on I Corinthians*, in loc.

[17] Calvin, *Institutes of the Christian Religion*, ed. John T. McNeil (Philadelphia: Westminster Press, 1960), I, xi, 13. Subsequent reference to the *Institutes* are to this edition.

space, what has been called a "sanctifying space": not an empty space, as commonly thought, but a space in which a particular saving grace shines forth in multiple ways that would propel believers to live out this grace in the world.[18] This is reflected in the visual structure of the typical Protestant church, where the elevated pulpit reflects the centrality of the preached word and the table resides below in front of the congregation.

For Calvin it was in the act of preaching that the "real" presence of Christ, and the summons of this presence, was set forth. But, I want to stress in this chapter, in the case of Calvin, the setting forth of the presence of Christ was *to the end of forming the congregation for living out the cross of Christ in the world* – it was perfected in its use, rather than in its performance. Of course, the performance of preaching in Geneva, accompanied and enhanced by the corporate prayers and singing of the Psalms, was also an aesthetic event – it was an oral and visual and, eventually, a dramatic event. But, as I will show, Calvin and his followers, unlike their medieval predecessors, were less interested in framing this as an aesthetic space. They had their eyes fixed on a larger dramatic performance.

The Theater of the World

Scholars have long recognized that the notion of theater played a significant role in Calvin's theological reflection and practice. William Bouwsma has shown "the theatrical metaphor for the human scene pervaded sixteenth-century discourse."[19] Using the search function on electronic versions of Calvin's works, one discovers seventy-nine references to theater in the *Commentaries* and seven in the *Institutes* – in addition to multiple instances of related words like "player," "spectator," and "spectacle." Many scholars have called attention to this – Michael Horton, Susan Shreiner, Kevin Vanhoozer, and Denis Crouzet most prominently.[20] Calvin's use of theater

---

[18] The notion of "sanctifying space" is argued in the recent dissertation of Edward Yang, "Sanctifying Space: A Reformed Theology of Places for Corporate Worship" (PhD dissertation, Fuller Theological Seminary, 2016).

[19] Bouwsma, *John Calvin: A Sixteenth-Century Portrait* (New York: Oxford University Press, 1988), p. 177. He notes its importance for Erasmus.

[20] Michael Horton, *Covenant and Eschatology: The Divine Drama* (Louisville, KY: Westminster John Knox Press, 2002); Susan Schreiner, *Theater of His Glory: Nature and the Natural Order in the Thought of John Calvin* (Grand Rapids, MI: Baker, 1995); Kevin Vanhoozer, *The Drama of Doctrine: A Canonical-Linquistic Approach to Christian Theology* (Louisville, KY: Westminster John Knox Press, 2005); Denis Crouzet, *Jean Calvin: Vies Parallèls* (Paris: Foyard, 2000); and see John Piper, David Mathis, and Julius Kim, eds., *With Calvin in the Theatre of God: The Glory of Christ and Everyday Life* (Wheaton: Crossways, 2010).

and human participation in the theater of the world had a long pre-history rooted in the classics and the Bible. But what exactly did "theater" mean at the time Calvin was writing, and what did *he* intend it to mean?

Drama and theater in the Renaissance reflect a recovery of classical drama, on the one hand, and a development of medieval traditions deriving from the Mass and mystery plays, on the other – both provide the context in which Calvin reflected on drama. Classical ideas of theater recovered in the Renaissance owe a debt to Aristotle's classic *Poetics*, where he develops the three-part drama – *protasis*, *epitasis*, and *catastrophe* (introduction, rising tension, and denouement).[21] Although classical plays were performed – Calvin approved of a performance of Terence in Geneva, and Martin Bucer acknowledged the value of classical dramatists – classical drama was not really recovered until the second half of the sixteenth century.[22] And, furthermore, there are important theological reasons why classical sources were not definitive for Calvin.

First, when it came to theatricality, Calvin was working with wholly different premises. His debt was to biblical categories and his own humanist heritage, rather than to the classical poets. The rhetoric Calvin employed, which we will discuss at length later, was dependent on his assumption that Scripture represented a living word (*la parole vive*) especially as this is enlivened by the Holy Spirit.[23] Erich Auerbach in his classic study of Western literature has contrasted the classical notion of drama with that of the New Testament. He notes the Greek storytellers looked down from above on the drama they are portraying; the Gospel writers are at the center of what is going on. The classical drama developed inexorably toward an end no one could change; for the Gospel writers, everything related effortlessly to Christ's presence with which they were personally involved. In the Gospel of Mark, Auerbach says, "the story becomes visually concrete. And the story speaks to everybody; everybody is urged and indeed required to take sides for or against it."[24] In classical drama the high and the low had been strictly separated; in the Gospel story they are merged (p. 151). Further,

---

[21] See Aristotle, *Poetics*, trans. S. H. Butcher (Mineola, NY: Dover, 1997), sections 14–16.

[22] Ruth Blackburn, *Biblical Drama under the Tudors* (The Hague: Mouton, 1971), p. 42; Howard B. Norland, *Drama in Early Tudor Britain: 1485–1558* (Lincoln: University of Nebraska Press, 1995), p. 142. Cf. David Bevington, "Nowhere in humanist drama before 1550 do we find classical five act structure, or the unities of time, place and action." *Medieval Drama* (Boston: Houghton-Mifflin, 1975), p. 96.

[23] See Olivier Millet, *Calvin et la dynamique de la Parole: Étude de rhétorque Réformé* (Geneva: Editions Slatkine, 1992), pp. 208–211.

[24] Auerbach, *Mimesis: The Representation of Reality in Western Literature*, trans. W. R. Trask (Princeton, NJ: Princeton University Press, 1953), pp. 46, 48. Quote at p. 48. Subsequent pages noted in the text are from this source.

in a reference directly applicable to Calvin's usage, Auerbach stipulates that for the gospel writers the categories of humble and sublime are theologico-ethical categories rather than aesthetic ones as in the classical writers (p. 153). In the Gospels as in Calvin, the theological categories were determinative, while, I argue, carrying deep aesthetic implications.

But the second reason the classical theater could not serve as a source for Calvin's understanding of drama is the history of dramatic performance that he would have inherited, especially as this was mediated through the humanist tradition. This tradition worked on the viewer in decidedly different ways from classical drama. To understand this difference, one needs to recall medieval notions of drama to which I referred earlier. By the early Middle Ages classical drama had been supplanted by the rise of the medieval liturgy. O. B. Hardison concluded that "religious ritual *was* the drama of the early Middle Ages, and had been ever since the decline of the classical theatre." Already in the ninth century, he notes, the Mass "was consciously interpreted as drama."[25] Hardison, in his classic treatment of these things, ascribes the ultimate source of this dramatic sensitivity to Pope Gregory the Great, who in the early seventh century formulated what became the dominant interpretation of the Mass. I quote Gregory's description in full, not only because of its influence on the Middle Ages but also because it bears centrally on Calvin's very different understanding of drama. Gregory writes in his *Dialogues*:

> See, then, how august the Sacrifice that is offered for us, ever reproducing in itself the passion of the only begotten Son for the remission of our sins. For, who of the faithful can have any doubt that at the moment of the immolation, at the sound of the priest's voice, the heavens stand open and the choirs of angels are present at the mystery of Jesus Christ. There at the altar the lowliest is united with the most sublime, earth is joined to heaven, the visible and invisible somehow merge into one.[26]

The Mass then in the medieval period was presented as a symbolic representation and elaborate drama of the renewal of redemption through the life, death, and resurrection of Christ. That drama, symbolized by the movement of the priest and the words of the liturgy, became the focus of the attention, and the emotions, of the medieval worshiper; it is in this liturgical drama

---

[25] Hardison, *Christian Rite and Christian Drama: Essays in the Origin and Early History of Modern Drama* (Baltimore, MD: Johns Hopkins University Press, 1965), p. viii. Emphasis in original. Quote that follows at p. 65.

[26] *Saint Gregory the Great Dialogues IV*, 60, trans. Odo John Zimmerman (New York: Fathers of the Church, 1959), vol. 39, p. 273.

itself that the high is merged with the humble. As Hardison describes this: "The elevation, which unites the role of the celebrant with the symbolism of the sacrament as Corpus Christi, provided a focus for the emotions of the medieval congregation. During the elevation, the body of the Savior was visibly suspended on the cross." And as believers see the elevated host, they visually participate in the sacred drama of Christ's death and resurrection. And the visual representation of this in multiple forms, and their reception, served as the animating center of medieval devotion and its related aesthetics.

There are significant aspects of the space of this performance and its time, to which I want to call attention. First, consider the location of the drama. Initially, it was circumscribed within the space of the churches. But as early as the tenth century, representational plays began to break away from this, and cycles of saints' plays and later mystery plays were developed out of this liturgy – as in the "Mystere d'Adam" and "Resurrecion."[27] But, Hardison stresses, in these representational plays (and later in the more secularized plays), the "ritual structure characteristic of the Mass ... carries over unchanged."[28] Still, as the drama moved out from the space of the church where the Mass was performed and the players mixed in with the people while the drama was acted out before them, the ritual was on the way to becoming a public drama.[29]

The object of these saints' plays, as of the Mass, was to call observers to participate in the recurring drama of redemption as this was described in Scripture and presented in the Mass – it represented an impulse to reform. Here the significance of time that we described earlier becomes clear. The dramatic structure of the Mass and these plays reflected a view of history as a single pattern of generation and return.[30]

As this was impacted by the Franciscan focus on emotional identification and later by the humanist movement, the observer was increasingly asked to participate in the dramatic action performed. As we noted in Chapter 1, the notion of "presence" was being transformed from its location in the Mass to the congregational response solicited. Developing devotional practices,

---

[27] James H. Forse points out that development of saints' plays was associated with a desire to reform the church. "Religious Drama and Ecclesiastical Reform in the Tenth Century," *Early Theatre*, 5/2 (2002): 47–70.

[28] *Christian Rite and Christian Drama*, p. 284.

[29] Cf. Edward Muir: "The Corpus Christi feast became one of the most important occasions for the transformation of ritual into drama." *Ritual in Early Modern England* (Cambridge: Cambridge University Press, 1997), p. 69.

[30] Marilyn Adams notes that in their present fallen state participating in this presence is the "positive occasion for humans to grow in deiformity." *Some Later Theories*, p. 291.

including the rosary and later Ignatian meditation, all had as their goal the spiritual movement of the believer into the movement represented by these sacred events. As we noted, the early modern period accelerated this process of subjectification, increasingly conferring agency on the viewer, who could become an initiator of action rather than a passive observer.[31] Kent Cartwright describes this audience engagement of humanist theater as this developed in the sixteenth century:

> Humanist theatre draws spectators inside [the self-contained world it evokes] as participants, respondents, and even fellow creators who incriminate themselves emotionally or imaginatively in the illusion.[32]

This notion of participation was very different from the way audiences were asked to participate in classical theater, and, when combined with the very different view of history that was developing during the Reformation, it led Calvin to a new understanding of drama.

Calvin and Theatricality

When the Reformers suppressed the Mass and medieval plays, they were certainly not taking issue with the drama of redemption these claimed to embody.[33] What they opposed was the restriction of this story, and the ensuing drama, to the Mass, and the sacred story this reenacted. In this chapter I underline two critical differences between Calvin and medieval drama. One has to do with the location, or space, of the dramatic events, the other with what we might call the direction of the dramatic movement and the impact this had on the sense of time.

First with respect to the location of the drama: Calvin moved the spectacle beyond the liturgy and into the city of Geneva and its world, even as he transferred the dramatic performance from the priest to the congregation. As we will emphasize in Chapter 4, the preaching and the teaching of Scripture for Calvin embodied a particular rhetorical structure that constituted a summons to respond to the call of God in the Gospel. The Lord's Supper, learning the catechism, and singing the Psalms all called for

---

[31] See Viviana Comensoli et al., "Subjectivity, Theory and Early Modern Drama," *Early Theatre*, 7/2 (2004): 89. She follows here the work of Louis Montrose.

[32] Kent Cartwright, *Theatre and Humanism: English Drama in the Sixteenth Century* (Cambridge: Cambridge University Press, 1999), p. 20.

[33] Hardison claims these plays were suppressed by the Reformers (p. 290). But as we have seen, this was not uniformly true.

participation and response, and this response involved centrally their life in the world. One can claim more specifically that Calvin's language implies that the Christian life is best understood as a dramatic embodiment of the redemptive work of God. Here the Renaissance *theatrum mundi* undergoes an important amplification. Calvin's use of the term subverts the received understanding. As this literary trope developed in the Western tradition from the Stoics (like Seneca, on whom Calvin had written) to contemporary Christian Platonists (like Marsilio Ficino), the metaphor portrayed humans as the principal actors in a play directed by the divine playwright. But the dominant theme was the vanity of human life and the failure of humans to play their roles. As Belden Lane argues in his discussion of the trope, "Calvin, in contrast, conceived of the world as a theater for the contemplation of divine beauty, with *God* assuming the central role at the heart of the action on the stage."[34]

The play that God is enabling encompasses the whole world. And believers are to contemplate creation, as Calvin liked to say, in order to see there evidence of the glory of God. Consider, for example, the first appearance of "theater" in the *Institutes*. Calvin is describing the knowledge of God visible in creation and in God's governance, and the Psalmist's description of the many ways God "wonderfully and beyond all hope succors the poor and almost lost." Calvin goes on: "But because most people, immersed in their own errors, are struck blind in such a dazzling theatre, [the Psalmist] exclaims that to weigh those works of God wisely is a matter of rare and singular wisdom."[35] Already it is clear that mankind, incited by God's works, is called to play a supporting role in this drama. Kevin Vanhoozer, who has given the clearest exposition of Calvin's dramatic intentions, describes this as Calvin's theo-drama: "God and humanity are alternately actor and audience. Better, life is divine-human interactive theater, and theology involves both what God has said and done for the world and what we must say and do in grateful response."[36] The emotional and dramatic response that medieval worshipers found in the elevation of the host, Calvin finds, in the first instance, in humankind's response to the beauty of God seen in the theater of creation. Notice that in both, the aesthetic dimension – the affective response of the viewer – is emphasized. But with Calvin the end toward which that response moves has been

---

[34] Lane, *Ravished by Beauty: The Surprising Legacy of Reformed Spirituality* (New York: Oxford University Press, 2011), p. 58. Emphasis in original.

[35] Calvin, *Institutes of the Christian Religion*, I, v, 8. He is referring to Ps. 107: 42, 43.

[36] Vanhoozer, *The Drama of Doctrine*, pp. 37, 38.

reframed. Whereas delight in beauty was to move the medieval worshiper toward spiritual union with God, worshipers in Geneva were meant to be drawn to praise and obedient living in the world.

Significantly, Calvin insisted this created beauty had supplanted the need for the images and ceremonies that accompanied the medieval drama of the Mass. In his commentary on Genesis 1:6, Calvin specifically contrasts the role the images of creation play with that of man-made images and statues. He writes: "Here the Spirit of God would teach all men without exception; and therefore what Gregory declares falsely and in vain respecting statues and pictures is truly applicable to the history of the creation, namely, that it is the book of the unlearned."[37] Thus the objects described in the creation account, Calvin goes on, "serve as the garniture of that theater which he places before our eyes." And this spectacle calls everyone, as he says: "Here the Spirit of God would teach all men without exception." This created spectacle, enlivened by the Spirit, comes alive as dazzling images that move the mind and emotions to the love of God. Similarly, in the commentary on Exodus 20 Calvin notes that one should not seek God's presence in any human attempt to devise any image of God, precisely because in the created order, wherever we cast our eyes, "God's glory shines on every side, and whatever is seen above or below invites us to the true God."[38]

The created order then provides a grand aesthetic spectacle that is visible to all. Calvin goes at great length to encourage the enjoyment of the goods of creation and strongly opposes any attempt to hinder this. In the context of using the goods of this present life as encouragements to us: "If we ponder to what end God created food, we shall find that he meant not only to provide for necessity but also for delight and good cheer." In elaborating such thinking, Calvin asks: "Has the Lord clothed flowers with the great beauty that greets our eyes, the sweetness of smell that is wafted upon our nostrils, and yet will it be unlawful for our eyes to be affected by that beauty, or our sense of smell by the sweetness of that odor? What? Did he not so distinguish colors as to make some more lovely than others?" He concludes with a reference that draws attention, specifically, to the aesthetic evaluation of these things: "Did he not, in short, render many things attractive to us, apart from their necessary use?" (III, x, 2). These things are given for enjoyment, pure and simple.

---

[37] Calvin, Gen. 1:6, *Commentaries on the First Book of Moses, Genesis*, trans. John King, in loc.

[38] Ex. 20:4–6, trans. C. W. Bingham, *Commentary* in loc. Jérôme Cottin argues that Calvin believed the Decalogue did not so much forbid all images as ethically regulate their aesthetic production. *Le Regard et la Parole*, 293.

Calvin's rhetorical purposes, as I will note in Chapter 4, included his desire to awaken the listener to the joy that creation exhibits and scriptures speak of. The encounter with creation is, consistently, a visual and aesthetic experience. And in describing this, Calvin employs a vocabulary heavy with visual and aesthetic implications: "Wherever you cast your eyes, there is no spot in the universe wherein you cannot discern at least some sparks of his glory. You cannot in one glance survey this most vast and beautiful system of the universe, in its wide expanse, without being completely overwhelmed by the boundless force of its brightness" (I, v. 1). As he says earlier in that section, referring to Psalm 104:2 ("[God is] clad with light as with a garment"), this splendor is the way God dresses himself, which Calvin goes on to describe in rich and dramatic detail: "Thereafter the Lord began to show himself in the visible splendor of his apparel, ever since the creation of the universe he brought forth those insignia whereby he shows his glory to us, whenever and wherever we cast our gaze."

Though Calvin will soon draw attention to the limitations of this exposure to God's wisdom, one should not underestimate the importance of this dramatic situation – it is basic to all that will follow in Calvin's dramatic scheme.[39] Viewers of this drama are not watching merely as spectators of this theater; they are called to become participants. As I will argue in Chapter 4, the response called for is fully embodied and participatory. This is because, for Calvin, the encounter with creation's beauty and drama is an encounter with God himself. In one place, Calvin, after exulting in the beauty and goodness of creation, goes so far as to admit: "I confess . . . that it can be said reverently, provided that it proceeds from a reverent mind, that nature is God."[40]

For Calvin, the end toward which the splendor of God's presence leads is the call to join creation in praising the great goodness of God. As Belden Lane has argued, Calvin's treatment of creation consists of a sustained invitation to join in its chorus of praise. Belden Lane has explored Calvin's teaching to uncover a neglected theme of Reformed spirituality. He describes

---

[39] And as will be argued in Chapter 4, Calvin's rhetorical purposes, in both his preaching and writing, is reflected here in the particular pedagogical and participatory structure of the *Institutes*. Cf. Michelle C. Sanchez, "Ritualized Doctrine? Rethinking Protestant Bodily Practice through Attention to Genre in Calvin's *Institutio*," Journal of the American Academy of Religion, 85/3 (2017): 755, 756.

[40] *Institutes*, I, v. 5. However, his belief that the world cannot hold God leads him to immediately qualify this by pointing out that "since nature is rather the order which has been established by God, it is harmful in such weighty matters, in which special devotion is due, to involve God confusedly in the inferior course of his works."

this as "the awakening of desire for a God of ravishing beauty mirrored so generously (and flagrantly) in the world of nature."[41] Calvin's consistent call to celebrate the beauty so lavishly displayed in creation suggests, Lane thinks, "the world is sustained by worship," that is, by the continued praise and celebration of God by his people.[42] "In extolling God's glory," Lane concludes, "the praise of the faithful helps restore the earth to its original order and wholeness." In extending then the range of pious attention to the whole of creation, Calvin, at the same time, expands the practices of worship – here joining in creation's praise of the creator – out into believers' lives in the world.

Significantly, though not everyone responds to this call to join creation's praise, it is issued to everyone. As Calvin says in his commentary on Romans 1, God's call is one that the person cannot evade, since the basis for it is "engraven on his own heart" – that is, built into the structure of creation. In his comments on v. 19, Calvin goes on to argue in words that recall John of Damascus' explanation of icons: "By saying God *manifested it* he means that man was formed to be a spectator of the created world, and that he was endowed with eyes for the purpose of his being led to God himself, the Author of the world, by contemplating so magnificent an image."[43]

My argument is that the medieval language of ascent to God with its vertical focus, in Calvin, has been supplanted by the imagery of invitation with a pointedly horizontal focus, encouraging believers to participate in God's work in the created order. But Calvin's comments on Romans 1:19 also suggest this may be construed as a reframing of Guigo's ladder, and the medieval journey of ascent to God. Julie Canlis, in fact, has argued that Calvin has intentionally reformulated the medieval ladder of ascent and descent in his theology of participation.[44] In Christ, she argues, God has come to humans to stand in for us (descent), so that as a human by the Spirit, Christ can lead us back to the Father (ascent). But significantly for our

---

[41] *Ravished by Beauty*, p. 18.

[42] *Ravished by Beauty*, p. 66. In Calvin's commentaries on Ps. 104:33 and Ps. 115:17, he notes the end for which humans are created is to celebrate and praise God's goodness. Subsequent quote is from Lane, *Ravished by Beauty*, p. 67. Lane goes on to draw out the ecological significance of this call; its aesthetic significance is obvious.

[43] Romans 1:19, *Calvin's Commentary on Romans and Thessalonians*, trans. Ross MacKenzie, in loc. Emphasis in original. Randall Zachman underlines the importance of this late (1556) insistence on the role of the spectator and the potential of contemplation of so beautiful an image to lead one to God. See *Image and Word in the Theology of John Calvin*, p. 33.

[44] Canlis, *Calvin's Ladder: A Spiritual Theology of Ascent and Ascension* (Grand Rapids, MI: Eerdmans, 2010), pp. 2–5.

purposes, the created order, Canlis thinks, represents both the ground and grammar of Calvin's ascent, implying that humans are called as spectators and actors into communion with God in the context of creation as the "place of communion" – with God, each other, and with creation itself.[45] Though often we perceive the world as disordered and confused, in Christ this order has been restored. In his commentary on Ephesians, Calvin writes: "The proper state of creatures is to cleave to God. Such an *Anakephalaiosis* [Greek, gathering together] as would bring us back to regular order, the apostle tells us, has been made in Christ. Formed into one body, we are united to God, and mutually conjoined with one other."[46] The key to this, Canlis argues, is to see that creation is ordered toward this communion, as the "Spirit acts to affirm creation's particularity and freedom, even as it is shepherded toward its *telos* of Trinitarian communion."[47]

The created order then has been shaped to draw those exposed to its splendor up to God. Notice that Calvin in laying out his theological program in the *Institutes*, which he shapes to reflect the theological structure of Scripture as he understood it, begins by describing this creational setting for the divine drama as its ground and its grammar. There is something going on in and through the intricate orders of creation that not only attracts human aesthetic attention, but calls for a response. But, we soon learn, there are things that we cannot know from observing creation as it is: that God is Father, for example, or that God calls us, specially, in the work of Christ.[48] At the beginning of Book II of the *Institutes*, Calvin again celebrates the wonders of creation. Referring to Paul's reference to wisdom in Corinthians 1, Calvin says:

> This magnificent theatre of heaven and earth, crammed with innumerable miracles, Paul calls the "wisdom of God." Contemplating it, we ought in wisdom to have known God. But because we have profited so little by it, he calls us to the faith of Christ, which, because it appears foolish, the unbelievers despise. (II, vi, 1)

Calvin tells us here, early in the second section of the *Institutes*, that there is a story embedded in creation that constitutes a kind of wisdom. And while it involves everyone in its purview, its drama is often missed. Like a

---

[45] *Calvin's Ladder*, pp. 53–60.   [46] *Commentary on Ephesians* 1:10, trans. T. H. L. Parker, in loc.

[47] *Calvin's Ladder*, p. 60.

[48] Susan Schreiner notes that it is important to keep in mind here the distinction Calvin made between nature and providence. It is harder to "see" God in the latter than in the former. "For Calvin, the disorder in history obstructed the view of providence more than did the disorder in nature." *The Theater of His Glory*, p. 113.

well-wrought play, the clue that ought to provide insight has been missed by the players, and they must suffer the consequences. Notice how again sight and contemplation – directed outward toward heaven and earth – are given a special place, though, again, their limits are soon apparent. And Calvin will come to highlight the journey to God through the hearing of the word. But hearing for Calvin will complement, not undermine, the visual spectacle of creation. This dialectic between seeing and hearing, central to Calvin, is evident at the very beginning of the *Institutes*. In discussing the visions and oracles that find their "public tablets" within the Old Testament, Calvin points to the Scriptures as providing a clearer way to God than exposure to creation alone:

> Therefore, however fitting it may be for man seriously to turn his eyes to contemplate God's works, since he has been placed in this most glorious theatre to be a spectator of them, it is fitting that he prick up his ears to the Word, the better to profit. (I, vi, 2)

For Calvin the special privilege accorded to the ear derives not from any special insight that organ provides in itself but from the fact that it is by the hearing of the word, that is, by preaching and teaching of Scripture, and as this is enlivened by the Spirit, that believers are persuaded of God's mercy in Christ, and are called to become players in the story.[49] As I will argue in Chapter 4, preaching and teaching represent a dynamic set of performances that are taken up into the dramatic situation I am describing.

The possibility of seeing God in what God has made Calvin recognizes and problematizes at the same time. Calvin here expresses the Renaissance assumption that the reality of the world is available for human inspection and will reliably repay careful scrutiny.[50] This is consistent with his insistence that the images of creation have supplanted artificial images and relics as vehicles of God's presence. In his *Inventory of Relics* Calvin is at pains to show that the longing for access to spiritual reality lies behind the search for power in relics; this longing, he thinks, leads one to pay them the honor due Christ. He concludes: "A longing for relics is never free from superstition, nay,

---

[49] Cf. Clark, *Vanities of the Eye*: "As has often been remarked, the general aim of many pre-Reformation and Protestant critics of the Church … was to replace eye-service with ear-service." However, he goes on to remark that Reformers went on to develop their own extensive image repertoire (p. 161).

[50] William Bouwsma argues that Calvin inherited the traditional epistemological optimism that believed the human mind is capable of knowing what exists as it really is, that in knowing the mind is joined with the thing known, and even that sight is a special guide to knowledge (Calvin was especially taken with the order illumined by astronomy). *John Calvin*, pp. 69–72.

what is worse it is the 'parent of idolatry.'"[51] But this is not in the first instance a spiritual problem, but one that is a simple betrayal of reason. A moment's reflection would show, Calvin thinks, that relics are mostly "spurious" – as even Erasmus had recognized. Calvin concludes: Let everyone "open his eyes, and exercise his judgment upon any relic … Let everyone be on guard and not allow himself to be led along like an irrational animal." Everyone then has the ability to make sense of the wisdom that God has placed in creation; there is no need to seek the divine in these special objects.[52] As Julie Canlis observes, if the goal is communion with God in and through the created order as the "trysting place," then idolatry obstructs this possibility by adding an intervening layer of mediation, and in the process belittles God's freedom.[53]

But the critical point for our purposes is that the openness of the world to exploration parallels and supports its availability to aesthetic attention. While God invites spectators to enjoy all that is presented before his eyes, this beauty should not be an end in itself. In his most expansive discussion of the matter, Calvin notes that painting and sculpture are gifts of God. They do not provide tools by which one can ascend to God, as medieval believers thought, but they do derive from God indirectly as a gift of the creator. And since their use should contribute to our well being, Calvin goes on, "only those things are to be sculpted and painted which the eyes are capable of seeing: let not God's majesty, which is far above the perception of the eyes, be debased through unseemly representations" (*Institutes*, I, xi, 12).[54] Taken in its context, however, and with the constructive suggestions of Calvin, I would argue this stipulation represents not a limitation but an expansion of potential subjects of artistic attention. There was plenty for the eye to see in the vast theater of the world, and so

---

[51] *Inventory of Relics*, trans H. Beveridge (Edinburgh: Calvin Translation Society, 1844), p. 290. Quote that follows at p. 340. Carlos Eire comments on this tract that for Calvin "man's blind search for spiritual values in the material world caused this betrayal of values." *War against Idols*, p. 211.

[52] Calvin's horror of the superstitious recourse to relics colors his attitude toward images in general. Cottin argues that Calvin is unable to distinguish images from icons and relics: he seems unable to see them simply as "signs." *Le Regard et la Parole*, pp. 288, 289.

[53] *Calvin's Ladder*, pp. 53, 69. "Trysting place" she borrows from Iain MacKenzie.

[54] In this passage he makes clear his reservations about images of "forms of the bodies" that have so often, he notes, been of a licentious sort. Though this may give pleasure, and contain nothing evil, "it still has no value for teaching." While this is not meant to dismiss pleasure as a legitimate end, as we have noted, it does seem to disconnect this from what we would call spiritual formation.

there were multiple ways in which this could be not only enjoyed and portrayed, but turned to good use.

Though Calvin will go on to argue that believers in particular are given fresh eyes to see and enjoy these gifts, this ability is not limited to the pious. In his Commentary on Genesis 4 he notes that the invention of arts "which serve to the common use and convenience of life, is a gift of God . . . the rays of divine light have shone on unbelieving nations, for the benefit of the present life; and we see, at the present time, that the excellent gifts of the Spirit are diffused through the whole human race."[55] To deny these gifts then is a kind of offense against the Holy Spirit.

But notice it is the theological grounding that opened up this broadened canvas. In his classic description of Calvin's aesthetic Léon Wencelius underlines this theological ground. Calvin, he writes, portrays God working out in creation the harmony that exists in the Trinity by creating "an immense fresco which unfolds itself across all of time."[56] Wencelius believes this promotes an artistic endeavor that "follows nature," thus encouraging a humility that best suits the human situation before God.[57] Moreover, as Wencelius goes on to argue, such a focus on the wonders of creation, given nature's capacity to express God's glory, ensures the arts' spiritual competence. If one traces the signs of divinity that God has placed in creation, Wencelius concludes, "it is unthinkable that art not be rich in spiritual possibilities."[58]

But, on the other hand, Calvin always circumscribes – and problematizes – the call to explore the beauty of God's world, by pointing to the blindness that keeps humans from seeing what is truly there.[59] Because of Adam's sin humans are naturally unable to take in this marvelous theater, or to properly discern the wisdom that is there. The problem is not that this knowledge is unavailable, but, Calvin believed, humans are so blinded by ignorance and malice that they cannot "see" this. Humans do not "apprehend God as he offers himself," Calvin writes, "but imagine him as they have fashioned him in their own presumption" (I, iv, 1).[60] In other words, the likeness of things

---

[55] Gen. 4:20, trans. John King, *Commentary* in loc.
[56] Wencelius, *L'Esthétique de Calvin* (Paris: Société d'Edition "Les Belles Lettres," n.d. [1937]), p. 94.
[57] *L'Esthétique de Calvin*, pp. 102–111.   [58] *L'Esthétique de Calvin*, p. 106.
[59] Though Calvin uses the image of blindness (for example, in his commentary on Heb. 11:3), he prefers to say the fall has weakened the sight so that it needs the spectacles of Scripture to see more clearly (cf. commentary on I Cor. 1:18 and 13:12).
[60] Calvin here, unlike Luther, seems unable to see any positive use of imagination in reflecting God's goodness. As Jérôme Cottin points out, human inclination toward idolatry begins with the images in the mind – there lie the seeds of idolatry. *Le Regard et la Parole*, p. 291.

has been distorted by false human imagining, what Calvin calls our diminished sight. The Fall for Calvin represented an aesthetic as well as theological rupture. Note, again, the problem is not that God's glory is invisible or that human eyes are not capable of seeing this; the problem is theological, not optical. And the solution itself involves a reorientation of our sight, involving both a vision of God and a corrected apprehension of the visible world – which is a recognition of its true likeness.

The Center of Calvin's Drama

In medieval spirituality, human life is imagined as a journey toward the *visio Dei* – the beatific vision of God in heaven. Calvin reverses this medieval journey toward God by insisting that one must *begin* with a vision of God: "It is certain that man never achieves a clear knowledge of himself unless he has first looked upon God's face and then descends from contemplating him to scrutinize himself (*sui notitiam*)" (*Institutes*, I, i, 2). And in a further distinction from the medieval journey, Calvin locates the vision of God firmly within the frame of created order: "This magnificent theater of heaven and earth, crammed with innumerable miracles, Paul calls the 'wisdom of God' [I Cor. 1.2]. Contemplating it, we ought in wisdom to have known God" (*Institutes* II, vi, 1; cf. I, vi, 4).[61]

But it is critical to understand how God has worked to reorient the gaze of believers. Here we return to the dramatic character of creation. The problem is not only that human blindness impedes a proper vision, but also that a vital part of the drama is not visible by even a careful examination of the theater of creation. This portion of the drama is expounded in Book II of the *Institutes*. Randall Zachman points out that, for Calvin, humans are not able truly to behold God until they have been humbled by the preaching of Christ crucified.[62] So there is a deeper dramatic encounter that Calvin's view of theater entails, and here the location of the drama becomes more complex: for while the drama is displayed throughout the entire order of creation, it is seen more particularly within specific events where God provides a remedy for human incapacity.

For Calvin, creation, as a whole, from beginning to end, has a particular dramatic shape – something is happening in creation; it is not simply for show. And as God's work in creation continues, there are particular places

---

[61] Michelle Sanchez notes also that here Calvin, while departing from medieval precedents, reflects more closely his Stoic influence, Epictetus in particular. "Ritualized Doctrine?," p. 762.

[62] Zachman, *Image and Word*, p. 35.

where this drama becomes especially visible: one of these is God's calling of Israel, another is in the Church, but centrally it is seen in the life and work of Christ.[63] In Book II of the *Institutes* Calvin develops at length the solution that Christ provides. Humans naturally have the sense that they are unable to find their way to God without help. In fact, Calvin says, "No one can descend into himself, and seriously consider what he is without feeling God's wrath and hostility toward him. Accordingly, he must anxiously seek ways and means to appease God – and this demands a satisfaction" (II, xvi, 1).[64] For this, God provides a solution, in the savior who is Christ. Following Augustine, Calvin will develop in Book II the role Christ will play in restoring our vision of God that creation intends. In Book I of *De Doctrina Christiana* Augustine notes that the goal of a properly oriented desire is to learn to enjoy God in all things and all things in God.[65] The truth about this is found in the Word, which became flesh and lived among us. Augustine goes on: "In fact, Christ, who chose to offer himself not only as a possession for those who come to their journey's end but also as a road for those who come to the beginning of ways, chose to become flesh." Though the whole of Christ's life is important as a path for Calvin as well, the climax of his life – and of his theater – comes at the cross. As Calvin goes on to say in this same chapter, though redemption follows from the whole course of Christ's obedience, it is "peculiar and proper" to his death – and it is here that Calvin uses his most dramatic language. The cross provides a blessing through what is cursed: "as if the cross, which was full of shame, had been changed into a triumphal chariot" (II, xvi, 6), it provides a satisfaction for sin, he goes on, a laver for washing, it delivers from death, and it is an instrument of mortification of our flesh.

The cross then is the climax of the drama. For in this single event God provides a remedy for all that keeps humans from seeing God, and its dramatic quality is underlined by Calvin: high and low are overturned; through what should be ignominious, God is glorified. The clearest expression of this comes in his commentary on John (13:31), and it is worth quoting in full:

---

[63] Kevin Vanhoozer argues that the drama comprises five "acts": Creation, call and response of Israel, Christ's words and actions, Christ sending the Spirit, and the Eschaton. Cf. *The Drama of Doctrine.*

[64] Notice in contrast to the journey of the soul proposed by Bonaventure, and much like Luther, for Calvin one turns inward not to ascend to God but to discover one's dependence on grace and the satisfaction Christ offers, which comes from outside ourselves (*extra nos*).

[65] *On Christian Teaching (De Doctrina Christiana)*, trans. R. P. H. Green (New York: Oxford University Press, 1999), Bk. I, p. 79, and for what follows, p. 81.

For in the cross of Christ, as in a splendid theater, the incomparable goodness of God is set before the whole world. The glory of God shines, indeed, in all creatures on high and below, but never more brightly than in the cross, in which there was a wonderful change of things (*admirabilis rerum conversio*) – the condemnation of all men was manifested, sin blotted out, salvation restored to men; in short, the whole world has been renewed, and all things restored to order.[66]

At this central point in the drama – in this "change of things" (French, *changement des choses*), Calvin comes closest to replicating Aristotle's notion of "reversal." Aristotle describes this as "a change by which the action veers round to its opposite."[67] This reversal, Aristotle goes on to say, must be accompanied by a corresponding "recognition" that produces either pity or fear. Similarly, Calvin avers of the one contemplating Christ's intervention: "will the man not then be even more moved by all these things which so vividly portray the greatness of the calamity from which he has been rescued?" (II, xvi, 2).

Notice this dramatic moment fulfills and elaborates the glory that is visible in the created order – it is not another story, but the climax of that same drama. Note also that it is in this moment that high things and low are together made vehicles of God's glory. At the very moment of this awful death, John insists – and Calvin after him – the glory of God is seen most clearly. Calvin continues here the focus of Western Christianity on the sacrifice of Christ's death as bringing about reconciliation – he is less interested, for example, in the saving potential of the Incarnation, as in the Eastern Church. It is the cross that represents the dramatic moment. But there is an important difference from the medieval drama: the drama not only extends beyond the liturgy into the city, as in the medieval Mystery plays, but it takes up the city and its people into its dramatic scope.

What is striking to someone reading Calvin after some exposure to medieval (and Renaissance) spirituality is the absence of any focus on the narrative of the cross and the details of Christ's final hours – all the mysteries elaborated consistently in the pictorial motifs of medieval art and recalled in the accompanying devotional practices. Nowhere in the *Institutes* does Calvin make any effort to describe the actual event; entire chapters that follow describe what the cross should mean for us, that is, how it should be enacted in our lives.

Calvin in the 1539 edition of the *Institutes* added a chapter, "The Christian Life," after his discussion of sanctification, which he subsequently reprinted

---

[66] Calvin, *Gospel of John*, 13:31, trans. T. H. L. Parker, in loc.

[67] *Poetics*, trans. S. H. Butcher (Mineola, NY: Dover, 1997), section 11, p. 20. Calvin never directly cites *Poetics* in the *Institutes*.

in later editions without change.[68] The development of this in Book III, chapters 6 through 9, recalls Luther's spiritual hermeneutic: the goal of the Christian life is to "manifest in the life of believers a harmony and agreement between God's righteousness and their obedience" (III, vi, 1); this process begins with the awareness that we are not our own, but we belong wholly to God (III, vii, 1). Then, at the center of this description, and before the chapter on the meditation on the future life (III, ix), lies a long chapter on bearing the cross (III, viii, 1–11), where Calvin goes to great length to explain what the cross *means*. He begins this chapter by noting that Christ calls disciples to "take up their cross" (Matt. 16:24). He explains:

> But it behooves the godly mind to climb still higher, to the height to which Christ calls his disciples: that each must bear his own cross (Matt. 16:24). For whomever the Lord has adopted and deemed worthy of his fellowship ought to prepare themselves for a hard, toilsome, and unquiet life crammed with very many and various kinds of evil. (*Institutes*, III, viii, 1)

The cross, Calvin says, that began with Christ, is now constituted in the lives of his followers. Here in the sections that follow Calvin describes the details of this cross-shaped life in the greatest detail: since Christ suffered, we too should not expect to escape; in this way God will teach us obedience and eventually patience;[69] he will reveal to us "that in the very act of afflicting us with the cross he is providing for our salvation ... thus it is clear how necessary it is that the bitterness of the cross be tempered with spiritual joy" (III, viii, 11). In other words, Calvin says, the drama of the cross becomes visible not in the actual details of Christ's death; indeed, for those standing around, these details contrived to conceal the meaning of the event. The drama is seen rather in the theater of the creation that has now been overturned (that is made right) and in the lives of Christ's followers who are enlisted into God's redemptive spectacle.

Something of the contrast with medieval teaching can be grasped by recalling the role that the cross came to play, for example, in the life of St. Francis (d. 1226). His prayer and meditation on the life of Christ and on the cross itself led to an experience of the stigmata – the wounds of Christ appearing on his body. Caroline Bynum observes that the iconography that came to surround the event suggests that in a sense Francis's body was *becoming a cross* – "an impressing of the crucifix into Francis's hands, feet, and side." She

---

[68] François Wendel, *Calvin: The Origins and Development of His Religious Thought* (London: Collins, 1965), p. 246. Wendel notes this explanation of regeneration preceded Calvin's discussion of justification by faith, which Calvin saw as logically distinct, both of which preceded any discussion of election.

[69] This recalls Luther's description that by our *tentatio* God will make a real doctor out of us.

10 Giotto di Bordone, *Francis Receiving the Stigmata*, c. 1300, tempera on panel.
Musée du Louvre, courtesy of Art Resource, New York.

continues: "Depictions of the event utilized black or red lines to indicate the
direction of impact, as if, like rays of light focused by a lens, the wounds of
Christ actually seared themselves into Francis's flesh," as in Giotto's depiction
of the event. (Figure 10).[70] Francis's example suggests Christians literally
undergo Christ's suffering – that is, enter this timeless *historia*. Calvin, by
contrast, encourages believers to live out the cross in their lives.

Calvin here reframes the *imitatio Christi* of the medieval period. In these
chapters Calvin does reflect on the emotional struggle and penitence that

[70] *Christian Materiality*, p. 113. She is referencing here the work of Chiara Frugoni.

following Christ entails, and the suffering the believers share. But this struggle is not the same as the spiritual struggle over faith that will characterize the literary heirs of this tradition that we explore below, nor does it directly anticipate the later Pietist movement. Further, unlike the medieval journey, and unlike Luther, true penitence *follows* faith; it does not precede it. As François Wendel explains: "One must already have faith to become aware of sin to perceive the necessity of penitence."[71] Though it is a deeply personal renunciation of oneself, this is for the sake of one's devotion to God, and it finds its locus in the Christian's life in the world, not in the interior life of the believer. Faith understood in this way is rich in aesthetic implications. Olivier Millet argues it is not simply knowledge but also "a movement of the soul by which the believer appropriates salvation," wrought by the Spirit's drawing of the affections.[72]

Seventeenth-century theologians often placed their focus on the examination of the conscience as to whether one belongs properly to the elect – something that Max Weber mistakenly identified as essential to "Calvinism." In the references we have examined in the *Institutes*, there is no such call to examination.[73] The emphasis is rather on the challenge to take one's place and calling in the world in obedience to God. And significantly in these pages on the Christian life, no ascetic practices are enjoined;[74] rather, like Christ, we are to expect persistent persecution and misery in the course of our life – afflicted, stripped of goods, even banished from our homes.[75] The believer's life in the world, then, is not meant as metaphor of salvation; rather, it is its metonym: Christian living does not symbolize redeemed action and relationships, it enacts them.

In arguing that Calvin relocates the dramatic events outside the liturgy, I do not want to give the impression that the liturgy – the sacraments, the preaching and singing of praise – played no role in this drama. In fact, it plays a critical role, which I will discuss in the next chapter. I will leave to one side whether and to what extent Calvin followed the structure of the Mass in his discussion of worship. What I do want to emphasize is the central role played by preaching in Calvin's dramatic sense. Both the performance and the substance of preaching mattered to Calvin – that is both the summons and

---

[71] *Calvin*, p. 248.   [72] *Calvin et la dynamique de la Parole*, p. 212.

[73] Nor is there such a call in the specific section that deals with election in Book III, chapters 21–24. There the call to obedience is repeated, something Calvin stresses throughout. See Max Weber, *The Protestant Ethic and the Spirit of Capitalism* (New York: Scribner, 1930). Although Weber admitted Calvin was unconcerned with this, he argued that the "recognizability of the state of grace necessarily became of absolutely dominant importance" among his followers (p. 110).

[74] On the refusal of asceticism, see Wendel, *Calvin*, p. 247

[75] See III, viii, 1 and 7. In this Calvin surely reflects his own experience of exile.

the response this called for. But I think it is critical to understand precisely the role of preaching in Calvin's drama.

The purpose of Calvin's drama was to hold up a mirror to the spectator, and in this respect it would anticipate Renaissance notions of drama, as we will show in Chapter 6. As Regina Schwartz notes, "the most common Renaissance theory of drama was that it offered an image of actual life: 'the purpose of playing . . . was and is to hold as 'twere a mirror up to nature.'"[76] But it does more than this: as this drama is brought to life by the Spirit it is meant to effect the transformation in the hearer that it represents, and in this way, in the Reformers' minds, it supplants the work of the Mass. For Calvin the image of the mirror indicated ways in which God makes himself known to the person, primarily via creation and Scripture. As Cornelius van der Kooi argues, "that the various mirrors are places where God becomes perceptible in his works is something that rests on God's order";[77] that is, it is built into the structure of creation. And it is in the proclamation of the living word that the mirror of Scripture enlists believers into this drama. One such mirror is represented by the sacraments, which are critical "images" – even for Calvin a painting. The sacraments, for example, are a visible word, "for the reason that it represents God's promises as painted in a picture and sets them before our sight, portrayed graphically and in the manner of images" (IV, xiv, 6).[78]

In the light of these comments, it is surprising that Calvin's discussion of worship uniformly eschews the language of drama, theater, and aesthetics in relation to the actual event of preaching, or indeed in the administration of the sacraments, in the congregation.[79] This is not to say that Calvin did not understand these events as formative, or, as I will argue in Chapter 4, as critical rhetorical tools; they were both. Calvin famously portrays worship

---

[76] *Sacramental Poetics*, p. 43. The last phrase is quoted from *Hamlet*, III.2.21, though it ultimately derives from Cicero.

[77] Van der Kooi, *As in a Mirror: John Calvin and Karl Barth on Knowing God*, trans. Donald Mader (Leiden: Brill, 2005), p. 59. The focus on God being "perceptible" is intentional. Van der Kooi believes Calvin intends here a "direct realization of God's presence," not an abstract demonstration (p. 60).

[78] The reference to painting is more graphic in Latin, which includes the Greek: "sub aspectus *graphiki eikonikos*." The likeness to visible words Calvin gets from Augustine.

[79] Significantly, David O. Taylor, in his laudable attempt to reconceive of the space of worship as an aesthetic space, using Calvin's categories, has to employ a reverse argument from creation: "If it is true, as Calvin maintains, that human beings 'cannot open their eyes without being compelled to see' God in creation, then this reality must also . . . be true of the faithful who gather in spaces built out of the material of creation." *The Theater of God's Glory: Calvin, Creation and the Liturgical Arts* (Grand Rapids, MI: Eerdmans, 2017), p. 86. Calvin's reticence to make this move surely reflects the polemics of his situation but also his intention to reframe the direction of worship.

(and our participation in the sacrament of communion) as our being lifted by the Spirit to be joined with Christ in the heavenlies. In his comments on Psalm 138:1 he notes "believers in drawing near to God are withdrawn from the world, and rise to heaven in the enjoyment of fellowship with angels."[80] That is certainly a dramatic reality! But, no doubt with the medieval abuse of such language in mind – perhaps even Gregory's dramatic description of the Eucharist we quoted – Calvin pointedly refrains from using dramatic language when describing the performance of these liturgical acts. He does refer to Church as theater on numerous occasions, but an examination of these passages show that it is not the spectacle of the liturgy he has in mind, but the response to Christ's righteousness in the people who compose the Church – and the evidence of this in their lives in the world, what he often calls the Christian's warfare.[81] Church and worship then both have their telos in the world and the redemptive work of Christ being played out there.

Drama and Time

Calvin then refocuses the drama within the liturgy in a way that embraces those in the congregation and includes their lives in the world. But the real contrast between Calvin's sense of drama and that of the medieval Mass is made clear in a further distinctive. The drama not only extends itself out into the world where the redemptive narrative is played out, but it introduces the significance of time in the dramatic situation. We noted earlier that the central moment of the medieval drama was the elevation of the host, which united "the role of the celebrant with the symbolism of the sacrament as

---

[80] Ps. 138:1, *Commentary on the Book of the Psalms*, trans. James Anderson, in loc. This passage comes the closest to describing these events as theater. Here he calls David's public solemn assembly as "so to speak, a heavenly theatre, graced by presence of attending angels." But he will go on to stress the goodness of God that is evident in the mercy and truth of the word spiritually apprehended, over against "those outward symbols which were the means then appointed." Believers in Christ had no need of these outward symbols, and thus of that theater. For a discussion of the issues surrounding the question of the believer being joined to Christ, see Julie Canlis, "Calvin, Osiander and Participation in God," *International Journal of Systematic Theology*, 6/2 (April 2004): 169–184.

[81] Cf. *Institutes*, I, v, 11; I, viii, 30. In his commentary on the Psalms, as we saw, Calvin does use dramatic language at times of Israel's worship, but this is relegated now to the period of "shadows and figures" that the church no longer needs. See, for example, Calvin's comments on praise offered with psaltery and harp: "To sing the praises of God upon the harp and psaltery unquestionably formed part of the training of the law, and the service of God under that dispensation of shadows and figures; but they are not now used in public thanksgiving." Ps. 71: 22, trans. James Anderson, *Commentary* in loc.

Corpus Christi,"[82] in the timeless participation in Christ's redemptive work. All the focus was to draw attention to this event and the redemptive reality of which it spoke. Indeed the entire arrangement of the cathedral, as well as the structured ritual of the Mass, and even the images of the altarpieces – everything was designed to exert its centripetal pull, drawing the worshipers into the reality of this event. This focus was so pronounced that it led to the notion of ocular communion, whose effect involved simply the sight of the raised host. And the understanding of contemplation that developed from this became the basis of many medieval practices, such as praying the rosary or prayer before devotional images (which developed in the fifteenth century) and, later, the Ignatian exercises.[83]

But notice how the orientation of Calvin's drama is exactly reversed. The dramatic movement is not toward the raising of the host as a symbol of the cross, but from the substance of that "astonishing change of things" outward, into the believers' lives – who, in Calvin's dramatic language, are called to play their own role in the theater of the Church. The movement was to be centrifugal. The dramatic movement of the performance of the liturgy is a dynamic impulse that directs believers' attention outward toward their life in the world; that is where the cross is enacted. At this point, as subsequent chapters will describe, the significance of Calvin's work becomes clear for the developing aesthetic situation. And here the contrast with the medieval (and Catholic) aesthetic situation is also clarified. Erwin Panofsky has characterized this difference by distinguishing between Protestant "absorption" and Ignatian "Ecstasy" – though he does not elaborate this difference.[84] Ignatian meditation asks believers to meditate on the events of Christ's life, to identify themselves with it "ecstatically," as though they were there; Protestants instructed by Calvin are to see themselves as "absorbed" into the story of redemption that Christ's work inaugurates, being played out in the streets of Geneva. But to properly assess the possible aesthetic contribution of Calvin, one must understand the larger significance of this move, which I will explore in more detail in Chapter 4. I argue that Calvin's construal of the created order in terms of God's presence and redemptive

---

[82] Hardison, *Christian Rite and Christian Drama*, p. 65.

[83] See Edwin Muir, *Ritual in Early Modern England* (Cambridge: Cambridge University Press, 1997). The classic treatment of the rise of the devotional image in the fifteenth century is Sixten Ringbom, *Icon to Narrative: The Rise of the Dramatic Close-Up in Fifteenth-Century Devotional Painting* (Åbo: Åbo Academi, 1965).

[84] "Comments on Art and Reformation," in Craig Harbison, ed., *Symbols in Transformation: Iconographic Themes at the Time of the Reformation* (Princeton, NJ: Art Museum of Princeton University, 1969), p. 14.

work, and the emphasis on the dramatic implications of this, was an imaginative and constructive project. We have seen that medieval theologians increasingly incorporated elements of the created order, which were believed to constitute *vestiges* of God – they could be used as the ladder by which one ascends to God. But Calvin has now completely reconfigured the structure of the project of creation in the light of God's creative and redemptive purposes – these decisive events, he argues, give creation its distinctive shape and quality. And the attraction the human spectator feels toward its splendor resides in and reflects this theological structure.

The major characteristic of Calvin's spirituality then is the call to live this out in one's concrete life in the world. Elsie McKee has argued that Calvin's special spirituality of time is best seen in his liturgical creation of the day of prayer service.[85] This liturgy was modeled after the Sunday liturgy, but was called in response to the particular needs of the community. The service, complete with its own printed liturgy, reveals Calvin's rejection of holy seasons and ordinary time in favor of seeing, as McKee notes, "the ordinary present as sacred time, providential time."[86] Natural disasters or persecuting powers – motivating special times of corporate prayer – are all within God's providence, and the believers' liturgical response can be both a means to call for God's intervention and a celebration of God's activity in the concrete events of sixteenth-century Geneva.

When one reviews Calvin's teaching on devotional and liturgical practice, there is much apparent overlap with medieval practices: there is baptism, Eucharist/Lord's Supper, prayers (even kneeling and lifting of hands), special occasions for repentance, and so on. But when examined carefully there is one central difference between these practices in Calvin's mind, and this has to do centrally with the changing view of time. These practices are no longer intended to integrate believers into the timeless and eternally recurring event, as the medieval practices were meant to do. Rather, they are firmly connected to the Christian's ongoing life in the world. Prayer services, confession, and penance now are enabled to reflect and support the Christian's warfare as this unfolds in time and history.

Notice the significance of this for time. The central focus of the transformation of things, Aristotle's change of something into its opposite (*Poetics*

---

[85] See McKee, ed., *John Calvin: Writings on Pastoral Piety* (Mahway, NJ: Paulist Press, 2001), pp. 157–193, summarized in "Spirituality," in H. J. Selderhuis, ed., *The Calvin Handbook* (Grand Rapids, MI: Eerdmans, 2009), p. 470.

[86] "Spirituality," p. 470. She notes how Calvin's notion of providence, God's fatherly care for his people, by contrast to his supposed emphasis on predestination, finds consistent expression in his instructions for corporate piety.

11), was transferred from a timeless and eternal recurrence into a particular set of events in the past: the death and resurrection of Christ and the gift of the Spirit. As Calvin's preference for specific prayer services and performances of penance indicates, this opened the way for the present and ongoing time to have new and dramatic meaning.[87] The drama of God's great work in Christ has transformed the way both space and time can be understood. Rather than being absorbed into the space and time of the ritual, for Calvin the drama, while beginning in the dynamic performance of preaching and sacrament, extends itself out into the city and its particular time, where believers are enlisted as players in the drama. This difference, I have argued elsewhere, has played an important role in the development of the (very different) Protestant and Catholic imaginations.[88] The Reformers are often accused of reducing the liturgy to language and song, but if what I am saying is true, one can also argue that they expanded greatly the dramatic potential of language, with great effect not only on theology but also on subsequent literary culture – not only playwriting and poetry but also attitudes toward the book in general. Recall Victor Turner's notion of an aesthetic mirror representing a movement in time; this captures nicely what Calvin attempted. And a movement in time not only became a spiritual calling but had a clear influence on what came to be known as realistic theater. But these developments, and the controversies surrounding them, while exploiting the expanded opportunities for aesthetic attention at the same time revealed – and often embodied – underlying tensions in the tradition.

One can see already in Calvin the embryo of these tensions. There is of course the problematic that Calvin saw in the visibility of the beauty of creation. It is there for all to see, but it is invisible to many. But this, Calvin insists, is because the dramatic character of creation cannot be read off from the surface of the dazzling display that one sees in mountain and seascapes; it is embodied in the story that constitutes the essential drama of the created order: the redemptive work of Christ in the cross and resurrection. There God truly is to be seen, and in embodying this reality, in taking up the cross, the believer becomes a player in the drama. Though one might wonder how this takes concrete aesthetic shape, Calvin offers no proposals; he suggests no implications of this for actual theatrical performance.

Nor did Calvin explore the inferences that may be drawn from his understanding of the theater of creation for the painter or sculptor, nor

---

[87] These paragraphs are dependent on the discussion in Zachman, *Image and Word*, pp. 355–367.

[88] See Dyrness, *Reformed Theology and Visual Culture* (Cambridge: Cambridge University Press, 2004), passim.

indeed for image-making of any kind. Though he could claim these skills were gifts of God, such artisans were mostly out of work in Geneva.[89] What he did do was promote the changes already under way in the multiple forms and use of language, not as a simple verbal transcription of Christian theology, as is often claimed, but as a potent and living weapon in the dramatic vision of the world he was forming – that is to say, he was on the way toward developing a notion of "representation" that might exist in addition to and alongside the sinuous display of the created order. And Calvin's development of this in particular forms of language includes important implications for forming readers (and hearers) by this vision. It is to a description and appraisal of these developments that we turn in the following chapter.

---

[89] In this respect Calvin may be said to share widespread attitudes of his Renaissance environment. Books in Geneva were often illustrated with suitable imagery that often owed no debt to the Reformer, and artifacts allowed in the *Institutes* (I, 11, 12): "stories in order to remember, or figures; or medallions of animals, cities or landscapes" were those regularly admired in the Renaissance. These were all profane in that they did not represent the divine or have a goal of forming people in faith. See O. Millet, "Art and Literature," in Selderhuis, ed., *The Calvin Handbook*, p. 423.

4

CALVIN, LANGUAGE, AND LITERARY CULTURE

A T THE BEGINNING OF 1518 MARTIN LUTHER BEGAN TO wonder if anyone would take notice of the 95 Theses he had published the previous year. He decided to publish a short defense of his teaching, the *Sermon on Indulgence and Grace*. The result was a revolution in the history of printing and, in one sense, the true origin of the Protestant Reformation.[1] There were sixteen editions of the pamphlet in the first year alone, published in five different cities; Luther had broken out of the obscurity of Wittenberg. This first best seller of the Reformation marked a milestone in the history of printing, but it also signaled a new importance for an older medium: preaching. This pamphlet was after all a sermon, barely 1,500 words long, one that would have taken only eight minutes to read out loud. But it was unlike any sermon anyone had ever preached – short and to the point. And the resulting pamphlet, this first publishing success, was addressed not to the usual audience of princes and university students and professors but, incredibly, to the larger reading public that, Andrew Pettegree observes, had not yet been discovered!

In the second decade of the sixteenth century, Lucien Febvre and Henri-Jean Martin claimed that everything changed for the book. As they note: "religious issues swiftly became questions of the foremost importance and unleashed the strongest passions."[2] Commentaries on Scriptures, versions of the Bible in the vernacular, pamphlets of sermons, and posters of

---

[1] Andrew Pettegree, "Calvin and Luther as Men of the Book," in K. Spierling, ed., *Calvin and the Book*, pp. 22–23. Whether the 95 Theses were actually published is not clear. See also his *Reformation and the Culture of Persuasion* (New York: Cambridge University Press, 2005), p. 8.

[2] Febvre and Martin, *The Coming of the Book: The Impact of Printing 1450–1800*, trans. David Gerard (London: NLB, 1976), p. 288. Subsequent quote at p. 291.

various kinds proliferated after 1517. Karl Schottenloher notes that, in the hands of Luther and Calvin, these became "forms of summons."[3] They carried this urgency and appeal, I will argue, because they embodied a dramatic rhetoric best seen and embodied in Reformation preaching. In what would become the first propaganda campaign carried on in the press, Febvre and Martin tell us, "all Germany caught fire." It took the rest of that century for rising literacy rates to allow the ordinary person to profit from this campaign,[4] but these developments would prove critical to the projects of Luther and Calvin. The printing of books of course was not a new thing, but it had not yet proven the change agent that many predicted. In fact, the study of the early history of the book has shown that, initially, books served to reinforce existing social norms.[5] But this was to change with the Reformation, when books were mobilized in the service of an emerging imaginary that would challenge long-standing assumptions about the world and God's presence (or absence) there. To explore this, I ask: Wherein lay the strength behind this Reformation "summons"? And what aesthetic potential did it hold? The answer to these questions lies in the larger story that this book intends to tell. In Chapter 3, I argued that Calvin's notion of the dramatic potential of everyday life was an opening for a new aesthetic mirror. In this chapter the focus shifts to the role of language as a unique carrier of these dramatic possibilities Calvin had proposed.

The clarity needed for players in this drama is found in a particular book, and, Calvin believed, in a particular reading of that book. Calvin placed the narrative of the Scriptures in the center of the dramatic action that God is directing. Denis Crouzet emphasizes that Calvin saw his own role, as an actor in God's theatre piece that he was to play with humility and sincerity, as a man of a book. At his conversion, Crouzet says, "another system of

---

[3] Schottenloher, *Books and the Western World: A Cultural History*, trans. W. D. Boyd and I. H. Wolfe (London: McFarland, 1968), p. 287.

[4] Febvre and Martin note that these materials "scarcely circulated outside the relatively restricted circles of educated clerics and of humanists" until the 1520s. *The Coming of the Book*, p. 288. But sermons were addressed to everyone, and as Andrew Pettegree notes, before 1526, 40 percent of Luther's publications were sermons.

[5] See Jonathan Green, *Printing and Prophecy: Prognostication and Media Change 1450–1550* (Ann Arbor: University of Michigan Press, 2012). "During the first century after Gutenberg ... a print history of prophetic works [is] ... largely the story of the printing press as an agent of the status quo" (p. 69). Cf. pp. 136, 137. And Pettegree, *Reformation and the Culture of Persuasion*: "The book had been an effective servant of traditional religion before the evangelical controversies broke out, and it would be again" (p. 8).

language is inaugurated, in which the man is thought (*est pensé*) by the words of *the book*, and does not speak or act except by this *book*."[6]

Scriptures are something like the Greek chorus that addresses the audience in Greek drama or the oracle that players consult. Yet, in preaching, its effect exceeded these, because in the hands of the Holy Spirit, Calvin believed, it could accomplish what it calls for – in its deployment in the Church it is taken up into that divine human drama around which everything else is played out. In contrast to the Greek dramas, as we noted in Chapter 3, the Gospels combine the high and the low, and place the reader (and hearer) in the midst of the action – listeners in Calvin's St. Pierre are required to take a position for or against the proposals set forth.[7] And, interestingly, the book itself becomes a character in the drama. For the progress of this book, from the first English translation by William Tyndale (begun in 1521), through the Coverdale Bible (1535) and the Geneva Bible (1553) to the greatest book in the English language, the King James Version (1611), becomes itself part of the drama the Scriptures embody. Its translators and publishers, seeking to make the Bible accessible to the plowboy, were often exiled or burned at the stake. This history itself incarnates the paradoxical overturning of high and low brought about by the cross, and that resulted in Paul's aggressive overturning of hierarchical standards, his exalting of the simple over the sublime, the humble over the noble (I Cor. 1:17–21).[8]

Earlier I have challenged the simplistic opposition of word and image as a misrepresentation of what was actually happening in the Reformation. In this chapter I want to contest – or at least nuance – the related charge that the Reformation exchanged an engaged contemplation of images with a passive reception of the literal word, and seeing with hearing. Hans Urs von Balthasar's charge is typical of this default perspective. He thinks the Protestant dismissal of aesthetics includes "the expulsion of contemplation from the act of faith; the exclusion of 'seeing' from 'hearing.'"[9]

---

[6] Crouzet, *Jean Calvin: Vies parallèls*, pp. 112, 113. Emphasis in original. For Calvin's sense of being an actor in God's drama, see p. 22.

[7] Auerbach, *Mimesis: The Representation of Reality in Western Literature*, trans. W. R. Trask (Princeton, NJ: Princeton University Press, 1953), pp. 46, 48.

[8] See Robert Pogue Harrison's review of books published during the 400-year anniversary of the KJV. The language of Paul "turns the cross into an agent of contradiction. In Paul's proclamation, 'this world' is a topsy-turvy one that Christ has turned upside down." "The Book from Which Our Literature Springs," *New York Review of Books*, February 9, 2012, pp. 40–45, here at p. 41.

[9] Balthasar, *The Glory of the Lord: A Theological Aesthetics*, trans. Erasmo Leiva Merikakis (San Francisco, CA: Ignatius Press, 1982), p. 70. And see Sergiusz Michalski, *The Reformation and the Visual Arts: The Protestant Image Question in Western and Eastern Europe* (New York: Routledge, 1993), pp. 64–65, who claims Calvin turned his discussion into an "apologia for hearing."

Such dismissals are overly simplistic. This is not to say that language, printing, and literal meanings did not play an increasingly important role for the Reformers. But these emphases must be seen as developments that were already in play in the previous century, on the one hand, and as compelling expressions of the emerging dramatic imaginary that we sketched in Chapter 3, on the other.

As we have seen, both Luther and Calvin were opposed to the simple destruction and removal of all images. They opposed rather the entire medieval project with its pilgrimages, novenas, and devotional images because in their minds this had become associated with pride and self-assertion. This medieval project was, Luther believed, the human attempt to build a ladder to heaven, rather than finding God's presence among us in the preached word. Calvin believed the abuses had so muted the voice of God that there could be no compromise. For Calvin the link assumed in medieval sacramentals was severed because of the finitude of the created order (*finitum non capax infiniti*)[10] but also, and more centrally, because of the human moral inability to imagine God aright. But as I will show, both their projects gave preaching, and thus reading and writing and the attendant apparatuses of printing and publishing, a new significance, one that opened up fresh scope for creativity. But this same expansion of aesthetic possibilities introduced its own tensions – and reactions – that call for attention.

Printing and literacy were important for Calvin, as for Luther, because eventually they would allow people to read Scripture for themselves. But initially both Reformers were hesitant to expose people indiscriminately to books and reading. There were two reasons for this. First, they understood Scripture not simply as a container of doctrine but as a dynamic Word from God that by the Spirit communicated the presence of God. But, second, this meant the most appropriate medium to communicate this presence was by preaching.[11] While Luther interpreted these goals in the context of his monastic heritage, as we have seen, Calvin will reflect more clearly his humanist heritage. And this heritage and its accompanying notion of rhetoric determined how books (and printing) eventually would be deployed and evaluated.

---

[10] *Institutes*, I, 5, i.

[11] Elsie McKee notes that Calvin, to oppose Anabaptist enthusiasm, did not give individual reading of Scripture a large role in the piety of the Genevan Church, preferring rather to encourage corporate worship and exposition of Scripture. "Spirituality," in Herman J. Selderhuis, ed., *The Calvin Handbook* (Grand Rapids, MI: Eermans, 2009), p. 467.

Preaching of course was not an invention of the Reformation. Eamon Duffy points out that already in the fifteenth century "lay people were enthusiastic sermon goers."[12] Indeed, listening to sermons had been a major pastime for people since the rise of the mendicant orders in the thirteenth century. Later, town magistrates competed with one another to attract the best preachers to their cathedrals. Calvin's regular preaching through books of the Bible may have changed the content of preaching but did not drastically alter the experience. What it did was significantly alter its appeal. The difference in the Reformers' mind lay in the fact that the act of preaching was meant to enact a dramatic situation that reflected both God's presence in the congregation and the significance of this for its members' own lives in the world. And because of this focus on preaching, language came to take on a central role in the shaping of affections and eventually making possible new arenas in which aesthetic properties would be displayed. John Bossy claims that Calvin did more than anyone to explore the use of word as "art." "He wrote more eloquently than was decent for a theologian," Bossy opines.[13] In Calvin the audible word of Luther became the visible quotable text.

A focus on language as formative of a new way of imagining and relating to the world cannot of course be separated from other media of communication. But it is important to my argument that we see a particular discourse emerging in the Reformation that changed the aesthetic situation. There was something happening in language, but I argue that there was also something happening *to* language that was to issue in new opportunities for aesthetic production. Scripture in the vernacular, commentaries on the Bible, pamphlets of sermons, and polemic posters made the message of the Reformers publicly available. And this availability coincided with, and further promoted, the growing subjectification we described earlier. With rising literacy rates ordinary people could become part of the larger religious debates – they were not addressed as passive bystanders, but were called to be active participants. Brian Cummings has argued that this change played a major role in the development of literary culture. While seeking to expound the literal (true) intent of Scripture, he argues, Protestants brought about a new process of interpretation resulting in a religion not of practices but of books, one that was to push language to the breaking point.[14]

---

[12] Duffy, *Stripping of the Altars 1400–1580* (New Haven, CT: Yale University Press, 1992), p. 57.

[13] Bossy, *Christianity in the West 1400–1700* (Oxford: Oxford University Press, 1985), p. 102.

[14] *The Literary Culture of the Reformation: Grammar and Grace* (Oxford University Press, 2007), pp. 5, 6, 51. I will argue later that this claim needs to be carefully nuanced.

Throughout the sixteenth century church attendance was required in Geneva, and preaching was the dominant medium of communication. Modern readers indifferent to religious observance, for whom "preaching" has taken on negative connotations, are apt to underestimate the significance of Reformation preaching. As Robert Wuthnow has argued, during the Reformation, preaching and teaching offered the most significant free spaces for intellectual inquiry and innovation on offer at the time. His comments are particularly pertinent: "Reformation discourse tended to favor the homily, the tract, and verse by verse commentary, all of which were suited to discrete observations about contemporary events, to a greater extent than the more systematically elaborated theological tome."[15] Indeed in an oral society preaching was the primary means of mass communication, especially when one recalls that church attendance was legally required of everyone.[16]

To properly evaluate the impact of preaching, one has to recall that Scripture first had to be rendered in the vernacular German or French. And this meant challenging the dominance of the Latin Vulgate text of Scripture. This challenge for some amounted to an attack not only on the power of the Church hierarchy but on the orthodoxy of the faith itself. Consider one telling incident Cummings recounts between William Tyndale and Catholic statesman and humanist Thomas More. Between 1529 and 1532 these opponents carried on a heated exchange that focused principally on language and the vernacular of Tyndale's translation of the New Testament. In his new translation based on the Greek, Tyndale translated "ekklesia" as "congregation," and this set More's teeth on edge. Modern readers would find this an unproblematic rendering of the underlying idea into a vernacular language. But for More the Latin "ecclesia" had already a received meaning that Tyndale's translation failed to accommodate. In a lengthy exchange More inveighed against the dangers inherent in reducing the majesty of church into something as accessible as "congregation." Cummings comments:

> As a social meaning, the Gr. *ekklnsia* has been occluded by the Latin *ecclesia* and is not recoverable in English. More's problem on the other hand, is that while he can easily support his doctrinal argument by reference to the [Latin] Vulgate, in English he is groundless.[17]

---

[15] This is argued in Wuthnow, *Communities of Discourse: Ideology and Social Structure in the Reformation, the Enlightenment and European Socialism* (Cambridge, MA: Harvard University Press, 1989), p. 552.

[16] Roger Haight, *Christian Communities in History: Comparative Ecclesiologies* (New York: Continuum, 2005), p. 121. Haight calls the pulpit the "major vehicle of mass communication."

[17] *The Literary Culture of the Reformation*, p. 193. To More, Tyndale's translation made the Church appear strange!

Grammar and language, Cummings argues, lay at the heart of the disputes of the Reformation. Luther, he thinks, finds the gift of grace first in language; the 95 Theses represent a new focus on textuality that was to put an unremitting strain on language.[18]

But I argue this reflected not simply a new focus on language but also a new way for the imagination to lay hold of the world. For More the Latin of the Vulgate reflected a pre-modern metaphysic in which language was part of a larger view of a world made up of signs waiting to be properly read. One's life in the Church was ordered by specific rituals that created, sustained, and celebrated unchanging and timeless relationships – the *historia* I described in earlier chapters. Language for More (and for medieval believers more generally) was embedded in this larger theory of signification – subordinated to visual forms and practices, embodying a process of signification that rested on Augustine's theory of signs and things.[19]

Tyndale's vernacular translation of Scripture, and the flood of polemic pamphlets and posters spawned by the Reformation, embodies the earliest stages of the development of a modern understanding of language, introducing a semiology that subverted this medieval consensus.[20] Catholic philosopher Charles Taylor has this development in mind in his book *The Language Animal*.[21] He argues that language does not simply designate objects in the world, but as something that straddles the boundary between mind and body, it actually constitutes human social and embodied life.[22] This more holistic view of language, which Taylor is commending, embraces three levels of language use: verbal, enactive, and what he calls portrayals (after the German *Darstellen*, which presents rather than designates and includes forms of art and ritual).[23] But Taylor believes our Western culture has come to

---

[18] *The Literary Culture of the Reformation*, pp. 15, 51.

[19] *On Christian Teaching (De Doctrina Christiana)*, trans. R. P. H. Green (New York: Oxford University Press, 1999), Book I. There signs are to be used to move us toward the love of God, a journey he lays out in Book II. Cf. pp. 29–34. This handbook for preachers is also considered to provide a radical reorientation of classical rhetoric to more theological ends. See Peter M. Candler, Jr., *Theology, Rhetoric, Manuduction, or Reading Scripture Together on the Path to God* (Grand Rapids, MI: Eerdmans, 2006), p. 54.

[20] Cf. Cummings: "Without reference to religion, the study of early modern writing is incomprehensible." *The Literary Culture of the Reformation*, p. 6.

[21] *The Language Animal: The Full Shape of Human Linguistic Capacity* (Cambridge, MA: Harvard University Press, 2016).

[22] Cf. his conclusion where he makes this argument, pp. 332ff.

[23] He finds this view best exemplified in Hamann, Herder, and Humboldt in the nineteenth century, thus his shorthand "HHH" for this view. Taylor admits that the designative view has come to play a central role in the rise of modern science and modernism more generally – including the ability to write coded languages that are so important to the development of technology.

accept an opposing, and increasingly widespread, view of language that is primarily designative, one that sees language use as a process of naming and encoding. Interestingly, he associates the rise of this view with Hobbes, Hume, and Condillac (in his shorthand HHC) – Hobbes and Hume not incidentally resident in Calvinist-influenced eighteenth-century Britain. Though he makes no reference to the Reformation heritage as the ultimate source of this view, one could easily argue that the view of language Taylor has in mind is glimpsed in its earliest stage in Tyndale's vernacular translation.[24]

In a point relevant to my argument, Taylor argues that the designative use of language is responsible for certain "structuring metaphors" that emerged in the modern period, which, when taken alone, blind us to destructive elements in our culture. One such metaphor is that "time is a resource to be used and not wasted," "time is money." Tellingly for our purposes, Taylor sees Puritan preaching especially exemplifying this ontology of time. He notes that though there is truth to this, which has become central to capitalist civilization, "what this frame can do is occlude other ways of relating to time, devalue, them and make them disappear for many people."[25]

Though Taylor does not do so directly, others have often pointed to the Reformation period as the origin of such deviations – as the period where embodied symbols have been replaced by a quest for literal truth. The Latin that More was evoking was constitutive of the ritual and drama of the liturgy; the language that Tyndale employed was liberated from the closed matrix of signs, and was seeking a truer designation of the world God had made – one in which language was verbal and enactive, but resisted "portrayal." (Taylor points out how resistant Locke and Hume were to metaphor and symbol, as a confounding of clear speech.) There is surely a connection to be made with Taylor's important argument. But what if the Puritan notion of time reflected a broader imagination in which time has taken on new significance – a new moral seriousness allowing for a new kind of portrayal? And what if this reflected a longer-term movement toward more accurate description and assessment of the objects of the world?

---

[24] Taylor has given an important role to the Reformation in its focus on everyday life in his earlier work, *Sources of the Self* (Cambridge, MA: Harvard University Press, 1989). In *The Language Animal* he has promised a follow-up book that will trace the rise of this constitutive view to the Romantic's recovery of the pre-modern view of language that I am describing. We may expect him to describe the role of the Reformation there.

[25] *The Language Animal*, pp. 163, 164. Interestingly, for his reference to Puritan preaching he cites Max Weber.

Something was changing surely, but is it fair to see here the emergence of all that Taylor dislikes in modern language use?[26] Clearly, this set of assumptions issued in a new imaginary, a new way of comprehending the created order, and it centrally involved a new way of seeing. This new alliance of text and image appears to comport with the evolving understanding of language as primarily designative. So, it is often argued, images are not meant to be contemplated as previously; they must now be interpreted, memorized, and enacted.

But this common charge leveled against the Reformation calls for closer scrutiny. As I have argued earlier, seeing contemplation replaced by Robert Scribner's "cold gaze" is overly reductive. On the one hand, insofar as this is true, I have argued that the Reformers inherited a larger cultural tendency toward investigation and careful description. We have seen ample evidence that, in this respect, the Reformation was simply continuing the development toward a more precise rendering of nature that was characteristic of the Renaissance more generally. But does this justify the simple conclusion that the engaged contemplation of images has been replaced with a passive reception of the literal word? And is aesthetics now necessarily reduced to the literary and the verbal? In order to explore an alternative explanation, I turn to the rhetorical strategies of Calvin's preaching and teaching as proposing a richer and more engaged interaction with the world than the default charge allows.

Scripture as Living Word

Calvin was emphatic that his *Institutes* were intended to provide a structured guide for the interpretation of Scripture, and in a more particular sense, an explication of the Word of God that is to be found there. Early in Book I (in chapter 6) of the *Institutes*, when he has demonstrated the limitation of the human response to creation, Calvin introduces his discussion of Scripture as God's provision for the dimness of human vision. Throughout this discussion the focus is on what one sees and does not see, and the language is dramatic. He begins chapter 6 of Book I:

---

[26] One sees a similarly reductive reading of the Reformation in Brad Gregory, *The Unintended Reformation: How a Religious Revolution Secularized Society* (Cambridge, MA: Belknap Press of Harvard University, 2012). "Because late medieval Christianity was an institutionalized world view, the Reformation affected all domains of human life in ways that have led over the long term and unintentionally to the situation [of hyper-pluralism and moral relativism] in which European and North Americans find themselves today" (loc. 319).

That brightness which is borne in upon the eyes of all men both in the heaven and on the earth is more than enough to withdraw all support from men's ingratitude – just as God, to involve the human race in the same guilt, sets forth to all without exception his presence portrayed in his creatures. Despite this, it is needful that another and better help be added to direct us aright to the very Creator of the universe. It was not in vain, then, that he added the light of his Word by which to become known unto salvation. (I, vi, I)[27]

Calvin then illustrates our situation with his famous simile: like an aged man, who with defective sight can only dimly make out what is written in any book, when given glasses to read can see clearly, "so scripture, gathering up the otherwise confused knowledge of God in our minds, having dispersed our dullness, clearly shows us the true God" (I, vi. I). The clarity of sight needed for the manifestation of the true God to whom worship is due is owed entirely to this gift to the Church, which is Scripture.

Calvin's humanist and legal training, moreover, led him to discern a particular rhetoric within Scripture that is critical to its aesthetic potential. Ever since Augustine theologians had been aware that Scripture embodied a rhetoric that was sensible to the architecture of a text and the structure of its narrative. This rhetoric was developed further by Renaissance and Reformation scholars who made use of the categories of classical rhetoric.[28] The biblical texts, Olivier Millet has argued, "are considered as the result of a project of persuasion, employing means that can be analyzed with resources provided by classical rhetoric." But these biblical scholars believed Scriptural rhetoric went beyond classical persuasion alone, toward putting the word into practice. They proposed that Scripture uses a style that is concretely didactic; that is, images and figures are employed for the purpose of making the word accessible and vivid and to encourage an active response in the reader. Calvin in particular saw in Scripture the accommodation of God to human blindness, as part of his larger project seeking to move the heart to action. In his commentary on Ps. 143:10, for example, Calvin calls special attention to David's prayer to "teach me to do your will." Calvin sees here a particular biblical rhetoric: "We are to mark carefully his way of expressing himself, for what he asks is not simply to be taught what the will of God is,

---

[27] Note this passage was added in the final (1559) edition of the *Institutes*, one we later note incorporates Calvin's definitive structured sense of the interpretation of Scripture.

[28] See Olivier Millet, *Calvin et la dynamique de la Parole: Étude de rhétorique Réformé* (Geneva: Slatkine, 1992), pp. 195–250. Millet notes especially the role of Erasmus, Bucer, and Guillaume Budé in developing this Scriptural rhetoric. Quote that follows at p. 195.

but to be taught and brought to the observance, and doing of it." Calvin consistently highlights Scriptures' call to draw out our affections toward God – leading us by the hand, as Calvin puts it. As he goes on to say in this passage: "by the inward motions of the Spirit . . . instructing us by his word, enlightening our minds by the Spirit and engraving instruction upon our hearts, so as to bring us to observe it with a true and cordial consent."[29]

In this respect, Calvin, following the earlier Renaissance scholars, saw that Scripture reflected and transcended classical categories. Adapting Cicero's three offices of the orator, Calvin saw in Scripture the ability to (1) teach and reason via the letter of the text (*docere*); (2) win over and persuade the reader (*conciliare*); and (3) move and bend the hearer by the attraction of the Holy Spirit to a new place (*movere*).[30] In the process Calvin will demonstrate that the horizontal reading of Scriptural texts, with their unique figures and vehemence, opens the way to the emergence of a new Protestant aesthetic.

Calvin famously avoided an allegorical reading of Scripture and any emphasis on its decorative ornaments.[31] In this he felt he was responding to God's intention of accommodating divine majesty to the dullness of human capacity. In his preaching and writing, Millet argues, the Reformer sought to accurately reflect what he saw as a "biblical eloquence," one that pursued both decorum and emotional impact. The unique rhetoric of preaching that Calvin would employ reflected the rhetorical structure of Scripture itself, as Calvin understood this. Throughout his commentaries, which were first given as sermons, Calvin highlights Scripture's rhetoric of excess, what he frequently calls its "vehemence." In accommodating to the limitations of human capacity, Calvin believed Scripture used irony and hyperbole, as well as pictures and personification, to amplify the exhortative character of the text. As Millet notes, these were employed "not as an ornament for the ear or imagination, but as a process that participates in the development of an argument and its psychological intention."[32] Consider Calvin's use of imagery in Matthew 2:18 (where he cites Jer. 31:15 "a voice was heard in Ramah" mourning the destruction of the tribe of Benjamin). Calvin describes the special role played by this imagery:

---

[29] Ps. 143:10, trans. James Anderson, *Commentary* in loc.

[30] Millet claims Calvin was clearly conscious of his debt to this threefold office. *Calvin et la dynamique de la Parole*, p. 223.

[31] Millet, *Calvin et la dynamique de la Parole*, pp. 292–349. Millet notes that with the 1539 and 1541 editions of the *Institutes* Calvin intentionally began to introduce similitudes, or figures of speech, to support his strategy.

[32] *Calvin et la dynamique de la Parole*, p. 318.

> That [Jeremiah] attributes the grief to the dead Rachel is a personification (*prosopoia*) to increase the sensation of emotion. Not that Jeremiah painted in rhetorical colors merely for the sake of decorating his speech, but because otherwise the hardness and apathy of the living could not be corrected, if somehow the dead were not recalled from their tombs, to mourn over the chastisement of God.[33]

Scripture, Calvin recognized, is filled with narrative and imagery, but its purpose, the exegete insisted, was not simply for decoration but for energy of tone. And it was carefully marshalled to shock listeners – to prick the conscience of hypocrites. It often comprised a literal "cry," either of the human sufferer, as in the Psalms, or, especially in the case of Hosea and Jeremiah, of God himself.[34]

Notice that Calvin's assumption is based on a particular view of what language was capable of doing. While appreciative of the orator's role as this was defined in classical rhetoric, he felt this did not properly account for the inherent limitations of language. The language of Scripture employs figure and emphasis (hyperbole, irony, simplicity, vehemence of tone) for a particular reason: these linguistic elements are stylistic signs that the passage in question is evoking realities that ordinary language is incapable of expressing. The figures of Scripture are meant to give concrete form and awaken conscience to a situation that transcends ordinary human experience, one that ordinary discourse is powerless to evoke. Scripture's particular use of language, in all its rich variety, Calvin believed, embodied the only efficacious language possible in the desperate situation in which humans find themselves.[35]

The nature of this situation, in Calvin's mind, was the characteristic blindness that keeps humans from recognizing their true status before God. Human language was limited not because of its inherent inability to express the ineffable but because of the human tendency to distort and resist God's approaches. As a result, the figures and images that Calvin employs play an entirely different role than poetic imagery in the medieval period. Consider Dante's frequent complaint of the limitations of language in his *Paradiso* (1308–1315). As he confesses to Beatrice in Canto I: "How speak of trans-human (*transumanar*) change to human sense? / Let the example speak until

---

[33] Matt. 2:18, trans. A. W. Morrison, *Commentary on a Harmony of the Gospels*, in loc.

[34] Millet refers to this as a grand style that does not comply with traditional notions of the sublime – less a style, he thinks, than sensitivity to a particular human and divine situation. *Calvin et la dynamique de la Parole*, pp. 327–328 and 349.

[35] *Calvin et la dynamique de la Parole*, pp. 351, 355.

God's grace / grants the pure spirit the experience."[36] Language cannot grasp the ineffable spectacle that Dante will experience in the beatific vision. As a result, Dante's rhetoric in this final canticle consciously subverts the literal description. As Peter Hawkins describes this, Dante's *Paradiso* has to "write itself out of existence." As Hawkins explains, Dante's rhetoric in this canticle subverts the literal: "Words about the ineffable sabotage their own literal meaning in order to draw attention to what cannot be spelled out in letters at all, but can only be attended to and longed for."[37] The experience that grace extends literally cannot be expressed in words. By contrast for Calvin the limitation of language relates primarily not to the inherent limitation of language but to the desperate situation of enmity humans find themselves in before God. For example, in his commentary on I Cor. 13:9, where Paul acknowledges that we know in part, the exegete notes that our partial knowledge "is owing to our imperfection." In I John 3:2 when John promises that when Christ appears we will see him as he is, Calvin avers that at present "we find always a hell within us," but at his appearing we will experience Christ as friend and not as judge. In I Cor. 2:9, 10 when Paul quotes Is. 64:4 about what humans are capable of seeing and understanding, Calvin immediately moves to the blindness to which human are subject (*Commentary* in loc.). The literal meaning, for Calvin, is enhanced rather than undermined by his figures, so that the dramatic intent of Scriptural rhetoric may be fully comprehended.

Millet highlights a further aspect of Calvin's use of especially the Old Testament (OT) that extends its aesthetic canvas. Part of Calvin's resistance to allegorizing OT passages, which are seen primarily as anticipations of Christ and the Church, involved his belief that the OT was not simply types and shadows of a future reality but a substantial body of "living pictures" of the lives of believers. That is, Calvin, consistent with the centrifugal impulse that we described in Chapter 3, undertakes a "horizontal reading" of the OT. For this exegete the Hebrew Scriptures constitute a true image of the life of believers living before the face of God. Addressed to the eyes of faith these images are not simply shadows but shocking counterweights to the vain spectacle of the world.[38] Calvin describes this treatment of OT examples in some detail in his commentary on I Cor. 10:11. Paul describes

---

[36] Dante Alighieri, *The Paradiso*, trans. John Ciardi. (New York: Signet/New American Library, 1961), I: 70–72.

[37] Hawkins, *Dante's Testaments: Essays in Scriptural Imagination* (Stanford, CA: Stanford University Press, 1999), quotes at pp. 223 and 216, respectively.

[38] *Calvin et la dynamique de la Parole*, pp. 369, 375. "Horizontal reading" is his term. See p. 289.

there the judgment of God on the sins of Israel, Calvin writes, "that they might be types to us – that is, examples, in which God places his judgment before our eyes ... that by these examples, like so many pictures, we are instructed what judgments of God are impending ... For they are lively pictures, representing God as angry on account of such sins."[39]

Now Scripture's impact, its energy, as we have seen, is made possible for Calvin by the attraction of the Holy Spirit; its narrative directs us to Christ, who enables the believer to properly see what God has done in creation. The description of this process Calvin developed at length in Book II of the *Institutes*. He clarifies the role played by this living word of Scripture, and its connection by the Spirit to Christ, in his extensive treatment of II Tim. 3:15–17. Timothy had been instructed from his infancy in Scripture, and this "strongly fortified [him] against every kind of deception." This is because Scriptures, as Paul's Letter to Timothy says, "direct us to the faith of Christ as the design, and therefore the sum of the Scriptures." The commentary goes on to affirm Scripture on account of its authority and also because of its utility, leading Calvin to assert, "absolutely, that the Scripture is sufficient for perfection."[40] Scriptures, in the hands of the Spirit, do the believers good, directing them to faith in Christ and thus fitting them to play their role in the theater of creation.

Kevin Vanhoozer describes Scripture as a kind of script for the theo-drama that God directs, calling it the Christian's "fiduciary framework."[41] This latter comment is helpful because in a sense it is not the script of the drama; rather, it is, as Vanhoozer also notes, theatrical directions and a description of the previous (and foundational) acts of the drama. It pointedly contains no lines for contemporary believers to read; rather, it proposes a drama that continues and that contemporary believers, in their place and time, are called to play out.

So the drama Calvin evoked includes a book that encapsulates the substance of this drama. When read, heard, tasted, contemplated, or memorized, Scriptures become light and life. Here Calvin vividly seeks a particular kind of reader, one who reflects and enhances his humanist training. As Anthony Grafton notes, scholastic readers often lived in a *hortus conclusus* – often

---

[39] *Commentary* in loc. Interestingly, Calvin goes on at some length to show how this also serves to discourage those who see the OT as only prefiguring the church rather than already embodying its reality. As he goes on to say, the Old Testament people are a "figure of the Christian Church" in such a way as to be at the same time "a true Church."

[40] II Tim. 3:15–17, trans. John King, *Commentaries on the Epistles to Timothy, Titus and Philemon*, in loc.

[41] *The Drama of Doctrine*, p. 259.

literally within cloistered spaces. Their texts similarly resided in a closed tradition of interpretation. But for humanists, Grafton thinks, books were to be treasured, copied out, even memorized – they were to be opened up. To that end readers added commentaries and glosses; books were to be chewed on and put to use.[42] Most importantly, they were to be deployed in what was still largely an oral rhetoric. Calvin developed these humanist notions in the service of his particular rhetoric of preaching and teaching.

Scripture as Preached Word

Scriptures could not do any of these things merely as a book; they needed to be set before people, the Reformers believed, in the act of preaching and the allied practices of teaching. The performance of preaching, for both Luther and Calvin, was the central ritual of corporate worship. But for Calvin in particular the way the language of Scripture was arrayed became critical to its impact on the senses and, eventually, to the expanding aesthetic options that artists and writers would later explore.

For Calvin (as for Luther) the focus of the space of the church came to rest on preaching – it was there Calvin believed that one could really see and hear God. Like Luther, Calvin stressed the external character of the preached word as the privileged vehicle of the divine presence. In the first chapter of Book IV, "On the Holy Catholic Church," he describes the external helps that God uses to bring people to faith, insisting that "The power to save rests with God [Rom. 1:16]; but . . . he displays and unfolds it in the preaching of the gospel" (IV, 1, 5).

But, notice, with its dramatic impact, accompanied and enhanced by the corporate prayers and singing of the Psalms, preaching was also an aesthetic event even if Calvin was hesitant to call attention to this fact.[43] And this configuration gave to language a new importance in corporate worship. Regina Schwartz has argued that while the Reformers opposed the reenactment of Christ's death in the liturgy, they came to believe that language – first in preaching, and later in Reformation poetry, could "carry the mystical force of sacramental re-enactment."[44] But the power of this reenactment

---

[42] "The Humanist as Reader," in Guglielmo Cavallo and Roger Chartier, eds., *A History of Reading in the West* (Amherst: University of Massachusetts, 1995), pp. 182, 197–204.

[43] Though later in VI, iv, 5, he could reference the earthly means of preaching, "as if to bear us up in chariots to his heavenly glory, a glory that fills all things."

[44] *Sacramental Poetics at the Dawn of Secularism: When God Left the World* (Stanford, CA: Stanford University Press, 2008), p. 120. Schwartz emphasizes here Calvin's focus on the sacraments as "acts."

was, in the first place, made manifest in the act of preaching. Calvin of course saw the Eucharist as a sign and seal of this preached word, and further as an *act* of God who alone can cause "such great mysteries of God to be concealed under such humble things" (IV, 19, 2). But it is primarily in the act of preaching that these mysteries and the summons they entailed were made clear, and to which the worshiper was meant to respond in faith. Here the corporate singing of psalms becomes a critical element in the drama, where the congregation together participates emotionally in the ritual of worship, something we will return to later.

Preaching and teaching of course did much to promote the importance of printing. But it is easy, in hindsight, to overemphasize the importance of printing during the Reformation. We need to remember that early modern culture was still, overwhelmingly, an oral culture. Initially, at least, print materials were incorporated into the dominant oral practices in play in late medieval culture – as the instance of Luther's pamphlet discussed at the beginning of this chapter illustrates.[45] Though the Reformation would eventually make the Bible available to a lay audience, this did not happen all at once. As I noted, both Calvin and Luther were initially hesitant to allow untutored access to Scripture. Calvin famously said that Scripture has a "thick crust" and should be given in small bites; Luther actually lamented that his works were being distributed so widely, wishing instead for more "living books," that is, preachers.

Preaching and teaching were still the privileged medium of providing access to God. Preaching, Calvin believed, is animated; it becomes attractive by means of the Holy Spirit who is present and active when the word is preached. Here is how he framed this:

> In the preaching of the word, the external minister holds forth the vocal word and it is received by the ears. The internal minister the Holy Spirit truly communicates the thing proclaimed through the word that is Christ to the souls of all who will, so that it is not necessary that Christ or for that matter his word be received through the organs of the body, but the Holy Spirit effects this union by his secret virtue, by creating faith in us by which he makes us living members of Christ.[46]

Though Calvin appears to belittle the human reception of this – it is not received through the organs of the body – it is still in the performance of preaching, as this is seen and heard, that this is accomplished.

---

[45] See for what follows Jean-François Gilmont, "Protestant Reformations and Reading," in Cavallo and Chartier, eds., *A History of Reading in the West*, pp. 213–237. As Gilmont notes: "Speech retained its primacy" (p. 224).

[46] Calvin, *Theological Treatises*, ed. J. K. S. Reid (London: SCM Press, 1953), p. 173.

What is the significance of this? Language has now become the privileged vehicle of spiritual mediation, supplanting the many sacramentals allowed by the medieval church.[47] But notice the focus is on language in a particular oral, visual, and dramatic setting. In preaching, the real presence of Christ, and the summons of this presence, was set forth. But here is what I want to underline: this performance, with its dramatic impact accompanied and enhanced by the corporate prayers and singing of the Psalms, was also an aesthetic and dramatic event. And what gave it this dramatic and aesthetic effect was the particular notion of rhetoric that Calvin employed.

Preaching and Performance

One danger in having recourse only to written (and subsequently published) sermons is that we forget they were originally intended to be experienced in a live worship service; they were first performed before they were recorded.[48] Consider again Calvin's expressed purposes in his teaching and preaching. His goal in his preaching as in his writing was the same: to move the heart to piety. Calvin, we have stressed, was deeply schooled in the humanist methods of Latin oratory, and the goal of its rhetoric to move in order to persuade. As we have seen, he adopted and adapted Cicero's threefold office of the orator. But along with the other Reformation scholars, he also adopted Augustine's adaptation of classical rhetoric to the goal of bringing hearers to the love of God. In this understanding of rhetoric, as Peter Candler notes, "words are not taken simply to name objects, but they point to the ends towards which they are ordered,"[49] that is, to move hearers along their journey to God.

We have described the way Calvin understood his *Institutes* as a guide to the proper understanding and ordering of Scripture. Thus in reflecting the rhetoric of Scripture itself, which we have briefly reviewed, the *Institutes* are structured to promote Calvin's larger rhetorical goals. One should not read the *Institutes* through the modern lens of a collection of theological beliefs. Recently, scholars have described in various ways how Calvin's rhetorical

---

[47] This is not to say the Eucharist did not mediate God's presence in some way, but for both Calvin and Luther this had to be accompanied by the promise of the Word.

[48] In fact, for this reason Calvin at first hesitated to publish his sermons. Gilmont, "Protestant Reformations and Reading," p. 235. Andrew Pettegree discusses the possible slippage of making published sermons our primary source as they were often edited for publication. *Reformation and the Culture of Persuasion*, pp. 11, 12.

[49] *Theology, Rhetoric, Manuduction*, p. 54. He makes use here of the work of Richard McKeon.

purposes are reflected in the very structure and order of the *Institutes*. Brian Cummings notes Calvin's conviction that the Bible constituted God's communication (cf. French, *accommodation*) to humans, and the purpose of the *Institutes* was to order the images of Scripture into *loci*, multiple words (even in multiple languages) directing the attention to a common word (*parole*), with a single meaning (*sensus*).[50] Catherine Randall has pointed to the way the *Institutes* provides an architectural treatment of theology that lays out a template for the ordering of the Church.[51]

An even more radical proposal for Calvin's structure of the *Institutes* is offered by Michelle C. Sanchez.[52] She proposes that the 1559 edition of the *Institutes* shows affinities to both the *enchiridion* (handbook) and *itinerarium* (pilgrimage guide), issuing in a kind of text that "in its written disposition, gives itself to be fully engaged and inhabited by an embodied reader in a concrete spatio-temporal location" (p. 747). Making use of what Peter Candler calls a "grammar of participation," she argues that the final (1559) structure of the *Institutes* embodies a proposed "itinerary" in which "candidates in sacred theology"[53] are meant to grasp the text's meaning holistically through participation in the proposed sequence (p. 765). This was laid out to Calvin's satisfaction by means of the four books of the final edition: through knowledge of the Creator (Book I), one moves to the knowledge of God the redeemer in Christ (Book II), by appropriating particular modes of obtaining this grace and its benefits (Book III), to the external helps offered by God in drawing us and keeping us in fellowship with Christ (Book IV) (pp. 755, 756).[54]

---

[50] *The Literary Culture of the Reformation*, p. 246. Cummings thinks Calvin's *Institutio* references Quintilian's *Institutio Oratorio*.

[51] Randall, *Building Codes: The Aesthetics of Calvinism in Early Modern Europe* (Philadelphia: University of Pennsylvania Press, 1999), pp. 26, 27.

[52] Michelle C. Sanchez, "Ritualized Doctrine? Rethinking Protestant Bodily Practice through Attention to Genre in Calvin's *Institutes*," *Journal of the American Academy of Religion*, 85/3 (2017): 746–774. Pages cited in the text are to this work.

[53] Calvin stipulates this primary audience in his note to the reader, *Institutes* (1960), p. 4. Calvin notes there also his complete satisfaction with this final arrangement reached in this 1559 edition (which was then translated into French in 1560).

[54] Sanchez notes these follow quite accurately theological *itineraria* described in Candler, though changing Candler's order. See Peter M. Candler, Jr., *Theology, Rhetoric and Manuduction*, pp. 5–7: one follows a route (*ductus*) heeding the specific guidance offered by the text, one that invokes the presence of a *traditio*, that moves the reader toward a particular aim (*scopus*). There is an irony in Sanchez's appropriation of his grammar of participation since Candler's book argues, in a way that recalls Taylor's view of language, that the sixteenth century (including Calvin) inaugurates the grammar of representation when books are simply read and interpreted, not embodied.

The ordering itself then moves readers toward the end (*scopus*), for which the work was undertaken. We have called attention already to Calvin's art of language and imagery, but it is important to hold in mind Calvin's larger formational goal. As Wayne Boulton has argued, Calvin's use of language, indeed the whole structure of his teaching, is ordered toward his rhetorical purpose: to move the heart in order to persuade. Boulton focuses in particular on the figurative language that Calvin frequently used, but applies his case more broadly.[55] Calvin, for example, liked to refer to God as "our enemy." In order to see God's mercy, Calvin writes, "we must see . . . how it can be said that God, who prevents us with his mercy, was our enemy until he was reconciled to us by Christ" (*Institutes*, II, 16, 2). Here Calvin meant to convey the boundless character of God's mercy, but this called for hyperbole. This mercy was so extraordinary that it called for a reading enhanced by expressive figures. These images, Boulton argues, cannot simply be "translated"; they must be experienced. So, Boulton argues, the figure – God is our enemy – is meant not simply to describe our lostness but to do something more visceral, more embodied, to move the believer toward *pietas*. The many images Calvin employs are all external aids – accommodation – to our blindness and intransigence, and to our limited capacities (*ad sensum nostrum*), and they are often achieved by a shock of contradiction. After quoting several passages in which sinners under a curse were reconciled by Christ, Calvin goes on to say: "Expressions of this sort have been accommodated to our capacity that we may better understand how miserable and ruinous our condition is apart from Christ." These formational purposes are woven throughout his teaching and preaching, so that, Boulton, argues, the best translation of *Institutes* is "deeply formative education."[56] One might say that Calvin's purpose involved creating a charged field that was meant to form believers, something Boulton describes as "A sphere in which by the Spirit's rhetorical engagement, disciples are cultivated, dispositionally and spiritually, into human beings fully alive and fittingly grateful." Boulton notes, however, one must have an ear for this music, just as in Orthodoxy one needs an eye for the icon.

Bouton's argument recalls the earlier treatment of Calvin's rhetoric by Olivier Millet, which we have reviewed. Millet goes further than Boulton in underlining the dramatic potential of this rhetoric but also in pointing out its

---

[55] "'Ever more deeply moved': Calvin on the Rhetorical, Formational Function of Scripture," in Karen Spierling, ed., *Calvin and the Book* (Gottingen: Vandenhoeck and Ruprecht, 2015), pp. 136–145.
[56] "Ever more deeply moved," p. 143. Quote that follows is at p. 145.

limitations. Millet notes Calvin's frequent use of pictures (*tableaux*) in his commentaries. In I Cor. 4:11, for example, Calvin notes how Paul portrays his condition in a picture ("we are poorly clothed and beaten and homeless"). Calvin notes: "Here the Apostle paints a vivid picture of his own circumstances, so that the Corinthians may learn from his example to give up their high-mindedness, and, submissive in heart, embrace the cross of Christ, along with him."[57] In Ps. 81:8 the Psalmist puts the reader into the scene where God speaks: "Hear, O my People, while I admonish you; O Israel if you would but listen to me." Millet notes that Calvin here wishes to transport the reader (or hearer) into a theater, whether the scene is historical or fictive.[58] As Calvin notes in his commentary on Is. 15:5: "It is customary with the prophet, however, to assume in this manner, the character of those whose conditions they foretell, and thus to exhibit their condition as it were on a stage."[59] This also, Millet notes, was surely meant to promote the role of the listener in the sacred drama.[60]

To see language as designative, or reduce human sight (or insight) to a cold, or intellectual, gaze does not do justice to these larger purposes of Calvin's use of language. The Reformer's focus on rhetoric and performance implies a participatory grammar and not merely a representational one. Further, Calvin sets the performance of worship within a congregational setting. He clearly sought to involve the whole congregation in worship as participants and not simply as spectators.

Something similar can be argued for Martin Luther, as we saw in Chapter 2. Though Luther was more favorably disposed toward religious images than Calvin, an openness that increased over his ministry, he is famously accused of moving images away from their contemplative function toward a more didactic and illustrative role. We recall that Joseph Koerner believes Luther's influence led his good friend Lucas Cranach to make his images into "confessional statements" rather than embodying the visceral sense of presence of, say, Hans Holbein.[61] But this common assumption has been challenged. Jérôme Cottin has argued that though Luther was opposed to the abuse associated with the late medieval *Andachtsbild*, or devotional image,

---

[57] I Cor. 4:11, trans. John Fraser, *Commentary* in loc.   [58] *Calvin et la dynamique de la Parole*, p. 362.

[59] Is. 15:5, trans. William Pringle, *Commentary* in loc. French, "on a stage": *comme sur un theatre*.

[60] *Calvin et la dynamique de la Parole*, pp. 365–366. Millet notes comparison with the theater was a staple of classical rhetoric and a permanent reference in Calvin's sensibility and culture.

[61] "Confessional Portraits," in Mark Roskill and John Oliver Hand, eds., *Hans Holbein: Paintings, Prints and Reception* (Washington, DC, and New Haven, CT: National Gallery and Yale University Press, 2001), p. 126. Quote that follows is at p. 130.

he was not against their devotional use in the service of the word.[62] Cottin admits (following Belting) that we see in Luther the emergence of a modern understanding of images that privileged their didactic function, but within this new semiological system defined by the word (*parole*) they could play a richly symbolic and even devotional function.[63] For Luther, Cottin argues, only the word and sacrament have a direct link to God, so the image can only be a sign of the gift of grace that is given in the word. But in this new theological framework it carries much of the resonance associated with medieval contemplation – Luther's own background as a monk was not lost. The key to understanding the continuing devotional function of imagery, as we argued earlier, lies in Luther's reinterpretation of medieval *lectio divina*, which he reinterprets in terms of *oratio*, *meditatio*, and *tentatio*. In this devotional itinerary (*ductus*) one seeks the comfort of God by a life of prayer, then one constantly meditates on the promise of God offered in the preached word, and finally one achieves understanding only when this is challenged through suffering of various kinds. As with Calvin, although there is movement toward modern designative language, there is still a critical role for the symbolic and imaginative.

Though Calvin can hold out this role for language, the use of actual images is still problematic. Millet notes that Calvin hesitates to develop biblical imagery, especially the parables, in any detail. "This betrays," he thinks, "a certain indifference to the art of visual representation on the part of the exegete, even if this discretion serves, again, to challenge allegorical readings which transform the details into so many symbols. Neither artistic nor symbolic, the biblical description seeks to move by quick visual suggestions and the exemplars it accumulates."[64] The images of creation display God's glory, indicating that beauty for Calvin has primarily a theological reference. Beauty is necessarily a work of God, not a human construction. It is present in creation to draw viewers toward the praise of God; but it is also present in the living images of corporate worship – the preaching, singing of hymns, and, above all, in the "visible words" of the sacraments. The language of worship and its allied practices suggest a different representational strategy than the one pursued by the medieval church. As Calvin says, quoting Augustine, the sacrament "represents God's promises as painted

---

[62] Jérôme Cottin, *Le Regard et le Parole: Une Théologie protestante de l'image* (Génève: Labor et Fides, 1994), p. 263. And see Matthew Rosebrock, "The Highest Art: Luther's Visual Theology in Oratio, Meditatio and Tentatio" (PhD dissertation, Fuller Theological Seminary, 2016).

[63] *Le Regard et le Parole*, p. 272. For what follows, see pp. 276–283. Cf. Hans Belting, *From Image to Art*.

[64] *Calvin et la dynamique de la Parole*, p. 368.

in a picture and sets them before our sight, portrayed graphically and in the manner of images."[65] But here too the power resides in the narrative enlivened by the Spirit's presence that structures the created order.

Outside these special places, human efforts to create beauty are bound to fall short. Millet thinks this offers the major challenge to a Christian aesthetic defined in these terms: How does one represent the visual and embodied elements of this economy of revelation, which in the nature of the case transcend human experience?[66] The single exception, Calvin allowed, lies in the potential of human language to carry a surplus of meaning, especially in preaching, and later in the singing of the congregation. For both Calvin and Luther, the point of language is its expressive power, as this is employed by the working of the Holy Spirit. Language now is constituted as a summons; preaching takes on a performative dimension. Language makes something happen. This allows for a new aesthetic situation to emerge that resides not in language or images alone but in the interaction of these and other factors. What was previously a sacred space, sanctified both by priestly dedication and by the presence of sacred objects – relics and altarpieces – was now a space animated by the call of God in the sermon, one in which the congregation becomes participants rather than observers. Calvin understood his entire vocation in this participatory way. As he writes, citing Augustine, at the end of his note to the reader in the *Institutes*: "I count myself one of the number of those who write as they learn and learn as they write."[67]

Still, to fully appreciate Calvin's contribution we need to locate his rhetorical purposes within the larger framework of the Christian's life in the world – as we noted in Chapter 3, his invitation toward a vision of God was located firmly within the framework of creation. For it was there that the entanglement of images, meaning, and desire was to be played out in the believers' lives. This issued in a new understanding of drama that emerged during this period, which we described and that deeply influenced the Protestant aesthetic. Building on Boulton and Millet's claim about the rhetorical structure not only of Calvin's preaching but of his *Institutes*, we might put matters this way: Calvin intended in his preaching and theology to project a world embodied in the narrative of creation and redemption, as mediated by Christ and the Spirit, as a world in which worshipers were called to account. But, as I pointed out in Chapter 3,

---

[65] *Institutes*, IV, 14, 6. As noted earlier, in Latin the graphic character is even more pronounced: *sub aspectus graphikē eikonikos.*

[66] *Calvin et la dynamique de la Parole*, p. 369.

[67] He is quoting from Augustine's *Letters*, 143, 2, in Calvin, *Institutes* (1960), p. 5.

though this opens up the way to think about aesthetic practices in a new way and will clearly have influence on subsequent generations, it does not directly reference any particular artifact – with one exception. There is one place one can point to where specific aesthetic artifacts are important to Calvin: the place and role of music, what one might call the musical poetics of language, in the Genevan experience of worship.

Music and Performance

There is a certain irony in Calvin's disinterest in the aesthetics of worship and his refusal to explore its potential in the way he did so expansively in his description of creation.[68] For the one place Calvin dealt extensively with what could be called art objects was in his exploration of the Psalms, and his promotion of singing the Psalms in congregational worship. The Psalms after all are instances of biblical poetry, and Calvin early in his career became enchanted with these Hebrew verses. In fact, I would argue that Calvin's love affair with the Psalms constituted his own aesthetic schooling, a process that eventually moved him to make them an important part of public worship. Though he did not publish his commentary on the Psalms until 1557 (in Latin; 1563 in French), he notes in the "Author's Preface" that he had "familiarly taught them" in his own household for a long time, and now, at the urging of many friends and colleagues, he finally allowed them to be published.[69] This preface itself offers precious insight into Calvin's own personal life in a way that is to be found in no other place. He calls this Hebrew poetry the "anatomy of all parts of the soul," wherein every emotion is brought to life by the Holy Spirit, and all our maladies (and their remedies) are laid out. All of this, he goes on, serves to teach us the true method of laying ourselves open to God in prayer. In this preface Calvin comes the closest to laying out the steps in the spiritual journey that he sought to embody in the structure of the *Institutes*. And it is, interestingly, in this preface where Calvin opens up for the reader his own pilgrimage that brought him to faith. After pursuing a career in law, he confesses, "God, by a sudden conversion subdued and brought my mind to a teachable frame."

---

[68] We have seen some of the historical and polemical reasons for Calvin's disinterest in the aesthetics of worship. Unravelling this unnecessary dichotomy is one of the purposes of David Taylor's book *The Theatre of God's Glory*. He finds the radical separation of material creation from public worship unpersuasive (p. 84).

[69] For what follows, see Calvin, "Author's Preface," in *Commentary on the Psalms* (trans. James Anderson).

Though Calvin was famously reticent about emotions that did not serve true piety, in encountering the emotional outbursts of the musician David, he finds his own soul opening up. This led to claims for music that he made for no other art: "Among other things fit to recreate man and give him pleasure, music is either first or one of the principal; and we must value it as a gift of God," even if we must be careful not to allow our ears to "be more attentive to the melody than our minds to the spiritual meaning of the words."[70]

It was surely this personal attraction that led him to see music's importance for corporate worship. Very early in Calvin's tenure in Geneva, Calvin outlined the importance of music in a letter to a colleague: "It is very expedient for the edification of the Church, to sing some psalms in the form of public prayer, by which one offers petitions to God or sings his praise, in order that the hearts of all may be moved and incited to compose similar prayers ... with the same affections."[71] Significant – and unprecedented – is the insistence that the whole congregation participates in this form of sung prayer. Calvin was famously suspicious of the emotions, but here he recognizes the role they can play in directing affections toward God – and he reflected on this frequently in his commentary on the Psalms. Apparently, he was unable to institute this practice before he left Geneva for Strasbourg in 1538. There he found Protestants had been singing psalms every morning in the cathedral since 1525. Calvin published there the first Reformed Psalter, in French, in 1539, and an enlarged version in 1542 following his return to Geneva in 1541. Some of the translations were his own, but most were by the best-known sixteenth-century French poet Clément Marot. In the introduction to the later edition, Calvin wrote: "We know by experience that singing has great strength and vigor to move and inflame the hearts of men to invoke and praise God with a more vehement and ardent zeal." In the preface to this collection, Calvin wrote that reading and singing the Psalms was not "*une chose morte*" (a dead thing); it was "*un mouvement*" (a movement) in the hands of the Spirit to form believers.[72]

In an important sense, as Stanford Reid points out, instructing the whole congregation to sing psalms in unison represented a revolution in popular music. Music here gave them a sense of unity and inspired them to go out to

---

[70] From the Epistle to the Geneva Service Book, quoted in Bouwsma, *John Calvin*, pp. 135, 225, respectively.

[71] Quoted in W. Stanford Reid, "The Battle Hymn of the Lord," in *Sixteenth Century Essays and Studies* (St. Louis, MO: Foundation for Reformation Research, 1971), vol. II, pp. 36–54, at p. 38. Next quote is at p. 39.

[72] This is quoted from Cummings, *The Literary Culture of the Reformation*, pp. 274, 275.

build the kingdom that they were singing about. Soon English and Dutch translations of the Genevan Psalter appeared. So popular was psalm-singing that it broke out of the confines of congregational worship and became "the defining activity of the Protestant insurgency."[73] In some places people would gather an hour before the service to sing hymns "after the Genevan fashion." Understandably, this aroused opposition and even ridicule — Queen Elizabeth famously called this music Genevan jigs.[74]

Though unison singing without instruments would not strike a modern reader as a particularly exciting innovation, in fact a tradition of popular music was born that has transformed Christian worship — and not just in the Reformed tradition. The innovation, as in other areas of the arts, lay not in the particular musical styles that Calvin encouraged but in the expansion of the aesthetic participation beyond the elite settings where Renaissance styles were developing and into the devotional lives of common believers.[75] One has only to recall the place of Isaac Watts's hymns in the Great Awakenings, or modern praise choruses in contemporary worship.[76] One question posed to Protestant respondents in my own contemporary research elicited an unexpected response. We asked Protestant worshipers: "At what point in the service are you moved to prayer, or experience the presence of God? What triggers this?" The overwhelming majority of responses indicated some form of music or song. No other category came close. This answer was particularly striking because our interview protocol had included no reference to music at all. This supports the argument that, though the story about what God has done in Christ is central to Protestant worship, as it was for Calvin, in

---

[73] Pettegree, *Reformation and the Culture of Persuasion*, p. 60. "Even in the years of persecution, the condemned evangelicals walked to their execution with the Psalms on their lips. The crowd often responded by singing with them in an embarrassed gesture of solidarity."

[74] "Battle Hymn," pp. 42, 43, 52. Ironically, though Clément Marot was commissioned by Calvin to compose some of the music, the Reformer was unsuccessful in getting a public stipend for the composer (though Marot did become successful in the court of Francis I where some of his psalms were sung). The work was completed later by Theodore Beza.

[75] In his cooperation with musician Guillaume Franc, Calvin chose musical styles that were neither sacred nor profane but simply part of the common melodies of the epoch, seeking only the coherence of melody with the biblical text, making the Psalms appropriate both for public worship and for use in "homes and fields." Cf. Olivier Millet, "Art and Literature," in Selderhuis, ed., *The Calvin Handbook*, p. 422.

[76] That this influence is still alive in the Protestant tradition became clear in research I concluded on the relative role of art and aesthetics in Christian, Buddhist, and Muslim worship. See William Dyrness, *Senses of Devotion: Interfaith Aesthetics in Buddhist and Muslim Communities* (Eugene, OR: Cascade Books, 2013), pp. 106, 107.

order for this to move the worshipers – for it to become a living image – it has to take on an aesthetic, in this case a musical, form.[77]

Conclusion: Projecting a Charged World

The true beauty and drama of God's creation is to be seen not in the church structures, but out in the wider world. That is where the drama of sin and redemption is being played out, and where believers are called to act out their parts. And precisely because this dramatic role is articulated in devotional and theological categories it is clearly mistaken to argue that this is simply the first expression of modern secularism; it is precisely because this narrative opens up onto something higher that it discloses new possibilities for aesthetic practices. This enlarged vision, I argue, would eventually open up new possibilities for the aesthetic object itself. Recall that medieval artistic artifacts fell for the most part into a range of specific objects that played some role in the liturgical and devotional life of believers – altarpieces, sculptures, later devotional images, and prayer books. As we have noted, their ontology as works of art was rooted firmly not only in the religious or devotional function they fulfilled, but more importantly in their place in the metaphysical ladder of increasing and decreasing spiritual being. As Bonaventure argued, art was meant to show the pattern of human life in its journey upward toward God. As Jeffrey Hamburger summed up this connection: "Medieval images give literal incarnation to the idea of God's creation as a ladder connecting the visible world to the invisible one."[78]

Calvin, by contrast, in his preaching and writing, appropriating the comprehensive detailing of the world and of nature, recognized at once the aesthetic potential of this enlarged landscape. He not only changed that direction of the dramatic movement, as I have argued, but gave human activity in time a new moral significance. Dramatic movement was centrifugal rather than centripetal; the impulse was horizontal rather than vertical. And in the performance of worship – preaching, teaching, corporate singing – he was seeking to project a world in which congregants were called to

---

[77] This is consistent with a study done by Peter Marsden that shows that, surprisingly, Protestants are significantly more likely than either Catholics or Jews to say that art brings them closer to God, since in his study music was included in the arts. Peter V. Marsden, "Religious Americans and the Arts in the 1990s," in Alberta Arthurs and Glenn Wallach, eds., *Crossroads: Art and Religion in American Life* (New York: New Press, 2001), p. 76. I believe this reflected the fact that when the Protestants were asked about "art" they naturally (and perhaps primarily) thought about music!

[78] "Introduction," in J. Hamburger and Anne Marie Bouché, *The Mind's Eye*, p. 8.

fresh responsibility.[79] His use of Scripture reflects a deep sense of the invitation embedded in the biblical narrative growing out of the imaginative restructuring of creation itself.

This movement then has issued in new aesthetic sensitivities and possibilities. But while they suggest new potential for language, they will not center on language alone, nor do they focus on visual images in any central way. Instead, they will all play out of a new understanding of a dramatic and aesthetic situation in which we find ourselves "called to account." Recently, scholars have emphasized that a focus on language or objects or practices by themselves will invariably distort the object of attention. Rather, these must be seen together in the way they project a world. In a recent summary of these developments, Sally Promey and Shira Brisman recognize the multiple factors making up our aesthetic situation:

> Objects, images, and a proliferation of materialities engage, shape, interact with human bodies, events, and ideas just as profoundly, subtly, and emphatically as the textual and literary "objects" with which scholars generally exercise more comfortable familiarities. Pictures and things surround us and people work with them – and they with people – in constructing selves, communities and worlds.[80]

This might be taken as a summary of the dramatic interconnections – both their potential and their limitation – made possible by the Reformation understanding of creation and redemption that was the focus of Calvin's preaching.

The triumph of designative use of language and the accompanying instrumental rationality, which Charles Taylor details, may owe something to this theological tradition. But one must also acknowledge what was made possible with this new imagination: the way is open for the present and ongoing time to have new dramatic meaning. As in the medieval period, worship and life in the world have an inseparable connection. But the changes in direction and emphasis made Calvin's rhetoric unique. One is summoned by the liturgy – by the preaching and sacraments to serve Christ out in the world; but this service in the world in turn has its reflexive

---

[79] For aesthetics understood as "projecting a world," see Nicholas Wolterstorff, *Works and Worlds of Art* (New York: Oxford University Press, 1980). This understanding of a work of art carrying with it a world, widely accepted in modern aesthetics, surely owes something to the tradition that we are describing.

[80] Sally M. Promey and Shira Brisman, "Sensory Cultures: Material and Visual Religion," in Philip Goff, ed., *The Blackwell Companion to Religion in America* (Malden, MA: Wiley-Blackwell, 2010), pp. 177–205, at p. 279.

influence on the liturgy: one calls special days of prayer or fasting for particular challenges, the preacher can call on the congregation to respond in faith to the challenges the world throws up. These together have the potential to enrich the narrative of the believers' lives. The liturgy calls them into the world, their life in the world throws them back into the liturgy and gives it fresh content. Rowan Williams, in his 2013 Gifford Lectures, describes the Eucharist this way:

> When Christians join in a celebration of Eucharist, they allow themselves to be interrogated by the story of Christ's self-sacrifice, to be questioned as to whether their present lives are recognizable linked with Christ's and to be reconnected with the story of Christ's death and resurrection by the renewing gift of the Holy Spirit.[81]

But his point in this chapter is to underline the connection between this experience and the broader pattern of our lives. This ritual "holds us to account" to that larger narrative, but it also is now connected in large and small ways to the narrative of my life in the world – where Calvin claims my pietas is experienced and lived out. That becomes part of the liturgy of our lives.

But this expansion constituted both a strength and a weakness. In refusing the limitations (and possibilities) imposed by either icons or – later – sacramentals as carriers of the sacred, artists would be free to turn their attention to a broader horizon, what Calvin called the theater of God's glory. But the same theological grounding that made this broader focus possible – that God's presence and working can be seen in the width and breadth of the creation – also eliminated particular places where that presence was clearly visible – *finitum non capax infiniti*. God's presence was to be experienced in the preaching and worship of the congregation – in preaching and song, but as we have noted, Calvin and his peers, for a variety of reasons, were not interested in considering this an aesthetically interesting space. As a result, while the "painting" of creation by which one can ascend to God, which Calvin describes in his commentary on I Romans, expands the aesthetic situation, no particular place is privileged or special, and thus no criterion for aesthetic judgment suggests itself.

Earlier I argued that Calvin's experience with music and especially with singing the Psalms represents his personal aesthetic development, and I want to return to this point in concluding this chapter. When compared with Calvin's treatment of creation as a theater for the glory of God,

---

[81] *The Edge of Words: God and the Habits of Language* (London: Bloomsbury, 2013), p. 85.

his more personal, even intimate, response to music represents a telling embodiment of the limitations of his aesthetics. Even if music played a lesser role than it did for Luther, Calvin understood the important role that music, especially corporate singing, could play in moving the heart to piety. The singing of psalms became for Calvin a crucial element in his rhetorical strategy. While wary of the way music moves the emotions, Calvin knew it was an element that the Spirit could use to move the soul. Music offered specific sites where humans can feel the beauty of God. But as I noted earlier, these sung prayers are human artifacts, the closest thing Calvin embraced to what we today would call works of art; and their performance, singing the Psalms, was the nearest approach to what we call an art practice. And although Calvin opened the way to seeing the potential for beauty in the broader canvas of the created order, he provided no instances of artwork that reflected that broader vision. While his language of this creational beauty could be expansive and even lyrical, his descriptions were general rather than particular – he pointed to every corner of the created order as a display of God's glory, but he offered no description of any particular corner. Despite casting a large vision of aesthetic attention, Calvin made only vague suggestions about how this might be embodied; and while he understood the potential of music to draw worshipers, together, to praise the creator, Calvin assigned the practice to a worship context he left aesthetically undeveloped. Unlike Dostoyevsky, Calvin did not believe beauty can save the world, but in its deployment in the created order, and in preaching and song, it is a sign that the world, in spite of its sufferings, is promised a complete redemption.[82]

Though Calvin himself did not pursue the possibilities his theology made possible, others would do so. For it is indisputable that this new attention to the wider world, animated by the summons of Calvin's rhetorical purposes, resulted in new aesthetic possibilities in places influenced by these ideas. These possibilities and the artifacts they made possible are the subject of the following chapters.

---

[82] Cottin, *Le Regard et la Parole*, p. 310.

5

PORTRAITS AND DRAMATIC CULTURE IN
SIXTEENTH-CENTURY ENGLAND

IN AUGUST 1552, THE YEAR BEFORE THE ACCESSION OF THE
Catholic Queen Mary in England, John Bale, the Protestant pastor and
polemicist, was appointed Bishop of Ossory in Ireland. At his installation,
he insisted on parading his Reformed sympathies: he refused to be vested in
cope, crozier, and miter, and insisted on wearing a black Geneva gown, while
his scandalized clergy followed, carrying his miter and crozier.[1] Bale was also
a skilled playwright and in his polarized religious world he instinctively
understood the role of theater in representing cultural tensions and, he
believed, theological fact. Bale's spectacle highlights the central themes of
this chapter. It underlines the role that pomp and display played in sixteenth-
century Britain. Processions, music, and ritual marked the calendars and filled
the town squares. As Alexandra Johnston says: "Life in early Tudor Britain
was one of ceremony and display ... mimetic activities were woven into all
aspects of British life."[2] But second, Bale's performance also illustrates a
transformation that would come about in the role of drama and theater
between the beginning and the end of that century. Bale himself, with the
help of his patron Thomas Cromwell, had been influential in moving
specifically dramatic performance out of its traditional setting in church and
court and into peoples' everyday lives. Bale in particular was skilled in using
these dramatic forms to attack the papacy and Catholic practices.[3]

---

[1] Vestments had become contentious during the reign of Edward. A ruling earlier that year had
simplified ministerial garb, but instructed bishops to wear a rochet. Even this was too much for
Bale. Peter Marshall, *Heretics and Believers* (New Haven, CT: Yale University Press, 2017), pp. 348,
354; Alexandra Johnston, "Tudor Drama, Theatre and Society," in Robert Tittler and Norman
Jones, eds., *A Companion to Tudor Britain* (Oxford: Blackwell, 2004), p. 431.
[2] "Tudor Drama," pp. 430, 433.
[3] Johnston comments: "Cromwell and Bale took the dramatic discourse out of the Court and into
the public domain" (p. 435).

In this chapter I continue my exploration of the changing aesthetic environment brought about by the Reformation by exploring this movement of drama into the civic life of people and, in particular, the influence of this on portraits and dramatic imagery. This will be examined alongside what seems to be a countermovement: the growing Protestant suspicion of visual representation. My main entry into these questions will be via a study of Elizabethan portraits, but I situate these within the larger backdrop of the mimetic society, or what might be called the symbolic structure of cultural life, one that reflects the influence of the theological emphases of Calvin that we have explored. While the extent of Calvin's influence on English culture has long been debated, scholars have now reached something of a consensus that Calvinism was "the dominant feature of the landscape of English political life from the accession of Elizabeth to the English revolution."[4] Though we have come to see that the transformation from Catholicism to Protestantism was not as sudden or as complete as was previously believed, I think we have not yet understood how those deeply held symbolic structures continued to influence religious believers, albeit in new ways that reflect the Calvinist impulses I have been describing. As this worked itself out in sixteenth-century England, I want to describe this in terms of the emerging Calvinist imagination, on the one hand, and the struggles and tension this produced in their attempt to construct a "godly commonwealth," on the other.

To get at this, I make use of categories that come from media studies, in addition to those of historians. As a theologian of culture, and of visual imagery in particular, I have struggled to apply prevailing text-based historical methods to the study of visual artifacts. I have been encouraged by John Elliot's similar struggle in his inquiries into seventeenth-century Spanish history. He has described his discovery of the importance of court art in a monarch's cultural program, especially in its attempts to solidify its reputation. Images provide, he thinks, "visual affirmation of the reputation to which the regime laid claim through its actions."[5] They reflect in ways printed material cannot the larger symbolic structures of Spanish life.

---

[4] Cummings, *The Literary Culture of the Reformation*, p. 282. He describes there the path scholars have taken to reach this point. As Adrian Streete points out, and as will become clear, this did not preclude the presence of a wide spectrum of beliefs and practice about aesthetic issues. *Protestantism and Drama in Early Modern England* (Cambridge: Cambridge University Press, 2009), p. 5.

[5] *History in the Making* (New Haven, CT: Yale University Press, 2012), p. 159. See also pp. 141–145. The weakness of using these materials, Elliott admits, is that they represented a language known only to the elite in its separate world, something that was overcome by the movement out of the court I want to highlight.

Here is where the categories of media studies prove helpful. Recently, media scholars have sought to go beyond thinking about media as simply the study of technology and communication, and even of the epistemologies these encourage. Lisa Gitelman, for example, thinks that one ought rather to focus, largely if not exclusively, on the job of "representation."[6] She finds it helpful to think of media as a kind of scientific instrument of society that one looks *through* to see what is really there – even if the information cannot easily be separated from the medium. This means seeing communication and media as a cultural practice, "a socially realized structure of communication." So the media does more than represent how a community imagines itself; they *mediate* that imagination and construct the underlying sensibilities.[7] In the case of our study, we might propose that portraits and accompanying protocol are social practices that seek to represent and organize popular perceptions about the monarchy. Moreover, as media they represent a transformation in the way visual images functioned. These images embody, in Gitelman's words, the "social experience of meaning as a material fact."[8] This attention to social (and political) experience is consistent with the focus of this work on what I am calling the expanded aesthetic situation made possible by Reformation worship.

Elizabethan Imagery and the English (Protestant) Imagination

The context in which I place the development of Elizabethan portraiture is the gradual triumph of Protestantism during her long reign, and its impact on the aesthetic situation and the emergent art practices and artifacts this made possible. The Elizabethan Settlement of 1559 called on clergy to "take away, utterly extinct [*sic*] and destroy all shrines . . . pictures, paintings and all other monuments . . . so that there remain no memory of the same in walls, glasses, windows or elsewhere within their churches or houses."[9] This impulse to efface the old imagery increased as the century wore on. In light of this iconoclastic impulse it might seem strange to focus on portraiture, but I argue that it is precisely in the development of these images that a kind

---

[6] *Always Already New: Media, History and the Data of Culture* (Cambridge, MA: MIT Press, 2008), pp. 4, 5. Quote at p. 7.

[7] See Talal Asad's discussion of modern nationalism and the media in *Formations of the Secular* (Stanford, CA: Stanford University Press, 2003), p. 5.

[8] *Always Already New*, p. 18.

[9] In Eamon Duffy, *Saints, Sacrilege and Sedition: Religion and Conflict in the Tudor Reformations* (London: Bloomsbury Publishing, 2012), p. 240.

of paradox in the Protestant imagination becomes evident, one that Calvin's aesthetic program made possible. And it is this paradox that issued in new ways of considering aesthetics and the production of art more generally.

Portraits turn out to be extremely important not only to Elizabeth herself but more centrally to the growing claims of the monarchy. In Chapter 2 we described the growing importance portraits played in Renaissance culture more generally. The tensions those portraits displayed over the nature of the sitter's presence will hover over the discussion in this chapter. During Elizabeth's reign there were royal portraits of all kinds – Roy Strong counts eighty, but that number may be too small.[10] In addition to painted portraits, there were group portraits, miniatures, and woodcuts (probably a couple dozen of each of these). A draft proclamation from 1563 found among state papers, framed to counter the rise of debased images of the Queen, specifies that "some special person that shall be by hir allowed shall have first fynihsed a portraicture thereof, after which finished, hir Majesty will be content that all other paynters, or grauors . . . shall and maye at their pleasure follow the sayd patron."[11] At this early stage in her reign this proclamation indicates not only that unauthorized images of the Queen were circulating but that these images were in great demand. As the proclamation goes on to say: "all sortes of subiectes and people both noble and meane" wish to have images of the Queen to exhibit in their houses.

But control of the Queen's image proved difficult. England was in a recession, and the Queen was a poor patron of the visual arts. She had no personal collection and, in the early stages of her reign, no official court painter.[12] All of this would be consistent with a developing Protestant consensus about the limitations and dangers of visual imagery. There were a number of factors that encouraged an antipathy toward visual display. After the death of Queen Mary, many Protestants, including the artist Nicholas Hilliard, returned from their exile in Geneva, bringing Calvin's notion of a holy community with them, but also his misgivings about visual imagery. In 1563 John Foxe published his influential *Acts and Monuments*, in a single folio volume, later expanded into two volumes and widely distributed, which recounted the story of Protestant martyrs under the reign of Queen

---

[10] Strong, *The Portraits of Queen Elizabeth* (Oxford: Clarendon Press, 1963), p. 5.

[11] *Portraits*, p. 5. Strong notes there is no evidence that this was ever put into effect, though he thinks it indicates that pattern drawings did exist. Quote that follows at p. 10.

[12] Strong, *The English Renaissance Miniature* (New York: Thames and Hudson, 1983), pp. 66, 67. Cf. Strong's assessment of the time: "few periods have been more inimical to the visual arts than the middle years of the sixteenth century." *The English Icon: Elizabethan and Jacobean Portraiture* (New York: Pantheon, 1969), p. 1.

Mary. In 1571 by action of the Bishops of the Church of England, chained volumes of Foxe's *Book of Martyrs* were placed in every church in England. Foxe's book probably did more than any other book to further the notion of England and its people being specially chosen by God – a development that will prove central to the rise of portraiture.[13]

In these developments John Bale (1495–1563) played a critical role. After thirty years as a Carmelite friar, in the 1530s he fell under the influence of the Reformation and turned his playwriting skills toward making contemporary miracle plays into biblical dramas.[14] I will assess his significance for the rise of English drama in Chapter 6, but here I call attention to his role in shaping England's view of itself as God's Israel. As a playwright he intuitively understood the possibilities of representation, in both theater and imagery, in promoting religious change – famously proclaiming that players, printers, and preachers would bring down the Pope.[15] His primary influence resulted from his popular book *Images of Both Churches* (1445/6), which interpreted the seals of Revelation in terms of the history and decline of the Church, and England's struggle with Rome. England, he felt, would lead to the final reformation of the Church, a work he came to feel Elizabeth was divinely appointed to undertake. As Leslie Fairfield notes, Bale helped supply England with a "usable past," one that animated the plays he wrote, and the visual culture that would develop. Bale and John Foxe were close friends, and it seems clear that the latter's work in *Acts and Monuments* was influenced by Bale's thinking.

The early part of Elizabeth's reign was marked by an increasing challenge to anything that resembled popish display, issuing in increasing tightening of visual imagery that continued into the 1570s. Paul White describes the dampening effect on drama and the visual in the churches: "By the 1570s the preaching of the word supplanted any dramatic performance of the word, and older notions of the visual supplementing the oral were falling away."[16] During this same period the medieval mystery plays were

---

[13] I have described developments of this period and the fate of visual culture in *Reformed Theology and Visual Culture*, chapter 4.

[14] Jesse W. Harris, *John Bale: A Study of the Minor Literature of the Reformation* (Urbana: University of Illinois, 1940), p. 129. Harris's work has been influential in a modern reassessment of Bale's significance for the rise of English drama. For what follows, see also Leslie P. Fairfield, *John Bale: Mythmaker of the English Reformation* (West Lafayette, IN: Purdue University Press, 1976), pp. 75, 109. Quote that follows is at p. ix.

[15] Paul W. White, *Theatre and Reformation: Protestantism, Patronage and Playing in Tudor England* (Cambridge: Cambridge University Press, 1993), p. 2.

[16] White, *Theatre and Reformation*, p. 168.

gradually dying out. The last Corpus Christi play in York was in 1569; in Coventry it stopped abruptly in 1580.[17] Patrick Collinson has been the most prominent in calling attention to the paradox in these developments. On the one hand, he notes, all of this represented a kind of secularization of society. Previously, public spaces were filled with religious processions and mystery and saints' plays; these were now banished. But, Collinson says, on the other hand, this "paradoxically involved the *sacralization* of the town, which now became self-consciously a godly commonwealth, its symbolic and mimetic codes replaced by a literally articulated, didactic religious discipline."[18] In these developments Calvin's influence was critical. The memory of a godly commonwealth brought back from Calvin's Geneva by the Marian exiles fired their imagination even as it fueled their civic rituals.

Accompanying this was a growing aversion to any visual portrayal of religious figures – even biblical themes were resisted. All images were banned from books published in Geneva after 1580.[19] But here, rather than seeing an effacement of the visual, we should see the emergence of a new aesthetic impulse, one now focusing not on the space of the church but on the home and town square. While it is true that the links to traditional forms of recreation and display were discouraged, as Tessa Watt notes, Protestants transferred their efforts to other forms of material culture: prayer books, psalters, sermons, handbooks of devotion, and popular prints.[20] This is not to say that people turned their attention from sacred imagery to secular ones – that would be to read back modern distinctions between the sacred and secular. For Protestants, moving drama and its visual display out of the church and into the larger world served clear religious purposes, as we argued in the last two chapters. Indeed, it represented a new understanding of the way God was at work in the world. It is in this context that I examine Elizabethan portraits.

Elizabeth and the Rise of the Royal Image

As we have seen, during the reign of Elizabeth, portraiture, as the visual arts generally, was in a state of decline. Hans Holbein had brought the latest

---

[17] Johnston, "Tudor Drama," p. 438.

[18] Collinson, *The Birthpangs of Protestant England: Religious and Cultural Change in the Sixteenth Century* (Basingstoke: Macmillan, 1988), p. 55, emphasis in original.

[19] Dyrness, *Reformed Theology and Visual Culture*, pp. 123, 124.

[20] Watt, *Cheap Prints and Popular Piety: 1550–1640* (Cambridge: Cambridge University Press, 1991), pp. 69, 70. Collinson sees the restrictions on imagery reaching a climax in 1580, but Watt thinks Collinson overemphasizes the "visual anorexia" of English culture during this period, stressing the role of both household and inns and alehouses in the promotion of a new visual culture.

Renaissance technique to the court of Henry VIII, but he was unable to spark a vital tradition of the visual arts. John Bettes continued Holbein's manner for a time, and Mary's court artist Hans Eworth also shows his influence. But during Elizabeth's reign it was Nicholas Hilliard and, later, George Gower, who carried the tradition of portraits forward, even though they never fully understood or appropriated the Renaissance techniques.[21]

Portraits had long been important means of defining the sitter's place in society and recording a person's likeness as they aged, as we saw in the case of Holbein. During the reign of Elizabeth they became important as gifts in diplomatic exchanges, and, in the 1570s, they played a prominent part in marriage negotiations. But portraits' symbolic and allegorical powers were also recognized and exploited. As Strong notes, "lessons of virtue and of vice were to be read from the countenances of the great."[22] Like art in general, portraits were to have instrumental value; they were to portray people (and events) not as they were but as they should be, thus inciting the viewer to worthy thoughts and deeds. And during the latter part of the sixteenth century, the symbolism of portraiture was increasingly pressed into the service of political ambitions. Portraits, like all the arts – state festivals, architectural complexes, even humanist poets – were being appropriated by the mechanisms of royal power, to sing the monarch's praises.[23] Frances Yates has argued that this development, which paralleled the revival of imperial imagery under Charles V in Germany, provides an important backdrop to the rise of the Elizabethan image.[24] Charles had claimed the mantle of Charlemagne, and thus gave fresh impulse to imperial ideas and spread them throughout Europe, especially, Yates thinks, in the symbolism of its propaganda.

We have seen that already in the 1560s images of the Queen were proliferating, sparking futile attempts to control their distribution. Clearly, influenced by Bale's apocalyptic interpretation of English history, the royal image almost from the beginning was deployed both for political *and* religious reasons, and it would have been available to people from all levels of society.[25]

---

[21] This is Roy Strong's assessment. Hilliard, he thinks, represented a recovery of an older medieval tradition – he was the last great medieval artist. *The English Renaissance Miniature*, pp. 135, 136.

[22] *The English Icon*, p. 46.

[23] Roy Strong, *Gloriana: The Portraits of Queen Elizabeth* (New York: Thames and Hudson, 1987), p. 10.

[24] Frances Yates, *Astraea: The Imperial Theme in the Sixteenth Century* (London: Routledge, Kegan and Paul, 1975), p. 1. She admits that the reality of Charles's rule was largely illusory, but its "phantom" nevertheless had a large impact especially on Elizabethan imagery.

[25] John Elliott's complaint that seventeenth-century images in Spain spoke a language only the elite could understand did not apply to Elizabethan imagery; Elizabeth's was a vernacular imagery.

11 Initial "C" (for Constantine) from John Foxe, *Acts and Monuments*, 1563.
RB 59840. Image courtesy of the Henry Huntington Library, San Marino, California.

In the 1563 edition of Foxe's *Acts and Monuments*, the opening "C" (the first
letter of the name "Constantine") features Elizabeth (possibly after a print of
Levina Teerlinc) seated on a throne, holding a sword in her right hand, with
her left hand on a globe and the pope under her feet (Figure 11). Elizabeth was
the new Constantine who had put a stop to Marian persecutions and restored
the true faith. The 1570 edition in the "C" with the same picture becomes the
first letter of Christ, which replaces the dedication to Constantine. Frances
Yates comments: "The initial 'C' is thus the climax of the whole book."[26]
As heir of imperial power Elizabeth can claim the right to throw off papal
suzerainty.

The earliest allegorical painting of Elizabeth is *Queen Elizabeth and the Three
Goddesses* (1569; Figure 12). The likely artist of this remake of the judgment of
Paris was Flemish artist Joris Hoefnagel, visiting from the continent, who
brought with him both the imperial allusion and the classical dress in which to
present this. To the left is Elizabeth with two of her ladies-in-waiting,

[26] Yates, *Astraea*, pp. 39, 44. John King thinks the three figures to the left, representing John Foxe,
John Day, and Thomas Norton, both served to underline her glorious rule and linked Elizabeth
to the Virgin Empress, recalling the visit of the magi to the Holy Family. John N. King, *Tudor
Royal Iconography: Literature and Art in an Age of Religious Crisis* (Princeton, NJ: Princeton
University Press, 1989), pp. 155, 156.

12 Jores Hoefnage, *Queen Elizabeth and the Three Goddesses/ The Judgement of Paris*, 1569. Hampton Court. Royal Collection Trust, copyright Her Majesty Queen Elizabeth II, 2018.

balanced on the right by the three goddesses, Juno, Minerva, and Venus embracing Cupid. The verses below explain the defeat of these goddesses by Elizabeth – with their scepter, quiver, and shoe (perhaps in respect of the holy ground). Juno points to heaven, possibly indicating that the reversal of the traditional judgment has now been decreed by heaven.[27] Hoefnagel belonged to a small circle of exiles from the Low Countries who came to England in the 1560s, and the picture may have been painted and presented as their expression of gratitude for Elizabeth's leadership of Protestant Europe and its triumph over Catholic power.

The earliest portraits by Nicholas Hilliard (1547–1619) came during 1572–1576 when he had completed his apprenticeship with Robert Brandon, the Queen's jeweler, and he became a semi-official court painter (though he did not receive an annuity until the 1590s). One of these early images, the "Pelican" portrait, by Hilliard (c. 1572) (Figure 13) shows the Queen already as a stylized icon, featuring a flat expression and elaborate clothes and jewelry. The absence of realism and natural expression in the face has led scholars to suppose there had been a pattern established that needed to be copied – as time went on the clothes and elaborate jewels became more ostentatious, and apparently more realistic, than the Queen's face.

This suspicion is further supported by the famous "Darnley" portrait, painted by Federigo Zuccaro, a visiting Italian Mannerist painter in 1575, surely the most influential portrait of Elizabeth ever painted (Figure 14). Zuccaro brought with him not only more advanced technique, but also the

[27] Strong, *Gloriana*, pp. 65, 66.

13 Nicholas Hilliard, *Elizabeth I: Pelican Portrait*, c. 1573–1575.
WAG 2994. Courtesy of the National Museums of Liverpool (Walker Art Gallery), Liverpool.

14 Attributed to Frederigo Zuccaro, *Elizabeth I: Darnley Portrait*, c. 1575.
Copyright the National Portrait Gallery, London.

formula for a sitter that had been perfected by great Italian painters like Titian. This composition would be used later by both Gower and Hilliard. More importantly, the face Zuccaro painted became the default pattern throughout the 1580s and even into the 1590s.[28]

These years proved to be decisive in the reign of Elizabeth. In 1576 Hilliard left for France in search of patronage that was lacking in Elizabeth's court and, as likely, further "knowledge" – training in the art of portraiture – and settled in the court of the Duke of Anjou, in Paris. The Duke was, not incidentally, Elizabeth's last suitor. While Hilliard was there these negotiations fell through and it became clear that Elizabeth would never marry. But the collapse of these negotiations represented a fresh opportunity for the expansion of Elizabethan imagery: she could now become the virgin queen. During her progress through East Anglia in 1578, plays were offered the Queen by Thomas Churchyard celebrating Elizabeth's virginity, with lavish references to Diana and the Virgin Mary.

This expansion of imagery is represented by an illustration to J. Case's *Sphaera Civitatis* published in 1588 (Figure 15). There the earth is surrounded by the Dantean spheres of the moon, sun, planets, and fixed stars, and Elizabeth is literally holding the world in her arms. Frances Yates thinks the key to this image is the imperialist argument for a single ruler: "As the heaven is regulated in all its parts ... by the one first mover who is God, so the world of men is at its best when it is ruled by one prince." Elizabeth then is Virgo-Astraea, the one monarch of this long medieval tradition who rules the world in justice.[29]

Around this time an engraving of Elizabeth by F. Delaram, after an image of Hilliard's (Figure 16), pushes the symbolism further into the religious realm. Here she is seated in glory with a crown of stars around her head, explicitly reclaiming the medieval imagery of the Virgin Mary. The original version of this print was accompanied by verses of Sir John Davies, famous for his Hymns of Astraea, the first lines of which, when read downward, spell ELISABETHA REGINA. These lines give some sense of Davies's intent:

---

[28] Strong, *Gloriana*. Strong thinks this reflects the increasing ability of the government to control the image of the Queen.

[29] Yates, *Astraea*, p. 64. In the dedication of his book to Christopher Hatton, Case explains the diagram showing the Prime Mover must be the Prince who represents the Deity. Yates notes how important "One" and "unique" were to Elizabethan symbolism. The Virgin Astraea derives from the fourth eclogue of Virgil that proclaimed the coming of the golden age ruled by the Virgin Astraea, or Justice (p. 4).

15 Engraving by J. Case, *Sphaera Civitatis*, 1588, frontispiece of Magistro Johanne Caso Oxoniensi, *Sphaera Civitatis*.

RB 46631. Image courtesy of Henry Huntington Library, San Marino, California.

E arly before the day doth spring
L et us awake my Muse, and sing;
I t is no time to slumber,
S o many ioyes this time doth bring,
A s Time will faile to number.

B ut whereto shall we bend our layes?
E ven up to Heauen, againe to raise
T he Mayd, which thence descended;
H ath brought againe the golden dayes
A nd all the world amended.[30]

Davies's vision of the starry virgin of the golden age returning to earth anticipates Edmund Spenser's famous *Faerie Queene* (1590), which can be read on one level as a celebration of the reign of Elizabeth.

---

[30] Quoted in Yates, *Astraea*, p. 66. Yates highlights the strange distance between the crude visual symbolism and the highly accomplished poetic imagery (p. 69).

16 Engraving by F. Delaram, after Hilliard (1617–1619), frontispiece of William Camden, *Historie of the Most Renowned and Victorious Princesse Elizabeth, Late Queen of England* (1630).
RB 97473. Image courtesy of Henry Huntington Library, San Marino, California.

But consistent with the Protestants' intent to move the dramatic imagery out of the court and into the everyday life of the people, Elizabeth's annual progress through her realm during this time took on ever more elaborate pomp, and in the process reanimated older medieval traditions. Formerly elaborate feast days, such as Corpus Christi, were celebrated with feasting and bell-ringing, festivities that ardent Protestants despised. But during this expansion of the idea of monarchy such festivities were reinstituted for November 17, the day of Elizabeth's Accession, the day she had succeeded her Catholic sister Mary. But now these older Catholic practices became the media of the social fact that Elizabeth represented, and the glow this was to extend over the whole of culture. The processions and pageants of Accession Day, as Roy Strong says, "were thus an adaptation of an old Catholic festival to the ethos of Protestantism."[31]

---

[31] For the description of these developments, I am dependent on Roy Strong, *The Cult of Elizabeth: Elizabethan Portraits and Pageantry* (Berkeley: University of California Press, 1977), pp. 117–121. Quote is at p. 118.

17 Attributed to George Gower, *Elizabeth I: Armada Portrait*, 1588.
Woburn Abbey and Gardens, courtesy of Bedford Estates.

With the defeat of the Spanish Armada in 1588, these state festivals
reached new heights of splendor. Her Accession Day that year was recognized as a special day of thanksgiving for the whole realm. Her procession
through the streets of London to St. Paul's recalled the Roman Emperors as
she rode in a symbolic chariot with her imperial crown placed on her head.
At St. Paul's she heard a sermon – a compulsory element of all Protestant
celebrations – praising God for his deliverance from their enemies.

This event was celebrated in the "Armada" portrait, by Elizabeth's
Serjeant Painter George Gower (1588; Figure 17), and based on a new sitting
that year. Through openings in the arcade behind her, the great sea victory is
recalled: on the left the fire ships are sent into the Armada; on the right
Spain's navy is driven by the winds onto the rocks. Though the portrait was
given to Sir Francis Drake in appreciation for his service, the subject is
Elizabeth's triumph, which is pictured as an imperial triumph. Her hand is
on the globe, in the fashion of the Roman Emperors, a theme emphasized
by the placement, just above, of the crown. The crown's four jeweled strips

18 Marcus Gheeraerts the Younger, *Elizabeth I: Ditchley Portrait*, 1592.
Copyright the National Portrait Gallery, London.

are gathered at the top, to indicate the equality of the Queen with the Holy
Roman Emperor.[32]

This theme reaches something of a climax in the "Ditchley" portrait, by
Marcus Gheeraerts the Younger (1561/2–1635) in 1592 (Figure 18). Gheeraerts,
though resident in England, was clearly trained in the Low Countries during the
1580s. Here is the first entrance of what was termed the "curious painting," which
allowed for light and shadows, called *chiaroscuro*, well established on the Continent
though unknown to Elizabeth (or to Hilliard).[33] Here reference to Elizabeth's
imperial rule becomes even clearer. Indeed, the crown, Queen, island, and the
globe on which she stands are all one. The first three books of Spenser's *Faerie
Queene* had just been published, and this must have had some influence on
Gheeraerts's symbolism. In Book II, lines 45–48, 46–49, Spenser writes:

---

[32] Strong, *Gloriana*, pp. 131, 132. Strong notes that whereas in previous portraits, especially the
famous "sieve" portraits, the globe was in the background, it has now been moved to the front.
[33] For discussion of this picture, see Strong, *Gloriana*, pp. 135–139. The Spenser quote is at p. 138.

> In widest Ocean she her throne does reare,
> That ouer all the earth it may be seene;
> As the morning Sunne her beams dispredden cleare,
> And in her face faire peace, and mercy doth appeare
>
> . . .
>
> That men beholding so great excellence
> And rare perfection in mortalitie,
> Do her adore with sacred reuerence,
> As th'Idole of her makers great magnificence.[34]

The literary and the visual tributes of this time were all connected to the larger dramatic presentation of the Queen endowed with both classical and sacred elements. The portrait itself, as in fact Spenser's epic, was influenced by the traditions of festival and chivalry, which were being reanimated in the service of the emerging nationalism, and even of England's pivotal role in God's program. Frances Yates calls this process the "imaginative re-feudalization," which "used the apparatus of chivalry and its religious traditions to focus fervent religious loyalty on the national monarch."[35]

But here is the paradox I want underline: at the very point imagery has been banned from churches and even printed books, visual display has been reinstated to its role of representing the truth that was also celebrated in verse – but now the truth is the glory of Elizabeth and the English nation. Indeed the literary and civic display and the portraiture are all mobilized in a common system of representation; they are media, in Lisa Gitelman's sense, of social practices that reorganize popular perceptions of power within a global order. Elizabeth's ascension – one is tempted to say, her divinization – is complete, so that it has become possible to refer to the "cult" of Elizabeth.[36]

But isn't this in many ways a strange and historically unexpected development? Patrick Collinson notes how Elizabeth began her life as a modest, demure young lady, in the 1550s dressing plainly without ostentatious jewelry – John Bale would surely have been pleased.[37] And yet in the 1570s and '80s, we find portraits with a symbol of a sieve held in her hand, identifying here with the vestal virgin Tuccia; her court becomes the center

[34] Edmund Spenser, *The Faerie Queene*, ed. Thomas P. Roche, Jr. (New Haven, CT: Yale University Press, 1978).

[35] *Astraea*, p. 108. See the discussion of the setting of Spenser and the Ditchley Portrait at pp. 104–108.

[36] Helen Hackett has questioned how accurate the attribution of a "cult" is in a purely religious sense, rightly pointing to Renaissance rhetoric and the older notion of sacred kingship that had been appropriated by Protestants. See *Virgin Mother, Maiden Queen: Elizabeth I and the Cult of the Virgin Mary* (New York: St. Martins, 1995), pp. 6–12.

[37] Collinson, "Elizabeth I," in *Oxford Dictionary of National Biography* (Oxford: Oxford University Press, 2004), pp. 96, 97.

of elaborate rituals, such as her daily procession to the Chapel Royal, in which Elizabeth could be seen wearing the dazzling contents of her enormous wardrobe. Though the face in her portraits was unchanging, her clothes and jewelry were portrayed in astonishing, and changing, naturalism. In 1596 a decision of the Privy Council ordered Serjent Painter George Gower to seek out and destroy all unseemly portraits of the Queen, which, they said, were "to her great offence." They had decided previously that the official "pattern" image of the Queen was to be of legendary and ageless beauty.[38] Notwithstanding this determination to pursue the policy of royal triumph, the 1590s found the people tired of war, suffering under high taxes and low wages, and with a corrupt and quarreling political system.

The Monarchy and Reformation Theology

One wonders: What did those returned exiles from Geneva make of this attempt of constructing a godly commonwealth? What would John Bale have said of these celebrations?[39] Were the returned exiles willing participants in the festivals that accompanied the Queen's annual progress through her realm? What did the devout Protestant Hilliard make of this? He certainly shaped the official image of the Queen, if anyone did, as the recreation of a medieval monarchy. Perhaps, Roy Strong thinks, his promotion of Elizabeth as Gloriana was not of his own volition: "We are looking at a government-promoted portrait," Strong thinks.[40] But in Hilliard's famous "Art of Limning" (1598–1599) there is no clue that he had anything but admiration for the Queen. Phillip Sidney's more famous "Defense of Poetry" (1595), which we will explore later, stays clear of politics altogether and avoids even mentioning the Queen.[41]

We must be careful of importing modern prejudices into this period, and approach these panegyrics with caution; they mostly represent conventional rhetoric. Protestants in general were not shy about appropriating biblical imagery for the godly ruler – even John Calvin does this, as Hackett points out.[42] Indeed for Calvin the role of the prince and magistrate is central to his larger dramatic vision. In his commentary on Ps. 82:1, "God sits in the

---

[38] Strong, *Gloriana*, p. 20, and Strong, *The English Renaissance Miniature*, pp. 81, 82.

[39] Bale had died in 1563. Though he would have supported Elizabeth's national aspirations, he did not see her as "crushing the dragon"; he looked to the return of Christ not to the triumph of England over her enemies. Fairfield, *John Bale*, pp. 109, 110.

[40] *The English Renaissance Miniature*, p. 118. See also p. 92.

[41] However, Hackett sees an indirect reference to Elizabethan imagery in Sidney's reference to the poet's attempt to describe a person to "make their images more lively," indicating that these panegyrics are not to be taken literally. *Virgin Mother*, pp. 125, 126.

[42] *Virgin Mother*, p. 21.

assembly of . . . the gods," Calvin writes that the "name of the Divine Being is applied to those who occupy the exalted station of princes, which there is afforded a peculiar manifestation of the majesty of God." He explains that "although the divine glory shines forth in every part of the world, yet when lawful government flourishes among men, it is reflected therefrom with pre-eminent lustre."[43] The Reformers, Hackett argues, actually worked to "enhance the sacred authority of secular rulers by attributing to them the power to protect the true Church and to defend it against papal ambition."[44] In the theater of the world that Calvin described, the ruler played a central role.

And Protestant theologians were eager to support this elevation. In his popular 1571 *Catechisme*, Protestant theologian Alexander Nowell could praise Elizabeth for "announcing [God's] religion and glory in her dominion and bringing peace to the consciences of her subiectes."[45] Thus while Protestant theologians were busy constructing long treatises in defense of the Protestant faith and in support of its iconoclasm, they were also busy shoring up their support of the Protestant queen. This pursuit of a sacred commonwealth after all found theological support in Calvin's notion that creation and our civic life and righteous rule could display the glory of God. But notice this proliferation of civic imagery was occurring just as their suspicion of religious imagery and drama was becoming more pronounced. This juxtaposition made it necessary for theologians to walk a fine line; Protestant suspicion of imagery in the Church sometimes sat uneasily with their promotion of royal imagery.

Consider an earlier (1560) catechism of Thomas Becon, a canon in Canterbury cathedral recently returned from exile, in the form of an exchange between father and son. The father notes that God spoke to Moses out of the bush. Moses saw no image; he heard a voice, Becon editorializes. This prompts the son to ask the father: "Is it lawfull in polltyke, civile, worldly matters to have images?"[46] The father responds that it is not forbidden, and calls on Christ's experience with Peter where the Lord asked whose image was on the coin. When Peter responds that it is the Emperor, Becon points out that Christ did not say that such images were wrong. Thus, Becon uses this biblical event to show both the utility of images of the sovereign and the way in which honor is to paid both to God and to the state. But the son asks the obvious follow-up question: If "in worldly things why not also in divine and holye things?" The father responds: "In the one, is no pearill, in the other, great danger, as we have learned to[o] much by experience."

---

[43] Ps. 82:1, trans. James Anderson, *Commentary on the Psalms*, in loc.   [44] *Virgin Mother*, p. 20.
[45] This panegyric is found in the preface of A. Nowell's *Catechisme* (London: John Daye, 1571), Aiiij.
[46] Becon, *The Worckes of Thomas Becon* (London: John Day, 1564), fols. 300.28 and 300.33.

Around this time, the Bishop of Salisbury, John Jewell, in his response to M. Harding (1564) offers the standard Protestant position on images. He praises the ancient Emperors for doing away with images, and saw the Tudor policy as a restoration of this ancient precedent. He did admit to his Catholic interlocutor that images could move the mind and affections, but this was all the more reason to keep them from the churches.[47] Jewell takes his stand throughout on the second commandment, even as he carefully allowed for the use of civic imagery. Catholic polemicists soon pointed out the inconsistency of this argument. Nicholas Sanders taunted Jewel: "Breake if you dare the Image of the Queenes Maiestie, or Armes of the Realme."[48]

Thomas Bilson continues Jewell's pamphlet warfare against Rome in a later work, and reflects a similar dis-ease. In his 1585 argument in defense of the Protestant faith, Bilson tries to clarify how images are dangerous, while some images are allowed.[49] Written in the form of a dialogue between the Catholic Philand and the Protestant Theophil, Bilson appeals to the ancient sources of the True Faith: What part of it is not ancient? he asks. Well, answers Philand, wasn't the use of images Catholic and ancient? Did not the Second Council of Nicea declare it so? No, many parts of the Church did not accept this, Theophil responds, and the Bishops at Constantinople condemned their use (pp. 546, 547). But, Philand notes, by worship we do not mean "godly honor," but simply gestures of outward submission" (p. 549). Theophil insists that any honoring, even holding up hands, "is such honor as [God] hath prohibited to be given to anything made with hands" (p. 551).

Philand again presses the obvious question: "For if the images of Princes may be reverenced and idolatrie not committed, much more the image of God." (p. 552). Theophil responds that we should not use earthly examples to overturn God's law: "The images of Princes may not be despited or abused least it be taken as a malicious hart against the Prince, but bowing the knee or lifting up the hand to the image is flat and inevitable idolatrie" (p. 552). That his own answer to this dilemma is unsatisfying even to himself appears in his return to this question a few pages later – after he has discussed, and dismissed, the traditional arguments in support of images. What about Princes? The question lingers. Theophil addresses it again, arguing, perhaps as much with himself as with the reader: "Princes can expect no more than a sober reverence due to their states, expressed by some decent gestures of the

---

[47] John Jewell, "Of Adoration of Images," in *The Works of John Jewell*, ed. John Ayre (Cambridge: The Parker Society and Cambridge University Press, 1847), vol. 24, pp. 644–688.

[48] Quoted in Strong, *Gloriana*, pp. 38, 39.

[49] Thomas Bilson, *The True Difference betweene Christian Subiection and UnChristian Rebellion* (Oxford: Joseph Barnes, 1585). Pages cited in the text are to this work.

body" (p. 560). Likewise with the arms and images. "In which case they that honour the Princes' throne, scepter, seale, swood [sic], token or image, honour not the things which they see, but the power that sent them." Though this is just about exactly the argument used by iconophils for the religious role of images, Theophil insists this in no way justifies the image of Christ. Why not? For Princes, Theophil says, we honor in their absence; Christ is always present with his people; he needs no image. Theophil concludes with the reminder that "you may not build any point of faith upon tradition, except the Scriptures confirm the same" (p. 578).

As the representations of the Queen became the media of royal power, Protestants were sometimes ambivalent about its imagery, but they were quick to celebrate the fruits of this power. Separating these was probably not even possible. Helen Hackett notes pointedly: "the apparatus of state power depended upon much the same use of symbolism and ceremony as did the Church."[50] Elizabeth, for her part, had to be nervous about the periodic religious iconoclasm. In 1575, for example, she came into conflict with her second Archbishop of Canterbury, Edmund Grindel, over the proliferation of prophesyings, a popular form of biblical exposition and preaching, which were a precursor to modern revivals. Elizabeth rightly recognized these rituals as competitive with her progressions, and unsuccessfully urged Grindel to outlaw them. When Grindel responded that he preferred to "offend your earthly majesty than offend against the heavenly majesty of God," Elizabeth suspended him for six months and saw to it that he was marginalized until his death in 1583.[51] Still for most Protestants, loyalty to the Queen, and the emerging state, had subtly determined how they thought about the visual trappings that spoke of its power. Patrick Collinson notes that in the 1580s, power in the Church passed from more progressive bishops to a new generation of bishops who were more comfortable with Elizabeth's via media, that is to say, with the status quo. Archbishop John Whitgift, who followed Grindal, reflected this conservative impulse and was more active in suppressing non-conformist Protestants. Elizabeth struggled both against the Papists on the right and with the Puritans on the left, though her campaigns against the latter were restrained and episodic.[52]

---

[50] *Virgin Mother*, p. 64. She notes recent studies that show that ritual and spectacle make up the very essence of political power.

[51] Susan Doran, *Queen Elizabeth I* (New York: New York University Press, 2003), pp. 108, 109. In his 6,000-word letter to the Queen, December 1576, Grindal had the temerity to point out that, in ancient times, bishops "were wont to judge emperors not emperors of bishops," reprising a hotly disputed point of view from the 1530s.

[52] Collinson, *The Elizabethan Puritan Movement* (Berkeley: University of California, 1967), p. 201. He notes that well into the 1580s the Puritans were convinced that Elizabeth was on their side in

Catholic recusants could be loyal, but their presence continued to pose a threat to the Protestant status quo. In 1580 Rome sponsored a group of Jesuits who crossed secretly into England from the continent, and that year a rebellion in Ireland sparked rumors that the Pope and King of Spain would raise an army to invade England; troops were even mustered in every county. Priests subject to Rome were believed to be secretly inciting rebellion under the seal of confessional, seeking "to draw the subjects from their allegiance and obedience to the Prince."[53] This may account for the particular hardening of attitudes around 1580 and the continuing support for the growing display in Elizabeth's reign.

But there is something larger going on here that transcends the religious debates of that century that I want to underline. This relates to the larger symbolic structure of the English imagination that I referenced earlier. To understand this, one must return to the period before the reign of Elizabeth. Thomas Cranmer, the Protestant archbishop and editor of successive versions of the *Book of Common Prayer*, had been famous for his support of the Divine Right of Kings. Since the King was Christ's vice-regent on earth, Cranmer had come to believe, he was necessarily above all earthly restraint. This fact is well known. But Cranmer's recent biographer, Diarmaid MacCulloch, has argued that Cranmer's hatred of the papacy was what came first; his view of divine kingship followed. When the Pope's authority was gone, MacCulloch argues, Cranmer was left with an "authority vacuum" that he filled with veneration for the monarchy.[54] This is suggestive for our period as well; with the Pope banished, Elizabeth filled the same authority vacuum for Protestants in general. We noted earlier Patrick Collinson's observation that the Protestant focus on town and family had

---

combating the abuses in the Church. He reminds us wisely in another place that no one in that century would have imagined that religious pluralism, as we understand it, would have been either possible or desirable. *Elizabethans* (New York: Hambledon and London, 2003), p. 228.

[53] William Camden, *The Historie of the Most Renowned and Victorious Princesse Elizabeth, the Late Queen of England* (London: Thomas Harper for Benjamin Fisher 1630), p. 107. On this period, see Marshall, *Heretics and Believers*, p. 530.

[54] MacCulloch, *Thomas Cranmer: A Life* (New Haven, CT: Yale University Press, 1997), p. 151. MacCulloch notes: "Cranmer came to hate the papacy, and therefore he needed the Royal Supremacy to fill the chasm of authority which had opened up in his thinking as a result." He goes on to cite a sermon in which Cranmer recounts his long-time desire for the popes' authority to be destroyed; now he thanked God that he had seen it in this realm. The term "authority vacuum" is Eamon Duffy's term, in *Saints, Sacrilege, and Sedition*, p. 186. John King's argument, a generation ago, that this iconography was simply inherited from medieval traditions, surely places too much emphasis on continuity. See *Tudor Royal Iconography* (Princeton, NJ: Princeton University Press, 1989).

the effect of sacralizing these settings. And for Protestants, as time went on, this sacralization came to be symbolized by the person of the Queen.[55]

But I would like to expand this metaphor of vacuum and suggest that, with the sweeping away of an old way of life – its festivals, rood screens, and processions – there remained not only an authority chasm but an "imaginative vacuum," a representational space that needed filling. As David Freedberg has argued, the impulse to image divinity is perennial; aniconic religion, he thinks, is impossible. Indeed the persistent attempts to suppress images are themselves testimony to the inevitable urge to picture.[56] And during this century the need to picture religious qualities was being forced out of the sanctuary and into the display and rituals of the state. This was a process that Calvin had not only suggested but developed in his aesthetic and political program in Geneva. There was no mystery in its attachment to the Queen. But one wonders whether its connection with Calvin's godly commonwealth has been weakened.

A helpful voice in filling out this suggestion is provided by the work of Eamon Duffy. His classic work, *Stripping of the Altars* (1992), encouraged scholars to rethink the sixteenth-century adoption of Protestantism.[57] In his more recent work, *Saints, Sacrilege and Sedition*, he has further pursued his reflection on the communal devastation resulting from the removal of the old practices and its visual culture. He argues that "these transformations of sacred space … had the effect of at once making invisible, and indeed abolishing, some of the social complexity of the parish."[58] What was being destroyed, he argues, was the symbolic structure of the people. I would like to suggest that, during the period of our study, what was going on was not so much destruction as displacement. With the withdrawal of the familiar religious practices and the comfortable furniture of worship, in both the sanctuary and the town, an imaginative vacuum was left that the cult of

[55] Regina Schwartz has observed a related dynamic in connection with the growing the veneration of the state. She thinks that it was giving up the doctrine of Christ's real presence in the Eucharist that created the space that was later filled by the Cult of Elizabeth. She writes: "At the time when the critique against the claims of transubstantiation was most vociferous, ironically the state appropriated substantialism. The logic of Eucharist – of embodying the supreme value – kept coming back in different forms: a substantial body became the way to figure the monarch, the state, and the nation." *Sacramental Poetics at the Dawn of Secularism: When God Left the World* (Stanford, CA: Stanford University Press, 2008), loc. 723.
[56] Freedberg, *The Power of Images: Studies in the History and Theory of Response* (Chicago: University of Chicago Press, 1989), pp. 54–65.
[57] See Eamon Duffy, *The Stripping of the Altars: Traditional Religion in England, c. 1400–1580* (New Haven, CT: Yale University Press, 1992).
[58] *Saints, Sacrilege and Sedition*, p. 101. For what follows, see p. 166.

Elizabeth was called on to fill. This did not reflect a conscious intention, nor was it true for everyone. But overall this displacement and replacement, I think, goes some way toward accounting for the otherwise mysterious paradox of Protestant iconoclasm coexisting with the cult of Elizabeth. The older symbolic structure, rather than being effaced, was simply displaced onto the larger mimetic structure of cultural and political life.

But there is a critical difference in this mobilization of imagery that is referenced by speaking of these portraits as media. The medium exemplified in this portraiture is rallied in support of a new way of relating to the world. Previously, imagery was *constitutive* of civic and religious relationships; during Elizabeth's reign it was becoming *representational* – a symbol that needed to be decoded. Medieval imagery was not a text in need of interpretation; it constituted an imaginative world in which believers dwelled. With the Reformation, imagery was on the way to becoming media, representing, but not embodying. Rather than contemplate it, we are meant to see "through it" to the sanctified world it celebrates.

Is There a Protestant Portraiture?

It is important to remember, however, that Calvin's rhetoric was also a call to action: listeners were meant to become players in this larger sanctified world. This dimension would come to play a key role in the emerging debate on the role of theater and the affective responses this solicited. But how does one assess the role Elizabethan portraits played in this emerging imagination? As we noted, one can see areas of overlap with Calvin's notion of the role of princes in the theater of God's glory. But there has also been a slippage. The prophetic call to work with God in restoring creation has been conflated with the view of England as God's Israel as a providential sign of the end of history. Significantly, John Bale had no sense that Christ's return would be delayed so that they might work to build the godly common-wealth.[59] In this respect Elizabeth's portraits served purposes at odds with an emerging notion of Protestant portraiture. We noted earlier that Calvin worked to replace what he called dead images (of the saints and holy persons) with living images of a people renewed after the image of Christ. Calvin's rhetoric called people to a new role in the theater of the world.

---

[59] Fairfield, *John Bale*, p. 113. But this also led him to resist attaching Elizabeth's reign to the promised culmination of history.

19 Anonymous woodcut of William Farel, from Theodore Beza, *Icones id est verae imagines virorum doctrina simul et pietate illstrium* (1580).
RB 601246. Courtesy of Henry Huntington Library, San Marino, California.

Zwingli's colleague, Leo Jud, captured this goal perfectly when he described portraits as "living images made by God, not by the hands of men."[60]

Something of this difference may be glimpsed by comparing these Elizabethan portraits with the use of portraits suggested by Calvin's successor, Theodore Beza. In 1580 Beza published a book of images, entitled *Icones id est verae Imagines Virorum Doctrina simul et pietate illustrium*.[61] This consisted of 90 biographical sketches, of which 38 are illustrated with woodcuts (with empty frames for 15 more – suggesting, R. M. Cummings thinks, haste in publishing the material). Dedicated to King James VI of Scotland, perhaps to remind him of his duty as a Protestant King, the collection represents emblems that highlight the virtues of a Christian man, in both prose and verse (Figure 19). Beza's intent was made clear in a cover letter to George Buchanan: "I can certainly say for myself that not only in reading the books of such great men, but *also in looking on their likenesses* I am as moved, I am as drawn to holy thoughts as if I were in their very presence, and with my own eyes saw them teaching, admonishing, chiding." Here Beza, tentatively, draws on long-standing traditions of images as standing in for a real presence, and places these in the service of the call to live life, as Calvin

---

[60] Quoted in Charles Garside, *Zwingli and the Arts* (New Haven, CT: Yale University Press, 1966), p. 182.

[61] Théodore de Bèze, *Icones 1580* (Menston: Scolar Press, 1971) (facsimile of volume *Icones id est verae Imagines Virorum Doctrina simul et pietate illustrium … quibus adiectae sunt nonullae picturae quas Emblemata vocant* published by Jean de Laon, Geneva, 1580), preface by R. M. Cummings, n.p. Beza's letter is quoted in this preface. Emphasis added.

would say, before the face of God (*coram Dei*), even if "looking on their likeness" in most cases involved reading their verbal portraits. Cummings suggests that Beza's work may have been a tardy response to his failure to collaborate with Jean Crespin's 1854 version of *The Book of Martyrs*. Though there is something of the medieval force of images standing in for their personal presence, like images in Foxe's book, Beza's "icons" are more a stimulus to emulation than contemplation.

The portraits of Elizabeth, however, serve distinctly different purposes, and, reflecting on them, Nicholas Sanders's taunt lingers in the mind: "Breake if you dare the Image of the Queenes Maiestie." Clearly, there were Protestants who worried about this imagery. Grindal dared to raise his voice; later William Perkins's writings reflected a Protestant concern; and some have seen an undercurrent of critique even in Spenser's *Fairie Queene*.[62] But overall prophetic voices raised against the excesses of the cult of Elizabeth were strangely muted. Despite this slippage between this visual imagery and Calvin's rhetoric, that theologian's portrayal of the drama of the world would continue to work its influence in the culture of England, especially in the areas of drama, literature, and music. Consistent with the emphasis on language, time, and drama that we have sketched, it is not hard to see why aesthetic production of this period came to be dominated by play-making, poetry, and music. It is to these practices and their particular contribution to a Reformed aesthetic that we turn in Chapter 6.

[62] See Hackett, *Virgin Mother*, pp. 190–205.

6

THE EMERGING AESTHETIC OF EARLY MODERN ENGLAND

A New World with Echoes of the Past

O N AUGUST 11, 1596, WILLIAM SHAKESPEARE TRAVELED TO Stratford for the burial of his eleven-year-old son Hamnet. As soil was thrown onto the casket, perhaps by William himself, the minister spoke words from the Protestant prayer book: "Forasmuch as it hath pleased Almighty God of his great mercy to take unto himself the soul of our dear brother here departed, we therefore commit his body to the ground, earth to earth, ashes to ashes, dust to dust; in sure and certain hope of the Resurrection to eternal life." Stephen Greenblatt, in his account of this event, wonders whether Shakespeare lamented the loss of the old comforting Catholic practices: candles burning, bells tolling, neighbors visiting to say a paternoster, alms distributed in memory of the dead, and priests paid to perform masses to ease the soul's passage through purgatory.[1] Whatever he thought at the time, Shakespeare must have brooded over this, Greenblatt thinks, when he sat down in 1600 or early 1601 to write the tragedy whose hero was named for his dead son, *Hamlet*. In this play, Greenblatt argues, Shakespeare succeeded – for the first time – in portraying an interiority that responded to deep unsatisfied cultural longings. The Reformation, this critic contends, offered the playwright an extraordinary gift, for it outlawed what had been a rich and comforting edifice, leaving a trail of "damaged rituals" that failed to assuage the confusion and dread people felt when facing death. So it is, Greenblatt concludes, that the great writer was left with a faith at home in neither Catholic or Anglican Churches, one situated in another institution: the theater. For only in the theatrical art could one "tap into the great reservoir of passionate feelings that, for him and for thousands of his contemporaries, no longer had a satisfactory outlet."

---

[1] Greenblatt, *Will in the World: How Shakespeare Became Shakespeare* (New York: Norton, 2004), p. 312. For what follows, see pp. 317–322. Quote that follows is at p. 321.

Greenblatt expresses here the common assumption that Shakespeare and other playwrights, deprived of the rituals and ceremonies of the old faith, turned to alternative (and mostly non-religious) forms of expression. But there is a growing consensus that conclusions of this sort tend to read back into this period modern assumptions about religious belief and practice, the same assumptions that have fueled debates about whether William (or his father John) were actually secret Catholic believers – debates that are as barren as they are impossible to settle.[2] More recent scholarship acknowledges that for most of the period under investigation, strict religious identities were in the process of formation, and boundaries were still frequently fluid – and for that reason hotly contested. This has led to a more non-sectarian investigation of, among other things, the rise of theater. Beatrice Groves, for example, argues that England's Catholic past did not disappear but continued to constitute an abiding presence even as the verbal texture of Protestantism with its sermons and Bible readings played an increasingly important role in the evolving shape of drama. Both, she argues, surely played their respective roles in Shakespeare's plays.[3]

Realistic Theater and the Godly Commonwealth

The mistake of Greenblatt and others is to focus too much on what was lost in the Reformation, rather than on the work of construction that it encouraged. Certainly, the familiar rituals and ceremonies, along with the material culture this made possible, were being challenged and displaced. But I argue that even if newly aroused suspicions about the role and efficacy of religious imagery made advance in that direction impossible, the larger world, now reconfigured in terms of the narrative of redemption, beckoned. What was one to make of this world? How was it to be negotiated? The use artists would make of that larger, reordered world opened up a broader aesthetic landscape and allowed the emergence of new aesthetic forms; the loss of the familiar resonance of bells, candles, and paternosters left open spaces in which new affective strategies could emerge.

Though play-making had a long history in England, the Reformation soon made its presence felt. Already in the 1530s, John Bale, under the

[2] A similar fruitless discussion revolves around whether, for example, John Donne or George Herbert were Anglican or Puritan writers. See Gene Edward Veith, Jr., *Reformation Spirituality: The Religion of George Herbert* (Lewisburg, PA: Bucknell University Press, 1985).
[3] Groves, *Texts and Traditions: Religion in Shakespeare 1592–1604* (Oxford: Clarendon Press, 2007). She argues for a synthesis rather than confrontation.

patronage of Thomas Cromwell, had begun to remake that tradition in terms of Reformation impulses. During that decade Bale and his troupe performed more than a dozen of Bale's plays, mostly biblical versions of morality plays. His play *King John* (c. 1533–1538) was significant for its introduction of a historical personage into a morality framework. Of this play Jesse Harris comments: "The introduction of persons from history was a step forward in the development of characterization; and the use of historical subject matter pointed toward the great historical dramas which were to grace the stage at the end of the century."[4] Bale's plays, however, were transitional, mostly reworking medieval forms, but the historical and personal realism suggests the influence of the Reformers and was an important precursor of later drama. Peter Happé argues that Bale's *Temptation of our Lord* (c. 1536–1538) shows the influence of Luther and the Reform in the dramatic encounter between Christ and Satan. By focusing on the life of Christ, Bale could hold up Christ's humanity while avoiding idolatry.[5] Bale's plays were important as transitions to more contemporary forms and reflected mainstream Protestant assumptions deriving from Tyndale or Luther. His major importance, in addition to his biblical historiography, was to promote interludes, that is, dramatic skits presented between acts of morality plays or, later, between elements of a worship service in churches, as important vehicles for religious teaching.

The flowering of these forms of Protestant play-making had to await the accession of Elizabeth in 1558. Contrary to common assumptions during the early years of her reign, Protestant consensus was positive toward drama, to the extent of encouraging dramatic performance even in the space of churches.[6] Between 1560 and 1580 dramatic performances were put on by touring troupes (of five to nine male players) that were often sponsored by Protestant nobles. Paul White argues that these participated easily with other publicists in disseminating Protestant teaching. In fact, of the 70 surviving plays from 1530 to 1580, he counts 40 that served homiletical purposes (p. 9). Early on the didactic purposes were underlined by the fact that every scene of every printed play of Bale was accompanied by verbal commentary that underlined its homiletic significance (p. 39). And with the return of exiles who had fled to Geneva during the reign of Mary, the influence of Calvin

[4] Harris, *John Bale: A Study in the Minor Literature of the Reformation* (Urbana: University of Illinois Press, 1940), p. 130.
[5] Peter Happé, *John Bale* (London: Prentice Hall, 1996), pp. 112, 115. For what follows, see p. 144.
[6] See Paul W. White, *Theatre and Reformation: Protestantism, Patronage and Playing in Tudor England* (Cambridge: Cambridge University Press, 1993), p. xiii. Pages cited in the text are to this work.

was making itself felt. Lewis Wagner's 1564 play *Mary Magdalene* draws entire sections of teaching directly from Calvin's *Institutes* (p. 60). White claims Wagner's play is "a dramatization of the process of religious conversion in specifically Calvinist terms" (p. 87), and it is particularly significant in that its prologue contains the first known defense of the stage by an English dramatist. Written by pastors or schoolteachers (professional playwrights did not yet exist), these pieces were performed in inns, taverns, outdoors, or in church. The popularity of these plays along with their explicit theological and ethical content gives some indication of the widespread commitment to the Reformation. While earlier the Reformation had been imposed from above, White points out, during the reign of Elizabeth it was increasingly embraced and encouraged by the people (p. 92).[7]

But acceptance of play-making – and even poetry, with which this was often associated – would become increasingly fraught as the century wore on. The conflicted discussions about royal imagery we have rehearsed in the 1570s made it inevitable that representation of all kinds, especially that which involved allegory and metaphor, called for justification. In the medieval period the ontology and function of aesthetic objects, as we noted earlier, reflected an underlying neo-platonic metaphysics – art objects could literally embody the ladder of spiritual reality. Calvin rejected this framework and replaced it with his robust theology of creation as the substantial sign and even the incarnation of spiritual reality, coming to the point where he could almost say nature is God. But the nature of the connection was tenuous and debated, as we have seen. Creation spoke of God but could not literally contain the divine; human sight was defective and could not properly discern God's presence in that larger theater. Both these difficulties were destined to create obstacles to a consistent theology of aesthetic objects.

While the proper (religious and political) use of imagery was being debated in the decade of the 1570s, a parallel conversation was taking place around both play-making and poetry. The setting for this was the growing suspicion of imagery that was taking place among Calvinist divines in the 1570s. It was only natural that this worry would be extended to play-making and poetry, aesthetic projects that were often related in the minds of theologians. Behind the continuing polemic against images emerging toward the end of the century, in the central period of Elizabeth's reign, lay a

---

[7] Though Peter Marshall argues that "from the very start the English Reformation as an 'act of state' and the English Reformation as a spiritual movement, were not remote and distant cousins, they were conjoined twins, dependent, sometimes resentfully, one upon the other." *Heretics and Believers*, p. 176.

gradual shifting of attitudes toward imagery and religious display. This was encouraged by the growing popularity of "prophesyings," referenced earlier, and their call to greater moral and religious rigor. Inevitably, these develop- ments drew attention to problems some conservative pastors had with play- making, and even drama more generally. The opening of public theaters in 1576 was a straw in the wind – indicative of the fact that the theater had become an institution no longer subject to clerical control. Wandering players had already been suppressed in 1572, four years before the establish- ment of public theaters, which were subject to licensing by the Mayor and Court of Alderman in London.[8]

One Reformed playwright soon registered his complaint. Stephen Gosson arrived in London from Oxford in 1576 and was dismayed by what he found. Gosson quickly published his protest, *The School of Abuse*, in 1579.[9] He lamented that poets had lost their ability to promote virtue – perhaps like the plays he had written earlier – and had become the "whetstones of wit," who mix honey with gall so that it goes down easier (p. 20). Piping (popular minstrels) and poetry are mostly abused, even in England; they no longer encouraged a martial virtue. Meanwhile people celebrate the Sabbath by flocking to the theaters, in breach of God's commandments (p. 35). Since none of this can be defended by Scripture, supporters defend themselves by taking refuge in antiquities (p. 42). He encourages the reader to "pull our feete back from resort to theaters, and turne our eyes from beholding vanitie, the greatest storme of abuse will be overblown and a fayre path trodden to amendment of life" (p. 44). Clearly, Gosson's judgments reflected a deepening concern that English society was not becoming the godly com- monwealth Protestant pastors had hoped for.

But Gosson's views did not go unchallenged. His diatribe was answered the following year by Thomas Lodge, who may be the first to offer a clear defense of play-making in Calvinist terms.[10] Lodge interestingly sets his

[8] David Bevington, "Literature and Theater," in David Loewenstein and Janel Mueller, eds., *The Cambridge History of Early Modern English Literature* (Cambridge University Press, 2002), p. 444. Raphael Falco argues that the anti-theatrical attacks actually sparked the opening of public theaters. "Medieval and Reformation Roots," in Arthur Kinney, ed., *A Companion to Renaissance Drama* (Oxford: Blackwell, 2002), p. 252.
[9] Stephen Gosson, *The School of Abuse*, ed. Edward Arber (London: Alex Murray, 1869 [1579]), introduction, pp. 1–16. Pages cited in the text are to this work. Interestingly, the work is inscribed to "Philip Sidney" and may have provided part of the motivation for Sidney's own work a few years later.
[10] *A Reply to Stephen Gosson's "School of Abuse" in Defence of Poetry, Musick and Stage Plays*, in *The Complete Works of Thomas Lodge* (London: Hunterian Club, 1883). Pages cited in the text are to this work.

defense of play-making within the larger frame of human ritual and play-making in history – that is, within the larger frame of the created order Calvin had developed. Play-making derives from an ancient ritual that had no other purpose than "to yeelde prayer unto God for happy harvests, or plentifull yeere" (p. 35). How is this a bad thing? How abuse? Or, often it was used to discover the follies of one's fellows, or oppose abuses. Even then, Lodge writes, "The good did hate al sinne for vertues' love / The bad for fear of shame did sinner remove" (p. 38). Not that play-making was in no need of reform – in ancient Rome and now. "I wish as zealously as the best that all abuse of playing were abolished, but for the thing, the antiquitie causeth me to allow it, so it be used as it should be" (p. 41). And this is so because, Lodge believed (anticipating Sidney's apology), "all the beginning of Poetrye proceeded from the Scripture" (p. 13), as Paul showed at Athens. Not that all "poets are holy but I affirm ye poetry is a heavenly gift" (p. 19). Lodge ends with a conventional dedication to the Peaceable Princes and Queen "that like Saba she may seeke Solomon: God confounde the imaginations of her enemies, and perfit [*sic*] his graces in her" (p. 48).

Striking in Lodge's defense is his ability to condemn abuse, while acknowledging the long-term cultural value of poetry and play-making. The conservative party, however, was unmoved. Their worry was more generally about the decline of society, what they saw as the loss of a righteous community. Philip Stubbes's *Anatomie of Abuses*, published in 1583, is especially interesting in this respect.[11] He asks the reader to consider a wide variety of practices: plays, gaming, dancing, and "such like," though he is opposed not to any kind of exercise but only to their abuses. When he comes to "stage-playes" he is emphatic that their wickedness – "bawdry, scurrility, wanton shewes and uncomely gestures" (p. 199) – cannot be mixed with the word of God and God's majesty, something that he goes on, interestingly, to describe in dramatic terms:

> All the company of Heaven … yea, the Devils themselves (as Saint James sayth) doe tremble and quake at the naming of God, and at the presence of his wrath: and doe these Mocker and flouters of his majesty, these dissembling Hypocrites … think to escape unpunished. (p. 199)

An array of Church Fathers is cited as witnesses against the evils of plays. Nothing can be learned from them but vice and blasphemy; those involved should "leave off that cursed kind of life, and give themselves to such honest

---

[11] Philip Stubbes, *The Anatomie of Abuses*, ed. Margaret Jane Kidnie (Tempe: Arizona Center for Medieval and Renaissance Studies, 2002 [1583]). Pages cited in the text to this edition.

exercises and godly mysteries, as God hath commanded them in his worde to get their livinges withal" (p. 205). The insistence on hypocrisy as the core problem for those who pretend to be what they are not speaks directly to issues of representation and metaphor. But at the same time, the dramatic vision that Stubbes extracts from Scripture is itself deployed in the service of an alternative social project that includes care for the poor, modest apparel, kindness toward neighbors, even humane treatment of animals. Stubbes found this social project compelling; he appeared uninterested in its aesthetic potential. Indeed he saw the artifacts on offer as obstacles to the performance of his social vision.[12]

As I argued in Chapter 3, performance of the Protestant ethical vision does not "stand in" for some higher reality. It is not a symbol of the new creation that God initiated in Christ; it is meant to literally enact this. Allegory and metaphor were suspect because they drew undue attention, and elevated weight, to the figure. As Adrian Streete points out, the shift of authority to representation is dangerous, "because this potentially then invests metaphor . . . with a degree of ontological truth."[13] As Calvin insisted, the truth of things lay out in the theater of the world, where God was performing the work of renewal. This work, as I argued earlier, constitutes a metonym, not a metaphor, and the difference would become critical.

Still, in addition to Thomas Lodge, there were voices anxious to draw out the aesthetic implications of the biblical drama Stubbes was so jealous to safeguard. The most influential of these was Sir Philip Sidney (1554–1586), the famous poet who served in the Court of Elizabeth. Already in 1582, perhaps prodded by the work (and dedication) of Gosson, he wrote his own defense, which he called *An Apologie for Poetrie*.[14] Sidney begins with a biblical allusion, noting those opposing poetry show ingratitude toward what is most noble in our history, indeed, our nation, "the first lightgiver to ignorance, and first Nurse, whose milk by little and little enabled them to feed afterwards of tougher knowledges" (pp. 2, 3). As with Lodge, this larger cultural contribution was to be embraced as

---

[12] For the cultural significance of this social project, see Dyrness, *Reformed Theology and Visual Culture*, pp. 126–127.

[13] Streete, *Protestantism and Drama in Early Modern England* (Cambridge: Cambridge University Press, 2009), p. 24.

[14] *An Apologie for Poetrie*, ed. Evelyn S. Shuckburgh (Cambridge: Cambridge University Press, 1891 [1595]). Pages cited in the text are to this edition. In this work, Brian Cummings claims, Sidney "makes perhaps the ultimate claims for a Protestant aesthetic of writing." *The Literary Culture of the Reformation*, p. 265.

good and even God-given. Though he acknowledges the debt to classical literature, he soon shows his Calvinist colors:

> There is no arte delivered to mankind, that hath not the works of Nature for his prinicpall object, without which they could not consist, and on which they so depend, as they become Actors and Players, as it were of what Nature will have set foorth. (p. 7)

All the "arts" depend on nature, but here the poet does nature one better: "Onley the Poet, disdaining to be tied to any such subjection, lifted up with the vigor of his owne invention, dooth growe in effect another nature, in making things either better than Nature bringeth forth, or, quite anewe, formes such as never were in Nature" (p. 8). There is a familiar strategy in this "erected wit" of the poet: to teach and delight. For since the sin of Adam results in our "infected wit," which keeps us from reaching what is higher, the poet's "erected wit maketh us know what perfection is" (p. 9). Following Aristotle (whom he cites), he notes the historian can only record the "foolish" story of human infected wit; the poet not only can show the way to virtue, but "giveth so sweet a prospect into the way, as will entice any man to enter into it" (p. 25). And this principle if followed makes plays, both comedies and tragedies, into potential engines of virtue (pp. 51, 52). Sidney here invests verse with the rhetoric of Calvin's sermons and, in the process, presses the reader to interrogate its imagery. If virtue is the resting place and goal of learning, "so Poetrie, being the most familiar to teach it, and the most princelie to move towards it, in the most excellent work is the most excellent workman" (p. 28).

Brian Cummings argues that for Sidney the creation of poetry – "another nature" – allows the emergence of new moral beings not subject to the consequences of the fall. The "wit" of the poet appears uncorrupted by the "infected will."[15] Sidney's defense, Cummings thinks, is borrowed from secular sources, and this tension would bedevil Protestant literature throughout the seventeenth century. But, I would argue, Cummings's complaint overlooks the precedent proposed by Calvin. Calvin's rhetorical purpose in his preaching and writing was in fact to project another nature, a new creation that, though not immune from the effects of the "infected will," proposes a story in which that will may be made whole. It was the gift of the poet, Sydney suggests, to imagine such a world.

But the worry over "infected wit" persisted among Calvin's followers. Fulke Greville, a lifelong friend of Sidney and promoter of his work,

---

[15] *The Literary Culture of the Reformation*, pp. 264–272, at 272.

harbored his own doubts about Sidney's claims. In a dedication to Sidney, Greville offers his gentle critique, and further nuances the emerging Calvinist sensibility. Though Greville affirms Sidney's (and Calvin's) goal of following nature, he felt his friend trusted his "erected wit" too well. He confessed in language that Calvin would have endorsed:

> For my own part, I found my creeping Genius more fixed upon the language of Life, than the Images of Wit, and therefore [I] chose ... to write to those only that are weather beaten in the sea of this world, as having lost sight of their Gardens, and Groves, study to saile on a right course among rocks and quick sands.[16]

Then Greville goes on, employing theatrical imagery, to press the question of the reader's role, recalling the rhetorical (and ethical) strategy of the Protestant project: "But he that will behold these acts upon their true stage, let him look on that stage whereon [he] himself is an actor, even the state he lives in, and for every part he may perchance find a player, and for every line (it may be) an instance of life." Greville underlines the fact that theater offers a mirror in which players and viewers are implicated; both are called to interrogate their own roles in the images played out on the stage. Indeed, during the earlier flowering of interlude plays of various kinds, the emphasis had always been on the benefits the drama provides. The theater that began to flourish in the established playhouses of the late 1570s did not always encourage visitors to appropriately interrogate their own roles, even if it could not escape the influence of the Reformation altogether.

But before turning to that part of the story, there is one play from this period that calls for special attention: Theodore Beza's *Abraham's Sacrifice*. Printed in Geneva in 1550, this was Beza's only play and one that Calvin would certainly have seen and approved of.[17] Staged in Lausanne and France "to great applause" (p. xxxviii), it was soon translated into Latin, Italian, and English (in 1575), going through ten editions in the sixteenth century and thirteen in the seventeenth century. Abraham's sacrifice of Isaac had been frequently treated by medieval mystery plays, later versions of which clearly influence Beza's work. The play's stunning popularity reflects its clear biblical message, but also the playwright's considerable literary skill. Significantly, Beza places the audience in the land of the Philistines in which Satan

---

[16] Greville, "A Dedication to Sir Philip Sidney," in *The Prose Works of Fulke Greville: Lord Brooke*, ed. John Gouws (Oxford: Clarendon, 1986 [1552]), p. 134. Quote that follows is at p. 135.

[17] See *A Tragedie of Abraham's Sacrifice*, English trans. Arthur Golding, 1575, ed. Malcolm Wallace (Toronto: University Library, 1906); for what follows, see the introduction. Quote from the conclusion at p. 63.

appears as a monk and an angel demands that Abraham sacrifice his son. Sparing of details, the action moves swiftly into a deeply involved psychological tragedy that moved audiences more immediately than its medieval or classical predecessors. Beza lays out his purposes in the conclusion. Both perversion and correction are there displayed before our eyes, to "make all of us to take such warnings by it as each of us may fare the better by the lively faith set foorth before our eyes." God of course makes no appearance in the play, but the figures represent well what Olivier Millet describes as Calvin's portrayal of Old Testament figures, not as shadows but as living pictures to instruct the faithful.[18] Abraham cries out to God, Satan tempts him, Sara laments her husband's absence. But it is Isaac that moves the heart: "Alas my father deere, upon my knees I humbly pray you here / My jouthful yeeres to pitie, if you may."[19] And Abraham replies: "Alas my sonne, God hath commanded me / to make an offering unto him of thee / to my great greef, to my great greef and pine /And endless wo" (p. 55). And Abraham's obedience, and God's deliverance of Isaac, becomes a sign of a deliverance to come: "And of thy bodie one shall come / By whom may blissing [sic] shall spred foorth / on all the nations of the earth ... / Because thou hast obeyed my mind" (p. 61). Beza's drama matches Calvin's attention to the exhortative intention of Old Testament figures, sensible to the affections rather than to rational theology – presenting not a symbol to decipher but an experience to discover.[20]

Since the play was not translated until 1575, it is difficult to argue for any influence on English play-making. References to it are scarce, and no one to my knowledge has made a study of the play and its impact. But its popularity argues for a widespread longing for theater that makes a comparable psychological appeal.

Calvin and Renaissance Theater

It would be hard to see how this growing focus on psychological and historical realism would not make some difference to developing attitudes to the theater. Despite the lively debate among the Calvinist divines, there is a growing scholarly consensus that the Calvinist religious framework that prevailed in England did in fact play a role the rise of Renaissance theater,

---

[18] *Calvin et la dynamique de la Parole*, p. 375. Millet references Beza's play as embodying Calvin's rhetoric in the form of a play (p. 276).

[19] *A Tragedie*, p. 54. Subsequent pages cited in the text are to this work.

[20] Millet, *Calvin et la dynamique de la Parole*, pp. 300, 423.

even if the precise nature of that influence is debated. A generation ago
O. B. Hardison argued that in Shakespeare we have a secular equivalent to
religious ritual.[21] Recently, Hardison's thesis has been elaborated in various
ways. We have noted that in the 1570s the last of the medieval religious
dramas died out. And by this time even biblical dramas, favored earlier by
Protestant playwrights, were being suppressed. But in terms of the larger
argument I am making in this book, this should not be surprising. Recall
that Calvin was emphatic that the dramatic focus was not on the religious
drama of the liturgy and its mystery play descendants – in this sense Beza's
play was an exception. Recall Calvin's reticence in elaborating biblical
stories as the object of the believer's intention, as the Franciscan tradition
proposed. The drama that interested him was the believer's call to enact the
drama of Christ's redemption out in the larger world. It was this call that
would serve as a touchstone for the development of realistic theater. G. K.
Hunter sums up the situation by noting: "The government requirement
that the writer avoid doctrinal matters (in a vocabulary still loaded with
doctrinal echoes) looks like an extraordinary boon, and may be one part of
the means by which Shakespeare was able to move into the 'modern'
world of psychological creativity."[22] Grace, repentance, mercy, forgiveness
are everywhere in Shakespeare's plays, he notes, but while they call for
theological glosses, they are embodied on the stage; they are experiences to
be discovered, not doctrines to be debated. And in late Elizabethan
England the extent of experiences to be discovered was expanding
dramatically, so that even the new alliances – both political and commercial – with the Ottoman empire and Morocco were soon reflected on
the English stage.[23]

    This influence then, however it is understood, reflects, I argue, the drastic
revision of what I have called the aesthetic situation occurring in the
Reformation period. As Huston Diehl put this in her ground-breaking
work: "Elizabethan and Jacobean drama is both a product of the Protestant
Reform – a reformed drama – and a producer of Protestant habits of

[21] *Christian Rite and Christian Drama*, p. 284. And cf. Peter Marshall: "Most educated English
Protestants were by the early 1570s 'Calvinists.'" *Heretics and Believers*, p. 497.
[22] "Shakespeare and the Church," in John M. Mucciolo, ed., *Shakespeare's Universe: Renaissance Ideas
and Conventions: Essays in Honor of W. R. Elton* (Aldershot: Scolar Press, 1996), p. 27.
[23] Tudor dramatists were eager "to exploit the ambivalent emotions created by English experiences
in the east as spectacular, captivating drama." Jerry Brotton, *The Sultan and the Queen: The Untold
Story of Elizabeth and Islam* (New York: Viking, 2016), loc. 2806. Brotton is emphatic on the role
that Protestant sensitivities played in these surprising alliances.

thought – a reforming drama."[24] Earlier descriptions of Calvinist influence
(by C. L. Barber and Louie Montrose) believed the efflorescence of drama
resulted from the suppression of Catholic ritual, so that the theatrical
"magic" was compensatory for the lost ritual, or, in terms I have used, the
old ritual was displaced onto the stage.[25] Huston Diehl and Deborah Shuger
argue that the Reformation rather created habits of thought that find a new
institutional home in the theater. Shuger describes these habits as "a culture's
interpretive categories and their internal relations, which underlie specific
beliefs, ideas and values."[26] But this is not altogether incompatible with the
notion that play-making represents a replacement of a lost ritual. As she goes
on to develop these cultural habits of thought, they throw light on the way
the theater provides an imaginative displacement for a lost ritual. As the
century wore on, Shuger sees the emergence of a modern hermeneutic, that
is, an increasing separation of the sign from the signified. Regina Schwartz
ties this trend to the Reformers' replacement of the real presence of Christ in
the Eucharist with *remembrance* of his death, which in turn opens the way to
see theater as a replacement ritual. Schwartz writes: "With its change from
sacrifice to remembrance, from transformation to representation, the Church
had embraced less the power of ritual than (ironically, given its opposition to
theater) the catharsis of spectacle."[27] But when understood as a reformulation of Calvin's rhetoric of summons, and the extension of this drama into
the larger world, the irony disappears. Schwartz thinks a craving for justice
and redemption lies at the heart of most of Shakespeare's plays, and this
craving is itself religious, not a sign that drama is now emptied of religion.[28]

Huston Diehl has discussed this influence in the context of what she calls
the deep distrust of the theatrical and imaginary of the Reformers. This
distrust led them to produce "their own dramatic forms to replace the
'idolatrous' spectacle and pomp of the Roman Church."[29] Her argument

---

[24] Diehl, *Staging Reform, Reforming the Stage: Protestantism and Popular Theater in Early Modern England* (Ithaca, NY: Cornell University Press, 1997), p. 1.

[25] See Anthony B. Dawson and Paul Yachnia, *The Culture of Playmaking in Shakespeare's England: A Collaborative Debate* (Cambridge: Cambridge University Press, 2001), who describe the various ways Calvinist influence on theater has been approached (pp. 27, 28).

[26] Shuger, *Habits of Thought in the English Renaissance: Religion, Politics and the Dominant Culture* (Berkeley: University of California Press, 1990), p. 9. These values and beliefs she thinks were "by and large religious." For what follows, see p. 37.

[27] *Sacramental Poetics at the Dawn of Secularism: When God Left the World* (Stanford, CA: Stanford University Press, 2008), loc. 1093.

[28] *Sacramental Poetics*, loc. 820. She mentions in particular Stephen Greenblatt's proposition that Shakespeare represents emptying life of religion.

[29] Diehl, *Staging Reform*, p. 5. For what follows, cf. pp. 13, 24.

underlines the fact that, so far from eliminating all imagery, Protestants placed a new interpretive focus on them. The theater could reflexively stage the conflict over images. While images were desacralized, they are now deployed in terms of a new rhetorical and ethical strategy. For Protestants, though the furniture of liturgy – font, pulpit – consisted only of "representational signs," not sacramental images, it is placed in the service of a larger rhetorical purpose. As she goes on to demonstrate through analysis of Shakespeare's tragedies, "by employing a revolutionary rhetoric that subverts and reinterprets older forms of theater while fostering new – Protestant – forms of seeing," viewers are asked to pay attention to their seeing.[30] By a reflexive attention to their own looking that recalls the plea of Greville, viewers were asked to become complicit in the narrative they were observing. The problem with medieval drama was not that it incited a devotional gaze or encouraged believers to meditation; these things were not wrong. Rather, these did not move worshipers to action. John Foxe in his *Acts and Monuments* had no time for the theatricality of the Roman Church, but, Diehl notes, he champions another kind of theater, substituting the theatrics of martyrdom for traditional pomp and pageantry. So, Foxe encourages readers to rewrite their past and, Diehl thinks, replace the devotional gaze with demystifying ceremonies. Diehl wants to contrast this new theatricality with liturgy, which she associates with the space of the church. But, while her argument overall is convincing, I believe hers is an overly narrow reading of liturgy. What Calvin sought was, rather, an expansion of the rhetoric of the liturgy, a reorientation of the drama to embrace the believers' life in the world – what Calvin called the Christian's warfare.

The intention of Calvin's drama to hold up a mirror to the spectator clearly resonated with the unfolding of Renaissance drama. The power of this developing dramatic sense lay in its reflection of ordinary life – its offer, as Regina Schwartz writes, of "an image of actual life: 'the purpose of playing ... was and is to hold as 'twere a mirror up to nature.'"[31] But it did more: in holding up a mirror, its very realism called spectators to attention. This is most famously seen in Hamlet's plan to stage a play within a play to "catch the conscience of the king" (III.I.582), that is, to trick the King into showing his guilt. The mirror that is placed before the spectator calls fresh attention to what is seen and what is not seen. As Huston Diehl

---

[30] *Staging Reform*, p. 65. As we saw in Chapter 2, she discusses the art of Cranach as an example of this project. On the theatrics of martyrdom, see p. 25.

[31] *Sacramental Poetics*, p. 43. The last phrase is quoted from *Hamlet*, III.2.21, though it ultimately derives from Cicero.

notes, Othello's handkerchief highlights the problematic of "seeing" and "not seeing." Shakespeare's portrayal of "lying signs" that keep one from noticing what is really there, Shuger thinks, is a direct application of Calvin's project of demystification of lying signs – a point to which I will return in Chapter 7.[32] Other scholars have pointed to the way the audience's lifelong experience with the liturgy, and the ritualistic efficacy of words, influenced playwrights' use of speech acts. Erika Lin, for example, argues: "By focusing the actual playhouse spectators to rely on spoken words to determine who [or what] counts as visible with the represented fiction, the scene [in Othello] serves as a warning to them not to rely too extensively on their eyes."[33] Audiences, whether Catholic or Protestant, were used to the idea that the Eucharist was made efficacious by the words of consecration. Religious practices thus infiltrated not only the representational strategy but the dynamics of performance as well.

Clearly seeing redemptive truth and, in the case of Foxe's book of martyrs, the drama of martyrdom actually played out in the world resonates with Calvin's liturgical goals. Public worship is not theater; it is not spectacle. For that we must lift our eyes to what God is doing in remaking creation. And this dramatic situation opened up new possibilities for realistic theater. As Regina Schwartz notes, even if "the theater cannot *do* anything to other humans, [or] *offer* anything to God," it can awaken our longing for redemption and forgiveness.[34] Shakespeare's plays represent not the secular absence of rituals, but rituals refilled with moral outrage, reflecting an influence of the Reformation narrative of sin and grace.[35]

Moreover, theater makes it possible for narrative, when seen and heard, to perform the rhetoric of Calvin. This is clearly seen in the subsequent defense

---

[32] *Staging Reform*, pp. 127–132.

[33] "'It is requir'd you do awake your faith': belief in Shakespeare's theater," in J. H. Degenhardt and Elizabeth Williamson, eds., *Religion and Drama in Early Modern England* (Burlington, VT: Ashgate, 2011), p. 111.

[34] "If in one sense, the Elizabethan theater competed with the Mass for an audience, in another, deeper sense, it replaced it, becoming the first truly Reformed church." *Sacramental Poetics*, loc. 793. Emphasis in original. Her argument is that the very elimination of the transformative work of the sacrament opened the way for later playwrights and poets to develop what she terms a sacramental poetics. Interestingly, these influences coincided with the progressive narrowing of the space of performance into specific and formal theatrical places. Cf Serene Jones, "Calvin's Common Reader," lecture, April 6, 2013, Calvin Studies Society, Princeton Theological Seminary.

[35] *Sacramental Poetics*, loc. 820, 864. Debora Shuger thinks this influence comes not only from Calvin but also from Luther via Tyndale, though she thinks the politics of Shakespeare has slipped from their Christian framework. "Subversive Fathers and Suffering Subjects," in Donna Hamilton and Richard Strier, eds., *Religion and Politics in Post-Reformation England: 1540–1688* (New York: Cambridge University Press, 1996), pp. 55–57.

of theater. In his *Apology for Actors*, published in 1612, Thomas Heywood, writing from the perspective of an actor, not a playwright, musters anti-theatrical arguments in support of the theater. Yes, the actors portray knaves as well as the righteous, because the theater holds up a mirror to all. We are all implicated in the common world the stage lays bare. "One man is ragged, and another brave. / All men have parts, and each man acts his owne / . . . and all finde Exits when their parts are done."[36] Heywood interprets this *theatrum mundi* in emphatically Calvinist terms: for it is God who sits in the gallery and watches the play:

> If then the world a theater present,
> As by the roundness it appars most fit,
> Built with starre-galleries of hye ascent,
> In which Jehove doth as spectator sit.
> And chiefe determiner to applaud the best.

And such performances, Heywood thinks, are far superior to painting, which simply represents its subject. Heywood insists princes can be formed by seeing the action of past heroes, just as Alexander the Great had been shaped by seeing the destruction of Troy acted out. Live action moves audiences better than other arts because it can serve as an enacted sermon. As Heywood explains: "Oratory is a kind of a speaking picture . . . painting likewise, is a dumbe oratory, therefore may we not as well by some curious *Pigmalion*, drawe their conquests to worke the like love in Princes towards these Worthyes by shewing them their pictures drawne to the life?" The viewer can indeed mistake the actor for the hero, but therein lies its power, its summons: "So bewitching a thing is lively and well spirited action, that it hath power to new mold the harts of the spectators and fashion them to the shape of any noble and notable attempt."[37] For Heywood, if you would deny theater, you "may as well deny a world to me."

But that influence, however construed, is not the whole story. For this same impulse could also contribute to the undoing of play-making. The defense of Heywood and the appreciations he includes suggest a lingering

---

[36] Heywood, *An Apology for Actors* (London: Nicholas Okes, 1612), p. A4v. Quote that follows is at this page.

[37] *Apology for Actors*, p. B4r. Quote that follows is at p. A4v. Here Heywood reverses the anti-theatrical argument: total engagement is not a danger, it is a "moral good." Although she goes on to note that recent scholarship has described the multiple ways in which audiences engaged with Renaissance theater, Erika T. Lin believes the religious call is still central. "'It is requir'd you do awake your faith'", in Degenhardt and Williamson, eds., *Religion and Drama*, pp. 89–113.

suspicion of eloquence and allure, and a preference for plainness. One hears, even in Heywood, echoes of Greville's worry over Sidney, and even of Stubbes's suspicions. The iconographic impulse had not disappeared, and it would eventually doom the theater, which Charles I finally closed in 1642.[38]

Though Shakespeare achieved unprecedented popular success in his lifetime, early critical appreciation of his work was sometimes more ambiguous. Samuel Johnson only grudgingly admitted him to the canon of great writers – as an honorary rustic. John Milton's faint praise sums up the common assumption: "Shakespear fancies childe, / Warble his native Wood-notes wilde."[39] In a sense such assessments reflect reigning assumptions, inherited from medieval drama, that sought to apply Aristotle's *Poetics* in a literal way – Shakespeare, on this reading, failed to follow the rules. Malcolm Guite has recently argued that it was not until Samuel Coleridge's famous lectures on Shakespeare that this conception was finally overturned, and Shakespeare's dramatic contribution recognized. In his lectures Coleridge argues that Shakespeare's genius lay in his recovery of the natural as opposed to the artificial:

> Nature the prime genial artist, inexhaustible in diverse powers, is equally inexhaustible in forms – each exterior is the physiognomy of the Being within, its true image reflected & thrown out from the concave mirror – and even such is the appropriate Excellence of her chosen poet, our own Shakespeare/himself a nature humanized.[40]

As we will see in the case of landscape painting, the decisive change brought about by the Reformed view of creation is to break down medieval notions of "unities" and open up the world not only to exploration but to celebration. As Guite says:

> The key to understanding the way imagination works in Shakespeare's art is not simply about art ... but about nature herself, ... Shakespeare's art is not simply the embroidering by fancy on the grave-clothes of the cold corpse of "dead" nature, as though nature ... only receives meaning from

[38] Diehl: "An iconoclastic theater eventually consumes itself." *Staging Reform*, p. 215. The closure of theaters proved of course to be a temporary measure; they were reopened by Charles II in 1660.

[39] Milton, *The Poetical Works of John Milton*, ed. H. C. Beeching (London: Henry Frowde, 1904), "L'Allegro," lines 134, 135, p. 23. "Honorary rustic" is Malcolm Guite's term. *Mariner: A Theological Voyage with Samuel Taylor Coleridge* (Downers Grove, IL: InterVarsity Press, 2018), p. 299. For what follows, see pp. 299–300.

[40] *The Collected Works of Samuel Taylor Coleridge; Lectures 1808–1819 on Literature*, ed. Kathleen Coburn (Princeton, NJ: Princeton University Press, 1987), vol. 5, p. 495. Cf. Guite, *Mariner*, pp. 299–300.

the "artificial" work of the poet, but rather it is the operation in and through Shakespeare as an artist of the very same power which itself gives nature life, and that power is the power of the Imagination.[41]

If Guite is right, the discovery of the hidden potential of creation and the theater of the world may not simply have influenced Shakespeare's dramatic strategy, but might have opened the way to more modern conceptions of imagination.

English Lyrical Poetry

Despite the suspicions of conservatives, or even *because* of them, scholars have argued that in the sixteenth and seventeenth centuries a uniquely Protestant way of reading and writing developed that reflected Reformation attitudes in general, and Calvin's theology in particular.[42] These attitudes were widely shared by Protestants in subsequent periods, especially in England and America, even by groups that were divided over other (non-literary) issues. This literary tradition, I would argue, finds its source both in the Calvinist vision of the world as theater, which I have developed, and in the particular developments in Calvinism around 1600 in England, which I explore in this chapter.[43]

While the decades around the turn of the seventeenth century were the most creative for an emerging English literature, they also marked a clear change in the developing Calvinist vision. England continued to exhibit the diversity of Calvinisms we have glimpsed, but there was one change that emerged during this period in particular. Since the classic article of Basil Hill in 1966, scholars have called attention to the fact that Calvinism underwent

---

[41] *Mariner*, p. 300.

[42] A thesis developed by a previous generation of scholars, but still widely influential. Cf John N. King, *English Reformation Literature: The Tudor Origin of the Protestant Tradition* (Princeton, NJ: Princeton University Press, 1982), and Barbara K. Lewalski, *Protestant Poetics and the Seventeenth-Century Lyric* (Princeton, NJ: Princeton University Press, 1979).

[43] Readers may complain that my discussion minimizes the difference between Anglican and Puritan parties during the period under investigation. As early as the 1960s Charles H. George, in *The Protestant Mind of the English Reformation: 1570–1640* (Princeton, NJ: Princeton University Press, 1961), argued that there was a broad theological agreement among Anglicans and Puritans. This consensus was corroborated and developed in the work of John N. King and Barbara Lewalski. As Nicholas Tyacke notes, the acceptance of the "indisputably Calvinist" Lambeth Articles in 1595 is an accurate index of this consensus. *Anti-Calvinists: The Rise of English Arminianism c. 1590–1640* (Oxford: Oxford University Press, 1990), p. 5.

major changes after the Reformer's death in 1564.[44] While Hill and subsequent scholars have been faulted for improperly assuming a normative status for Calvin's writings and focusing on particular doctrinal issues – such as the place of predestination in Calvin's thinking – several changes may be signaled that were to have profound implications on the emerging poetics of Protestantism.

As we have seen, Calvin's final structuring of the *Institutes* in 1559 generally laid out a narrative of biblical teaching that roughly followed the Apostles' Creed. It was this biblical narrative and the careful exegesis that supported it that was central for Calvin, and he expressed satisfaction that it was appropriately laid out in this final edition. In the preface to the 1559 edition of the *Institutes* he writes: "Although I did not regret the labor spent [on previous editions], I was never satisfied until the work had been arranged in the order now set forth. Now I trust that I have provided something that all of you will approve."[45] This involved the dramatic program that we have noted, beginning with the created order and the evidences of God's glory found there in Book I, moving to the work of Christ in redeeming humanity's propensity to self-promotion in Book II, and finally describing the means by which this grace is received both internally and externally in Books III and IV. Calvin's followers, however, would not follow this narrative structure. Theodore Beza, Calvin's successor in Geneva, was more interested in systematically laying out the flow of doctrine that focused on God's electing purposes than in developing the movement from creation to new creation that Calvin had proposed.[46] Toward the end of the century the teaching of classical rhetoric waned, and a revival of scholastic logic influenced by Peter Ramus became influential – particularly in England.[47] In the 1590s this quest for clear guidance and certainty led to the development of what was called practical divinity. Richard Hooker and William Perkins, in particular, placed the emphasis more on what Perkins called experimental theology. This had two sides that might be thought antithetical to each other. On the

[44] Basil Hill, "Calvin against the Calvinists," in G. E. Duffield, ed., *John Calvin Courtenay Studies in Reformation Theology* (Appleford: Sutton Courtenay Press, 1966). See the summary and response in Carl Trueman, "Calvin and Calvinism," in Donald McKim, ed., *The Cambridge Companion to John Calvin* (Cambridge: Cambridge University Press, 2004), pp. 225–244.

[45] *Institutes*, ed. John McNeill, p. 3.

[46] In addition to sources cited above, see Philip Benedict, *Christ's Churches Purely Reformed: A Social History of Calvinism* (New Haven, CT: Yale University Press, 2002), pp. 300–303. Aristotle's influence is apparent in Beza in a way not true for Calvin. This is not to say Calvin did not believe and teach God's electing purposes – this had been orthodox Christian teaching since Augustine – but this was not central to his thought in the way it was for many of his successors.

[47] On Ramus's influence in England, see Dyrness, *Reformed Theology and Visual Culture*, pp. 133–137.

one hand, Hooker represents further support for the Renaissance appeal to reason and evidence over against all (papist) forms of emotional delusion. Debora Shuger has described the transformation that Hooker represents in terms of an emerging individualism. Whereas medieval Eucharistic teaching focused on the real presence of Christ in the elements, for Calvin and the English Puritans, she argues, "the locus of presence transfers to the faithful community; in Hooker it transfers to the individual." The relation between God and the individual is privatized in Hooker, she thinks, loosed from its institutional and communal moorings.[48] Accompanying this, on the other hand, was an increasingly inward and emotional quest for the assurance of salvation. Whereas Calvin subordinated individual feelings to a focus on Scripture, Christ, and the sacraments, Perkins will write that "you should pray so that you feel inwardly . . . signs and testimonies in yourself."[49] As the nonconformist divine Richard Rogers would write in 1603: "Give no rest to yourselves, till you can prove that you be in the estate of salvation."[50]

Notice the significant transformation of the focus of attention. Calvin's rhetoric called believers to play their role in the theater of the world, to bear patiently the hardships that would come; now the struggle has become an inward and personal search for the assurance of grace. The focus of aesthetic attention now rests not on the theater of the world but on the inner struggle of the soul. At the turn of the century, popular manuals promoting the spiritual life proliferated; and major poets, George Herbert and John Donne themselves pastors, wrote lyrics that illumined the soul's terrible and wonderful struggle over God's presence and forgiveness.

One of the enduring questions faced by students of this period is: What caused this change, what prompted this inward turn? Debora Shuger thinks the seventeenth-century focus on the inner life of the spirit was partly a reaction against the polemics of politics and Church.[51] But it is also, as she recognizes, a continuation of the subjectification that was beginning

---

[48] Shuger, *Habits of Thought*, pp. 39–40. She sees in Hooker the emergence of a modern hermeneutic. She notes that while Calvin insisted on a public penance, now it will become inward and personal. Christopher Hill long ago had noticed this change and saw it accompanying the transfer of religious focus from the parish to the home: from the 1590s "the preachers stressed an individual pietism, with the household as its essential unit rather than the parish." *Society and Puritanism in Pre-Revolutionary England* (London: Secker and Warburg, 1964), p. 502.

[49] Quoted in Hill, "Calvin against the Calvinists," p. 30.

[50] Quoted in Benedict, *Christ's Churches*, p. 321. That this represents a radical change in focus has been questioned most prominently by Richard Muller, *The Unaccommodated Calvin* (New York: Oxford University Press, 2000).

[51] "Literature and the Church," in Loewenstein and Mueller, eds., *Cambridge History of Early Modern English Literature*, pp. 521, 522.

already in the medieval period – which we have traced – and a revival of a particularly Augustinian conception of the Christian life.[52] But more to our purposes, as Brian Cummings points out, there was a battle over representation driving this inner vision, a process in which poetry itself became an active participant.[53] One is tempted here to see evidence of the common assumption that the word, now in a literary form, is replacing images and relics that prevailed in the earlier period. But as Cummings insists, things were not so simple. The episodes and debates over images were about communication of spiritual power, but they were also about the operative signifying system. Cummings argues that the "significance of the image lies only in its signification." As Tyndale's exchange with More made clear, words now take the place and expand on pictures, and these "images" will now be read as "literature." In ways that have yet to be fully acknowledged, I believe this move opens the way for the modern notion of literature as the carrier of a people's soul. Barbara Lewalski pointed out a generation ago that Protestant poets appropriated biblical material – as both source and model – to form a body of lyrical poetry for the "pains-taking analysis of the religious life."[54] The insistence on biblical material and style is a telling sign of the continuing influence of Calvin. And the focus of their "arte," though now directed on the experience of grace, was still oriented by the narrative of sin and redemption that Calvin had elaborated in scriptural terms. Imagery is still a central concern, but now the images are verbal. And these images still carry the rhetoric of Calvin's summons.

The generation alive at the beginning of the seventeenth century saw an explosion of printed devotional materials of all kinds – bibles, psalters (more than a million of these were printed), sermons, emblem books, poetry, and spiritual biographies. Many of these went into ten or twenty printings; whereas, by contrast, the very few non-religious titles seldom reached even ten printings.[55] This tidal wave indicates a highly literate culture – having

---

[52] An aspect of this continuity was also a recovery of late medieval mystical theology represented, for example, by Johann Arnold's wildly popular *True Christianity* (1605).

[53] Cummings, "Iconoclasm and Bibliophobia in the English Reformation, 1521–1558," in Jeremy Dimmick et al., eds., *Images, Idolatry and Iconoclasm in Late Medieval England* (Oxford: Oxford University Press, 2002), pp. 187–200. Quote at p. 190.

[54] Lewalski, *Protestant Poetics and the Seventeenth-Century Religious Lyric* (Princeton, NJ: Princeton University Press, 1979), p. 13. Of her focus on five poets to study (Donne, Herbert, Traherne, Tayulor, and Vaughan), only Henry Vaughan was not a clergyman!

[55] Susan Tara Brown, *Singing and the Imagination of Devotion* (Colorado Springs, CO: Paternoster Press, 2008), pp. 31, 32.

reached 80 percent in England at the beginning of the new century – but also a deep spiritual longing these materials were meant to satisfy.

Earlier we saw two characteristics of the poetry of this period that seemed to be in tension: the desire to define and specify the theological truth of God's saving presence and care, and at the same time the emotional quest for personal assurance, and the personal appropriation of this presence. In many respects both of these characteristics define these Protestant lyrics. Much of the preaching and poetry of this period embodied the attempt to work out the intricate meaning of the narrative of sin and salvation, and also to know it experimentally. As Brian Cummings put this, both preachers and poets exhibited a "writing and rewriting of the self and of society ... as part of the practice and experience of doctrine." These were, he thinks, "intersecting speech acts."[56] The poetry especially wrestles with truth sometimes through a long night – like Jacob – eager to receive a blessing. The poem itself becomes a participant in forming belief.

In 1592 William Perkins, preacher and teacher at Cambridge University, wrote a treatise entitled *The Arte of Prophesying*.[57] Perkins wanted to stress the "art" that is the constructed and attractive character of the sermon, which here he calls "prophesying." The sermon is both a reading and an exposition of the text, interpreted by itself, and, second, an application "whereby the doctrine rightly collected is diversely fitted according as place, time and person doe require" (p. 664). This can be intellectual, for information, or practical, for instruction and correction, and will be represented and delivered in the sermon. And though the preacher is free to use any study materials available, when he (it was always "he") preaches, "he ought in publicke to conceale all these from the people" (p. 670). The reason for this is theological – the true power of this is meant to be the Holy Spirit and not human eloquence, but it is also, in Perkins's terms, aesthetic – *artis etiam est celare artem* (It is [a point of] art to conceal art). So the preacher is to apply the doctrine rightly collected from Scripture, to the life and manners of men in a "simple and plaine speech" (p. 673).

Nothing could better define the emerging Protestant aesthetic – and the poetry that expressed it – than this famous expression of Ovid. Note the style Perkins promotes is a common speech for common people – those addressed in sermons, the same audience addressed in plays and poetry. And the eschewal of decoration is both a theological assertion and an aesthetic

---

[56] *The Literary Culture of the Reformation*, p. 285.
[57] *The Arte of Prophesying: The Works of That Famous and Worthy William Perkins* (London: John Legatt, 1631 [1592]), vol. II, pp. 646–673. Pages cited in the text are to this work.

decision; plain speech is meant to open a space for God. George Herbert captures this considered strategy in a stanza of "A True Hymn":

> Whereas if th' heart be moved,
> Although the verse be somewhat scant,
> God doth supply the want,
> As when th' heart says (sighing to be approved)
> "O could I love" and stops; God writeth "Loved."[58]

While suspicion of the senses was widespread in this tradition, this very apprehension could be appropriated and put to use by poets. Ernest Gilman goes so far as to argue that the iconoclastic temperament of the Reformation *created* the splendor of seventeenth-century poetry. For since the imagining power of the mind was tainted by pride and sensuality, these writers realized that "the word was the bulwark of the spirit against the carnal enticements of the image."[59] Consider this Holy Sonnet of John Donne:

> When senses, which thy souldiers are,
> Wee arme against thee and they fight for sinne ...
> When plenty, Gods image and seale
>   Makes us Idolatrous,
> And love it, not him, whom it should reveale,
> When we are mov'd to seeme religious
> Only to vent wit, Lord deliver us.[60]

Despite this mistrust, Donne can draw from the biblical narrative powerful images that feed the imagination. Because it distrusted vain display and sensuality, this poetry was not intended to be artless; rather, following William Perkins it sought an "art whose precepts may be derived, and whose stylistic features may be imitated, from the Scriptures."[61]

Though the focus of attention is now the believer's life before God, rather than his or her larger calling to serve God in the theater of creation, as Calvin proposed, one can still see the influence of that theologian on the developing aesthetic. Calvin's understanding of biblical rhetoric, which we described in Chapter 4, is still determinative. The biblical drama was to be personally appropriated by believers' identification with the story – something that we

---

[58] *The Works of George Herbert in Prose and Verse* (London: Frederick Warne, n.d.), p. 232.

[59] Ernest B. Gilman, *Iconoclasm and Poetry in the English Reformation* (Chicago: University of Chicago Press, 1986), p. 1 and see pp. 5, 6.

[60] John Donne: *The Divine Poems*, ed. Helen Gardner (Oxford: Clarendon Press, 1978), "A Litanie," xxi, p. 23.

[61] Lewalski, *Protestant Poetics*, p. 219. She also discusses Perkins's instructions for preachers as an important source for this aesthetic disposition.

saw demonstrated in Beza's *Tragedie of Abraham*. As Olivier Millet puts this: "The proximity of biblical figures, even the identification with them, can be translated, in Reformed literature, into epic recitations, edifying biographies, and moving lyricism."[62] This short-circuits, Millet thinks, the traditional Christian symbolism in favor of psychological exactness of biblical examples, a practice that underlines their human density and their universal reach. This personal identification with biblical material characterizes the Reformed lyric poetry of this period.

Taking the Bible literally, rather than reading it symbolically, also meant interpreting its story typologically. That is, Old Testament figures anticipated New Testament fulfillment, which in turn anticipated the struggle of contemporary believers. Ira Clark has argued that this historical interpretation of Scripture instigated in Reformed believers a lyric persona. That is, the Reformed believer should not seek to presumptuously imitate Christ directly as medieval believers sought to do. Rather, the lyric persona, Clark claims, would "humbly embody the individuality and failure of a type and thereby realize salvation through Christ, the anti-type."[63] What gives this literature its power, Clark thinks, is the expressive potential of typology. "These poets were unique in imitating types to such an extent that they were remaking themselves into their typological past."

With all of its variety, the primary characteristic of this body of poetry is consistent. These poets and lyricists sought to rewrite the narrative of their own lives in terms of the biblical narrative of sin and salvation – to literally write themselves into the poetry. In other words, they sought to project a world in which they were called to account. William Ames in his *Conscience* identified our process of sanctification with the nailing of Christ on the cross. He wrote: "The nailes whereby in this application sinne is fastened to the cross, are the very same with those whereby Christ was fastened to the cross."[64] John Donne can interpret the cross in terms of his life as a sinner, as I argued in Chapter 3, living out the meaning of the cross in his world:

> Spit in my face . . . and pierce my side,
> Buffet, and scoffe, scourge and crucifie mee . . .
> They kill'd once an inglorious man, but I
> Crucifie him daily, being now glorified.[65]

[62] *Calvin et la dynamique de la Parole*, p. 376.

[63] Clark, *Christ Revealed: The History of the Neo-Typological Lyric in the English Renaissance* (Gainesville: University Presses of Florida, 1982), p. 21. Quote that follows is at p. 28.

[64] *Conscience with Power and Cases*, Book 2, p. 26. Cf. discussion in Dyrness, *Reformed Theology*, p. 195.

[65] Donne, *The Divine Poems*, "Holy Sonnet," vii, p. 9.

Here one might say the rhetorical purposes of Calvin's preaching have been embedded in a uniquely dramatic (and theological) literary structure.

Music and the Emerging Protestant Aesthetic

As has become clear, the literature common to this period, rather than being designed for use in church or university, was primarily written to be read at home, in personal and domestic settings. Its immense popularity speaks to the fact that this literature was part of the long process of working the Reformation faith and teaching down into the fabric of everyday life.[66] And, arguably, a major driver of that process was the practice of singing, first Scripture, and later devotional lyrics.

In Chapter 4 I argued that the definitive aesthetic experience for Calvin likely came from his encounter with music. While he could praise the beauty of the created order as evidence of God's glory, it was not until he experienced the power of singing the Psalms – poetry that, he felt, embodied the anatomy of the soul, that he came to appreciate the affective potential of aesthetic artifacts. It is not surprising, then, that those following his teaching in England should place a similar emphasis on the role of music.

At the Reformation, England was heir to a rich tradition of church music and it is not surprising that its adaptation of existing Sarum melodies, along with Lutheran and Calvinist sources, led to the forging of one the finest traditions of Christian music.[67] Already in the 1530s Miles Coverdale published *Goostly Psalms* (c. 1534), which Thomas Cromwell promoted as an early attempt to encourage the singing of psalms in the vernacular. These mostly made use of inherited plainsong melodies and Lutheran imports. Music, in England as on the continent, depended largely on royal and noble patronage, so this initiative faded when Cromwell fell from favor. But royal patronage continued to support the Chapel Royal with its residential chorale and composers, an institution that was responsible for some of the most important musical developments of the Renaissance in England. Its influence was felt especially in the cathedral tradition of church music, which

---

[66] Cf. Peter Marshall: The English "'Reformation' was a journey; a continual striving after elusive perfection, in the world and in oneself." *Heretics and Believers*, p. 434.

[67] This tradition has been the subject of important recent scholarship. See Andrew Gant, *O Sing unto the Lord: A History of English Church Music* (Chicago: University of Chicago Press, 2017); Susan Tara Brown, *Singing and the Imagination of Devotion: Vocal Aesthetics in Early Protestant Culture* (Colorado Springs, CO: Paternoster Press, 2008); Jonathan P. Willis, *Church Music and Protestantism in Early Modern England* (London: Routledge, 2010).

prospered in the cities, where trained choirs ventured into more advanced polyphonic styles emanating from the Chapel Royal.

But alongside this tradition there arose a more indigenous style of music more directly influenced by Calvin's practice of psalm-singing and centered in rural parishes. These melodies were often led by unschooled parish clerks and represented the only form of music that most people would experience at the local level.[68] Both these traditions developed especially during the reign of Elizabeth, who turned out to be a more enthusiastic promoter of music than she was of the visual arts or theater. Significant in this process was the publication by John Day of *The Whole Book of Psalms Collected into English Metre* in 1562. Many of these psalms had been translated by William Whittingham in Geneva, and brought back to England by the returning exiles. The diary of Henry Machyn offers what was perhaps the first record of congregational singing of these tunes, and the freedom this expressed, on September 21, 1559: "The new morning prayer ... after Geneva fashion – began to ring at 5 in the morning; men and women all do sing, and boys." Later he recorded: "After the sermone done they songe all, old and yong, a salme in myter, a the tune of Genevay ways."[69] The singing, initially at least, was lively and quick. The Geneva revolution in popular music was to work its decisive influence on English music. The popularity of the practice is indicated by the fact that *The Whole Book of Psalms* (popularly known as Sternhold and Hopkins, after two of its translators) went through more than 200 printings before 1640. Often these psalms were printed along with the catechism so that it could be used at home and at church. That it was meant to be widely used by a population untrained in music presented a problem that was addressed in early editions. In the introduction to early editions, Thomas Sternholde included what he called a "plaine map and rule" of music, so that even the "rude and ignorant" could learn to offer praise to God. Sternholde assured the reader that "every man in a few days, yea in a few hours easelye with out all payn, and that also without ... helpe of any teacher, attayne to a sufficiente knowledge to syng any Psalme contained in this book."[70] There follows some simple instructions on scales and singing that surely represented a milestone in popular music education.

---

[68] The concern to develop competence in singing was evident in the fact that the introduction to Sternhold and Hopkins, the most commonly used Psalter, included basic instruction in singing.

[69] Gant, *O Sing unto the Lord*, loc. 1983.

[70] Thomas Sternholde, *The First Parte of the Psalms Collected into English Meter* (London: John Day, 1564), n.p.

The significance of this popularity lies in the fact these books were clearly designed for widespread and intergenerational use in domestic settings and in church. Early in Elizabeth's reign this tradition of psalm-singing flourished alongside developments in more florid styles, which like the dramatic performances of the time were supported by noble patronage and largely approved by the growing Protestant majority. But as with drama and visual arts, a growing suspicion of decorative styles that did not contribute to clarity and teaching led to the suppression of more elaborate music and even at times of choirs. The struggle reflected a familiar debate: Should music be allowed to develop for its own sake, as in the increasingly rich polyphony of Renaissance styles influenced especially by music from Italy, that musicians supported by the Queen and cathedrals preferred? Or should music be simple and clear – one note per syllable – in order to promote clarity of understanding, as the parish tradition and more conservative Puritans wanted? As Andrew Gant sagely notes, this struggle was not new either to England or to the Christian tradition more generally. Rather, it "plugged into a running commentary that was already many centuries old, and had many more to run. The imagery of this dialectic remains remarkably consistent: the pros [i.e., Puritans] wanted to hear the words, not the music for its own sake, and think elaborate music is effeminate, theatrical and bawdy; the antis [i.e., cathedral school] think that beauty in worship and skill in art are things of God."[71] Calvin was convinced music was a gift of God, but he also worried that, used improperly – with instrumental accompaniment, for example – it might distract the mind from growth in piety.

The rhetorical focus of Calvin that we explored earlier led to an aesthetic surface that was simple and focused, but that also contributed to his goals of moving the heart to the love and praise of God. It is not hard to see that these goals were well served, aesthetically, by the practice of congregational singing of psalms, and later of hymns deriving from the proliferating devotion literature. Andrew Gant argues that this influence nurtured a distinctively English tradition of religious music. In both the parish and court, composers absorbed and worked with this new style of music. When borrowed tunes and traditional melodies were set in the English vernacular, they took on, Gant thinks, a "distinctively English musical signature." Simplicity of language did not keep this adaptation from making its unique contribution to musical styles. Gant concludes: "The reformed style is plain,

---

[71] *O Sing unto the Lord*, loc. 2486. He gives examples from the eleventh and twelfth century of similar struggles over musical styles; contemporary battles will be familiar to any churchgoer today.

direct, and, at its best, has a simplicity and elegance which Latin Catholic music never achieved."[72]

But the fact that the primary musical styles were designed to be sung, in both ecclesial and domestic settings, carries further implications for the developing aesthetic situation. As we have observed, this was music that called for conscious participation – the focus shifted from patronage to consumption, from passive listening to personal appropriation. And singing together with family or congregation was also an embodied experience that carried deep implications, not only for new devotional practices but also for a developing musical aesthetics. Susan Tara Brown has argued that vocal participation in singing made possible a self-expression that allowed believers to relive the experiences of the Psalmist, and thus allowed them to personally participate in the drama of sin and salvation that poet recounted.[73] Calvin recognized that singing allowed believers to experience emotions that kindled love for God. As Brown argues, the particularly embodied character of vocal music provides a space where psychological states could be created. She goes on to note that the struggle over use of instruments in worship – a debate that strikes modern readers as strange – is deeply connected to the fact that, for sixteenth-century congregations, only vocal music, tied as it was to the personal affective appropriation of the biblical text, had true efficacy (pp. 59–60). Following an ancient tradition, the early modern period saw music and poetry as closely related. Recall this was still largely an oral culture, and even poetry was designed to be read aloud, and eventually sung (pp. 62, 66).

Nathanael Homes, writing in the seventeenth century, offers supporting evidence. He expressed a common assumption when he argued that singing improved the words, celebrating them with more glory.[74] He notes this corporate practice has become characteristic of all Reformed churches and has as its goal to promote what we are to perform or leave undone. "How do we celebrate a day of praise, and deliverance, according to the Scripture," he writes, "unless we have Psalms and hymns of praise?" (p. 7). Homes goes on to stress that this leads especially to the personal appropriation that Brown has highlighted. "Singing is the making in a special manner man's tongue to be his glory ... every man quickening himself and others by symphonie and singing concent together" (p. 9). By singing

---

[72] *O Sing unto the Lord*, loc. 2037.

[73] Brown, *Singing and the Imagination of Devotion*, p. 47. Subsequent pages cited in the text are to this work.

[74] Nathanael Homes, *Gospel Musick or the Singing of David's Psalms in the Publick Congregations or Private Families Asserted and Vindicated* (London: Henry Overton, 1644), pp. 2, 3. Pages cited in the text are to this work.

we are drawn deeper into faith (pp. 10–11). He concludes: "By singing we present unto our sences and mind a lively type of heavenly joys" (p. 11).

Music, then, in this tradition becomes a personal and bodily engagement with the experiences of trial and deliverance recounted in the Psalms, with critical implications for use of the senses. More importantly, it becomes a vehicle of the horizontal extension of spiritual and aesthetic experience out into the family and community. As with the devotional poets we have described, these believers are singing themselves into the music and becoming an instance of the drama of sin and salvation that structures the biblical narrative.

But this horizontal impetus did more than simply bond together the faithful while they worshipped; it pushed them to reconsider their responsibilities in the larger world. While this impulse has mostly been discussed in terms of whether or not Calvinism contributed to an emerging capitalist economy, it would also have deep implications for aesthetic reflection as well. It is to these possibilities that we turn in Chapter 7.

7

THE NEW VISUAL CULTURE OF REFORMED
HOLLAND AND FRANCE

IN NOVEMBER 1525, THE ZURICH TOWN COUNCIL ANNOUNCED that all gravestones in the city should be removed within one month, after which they would be confiscated and used for building materials.[1] This incident provides a metaphor both for the reach of the Reformation into the everyday life of people and their connection with the past and for the urgency with which the cleansing was carried out. This act, surely considered by some an act of impiety toward one's ancestors, was to be completed in a single month. And while carrying deeply contested religious resonances, the decision was taken by the town council rather than any religious body, with the civic – and very practical – result that further building materials would become available.

From Iconoclasm to Reconstruction

While not relating directly to developments in aesthetics, such events – and the new attention being paid to them by scholars interested in broader cultural issues – reflect the newly awakened attention to the social world of the Reformation and its look and feel. In this chapter we explore in particular the changing structure that offered this new setting for the senses, and the implications of this for aesthetics. As we have seen, when Calvin arrived in Geneva in August 1536 much of what we associate with the Reformation was already accomplished. The civic leaders of Geneva, like other Swiss cities, had begun to institute economic and social reforms; they sought out preachers who would edify the people; they fought heresy;

---

[1] Robert W. Scribner, *Religion and Culture in Germany (1400–1800)* (Leiden: Brill, 2001), p. 275. The council had voted earlier in the year to abolish the Mass. Philip Benedict, *Christ's Churches Purely Reformed: A Social History of the Reformation* (New Haven, CT: Yale University Press, 2002), p. 30.

and they sided with the people in agreeing to abolish the Mass and seize church property – with proceeds to be used in caring for the poor.[2] The first hospital had already been established in 1535, which was to care for the poor and refugees, as well as the sick, all at public expense.[3] On May 21, 1536, the General Council of Geneva (those men who had the right to vote) agreed unanimously to "live according to the Gospel and the Word of God ... wishing to give up all Masses and other papal ceremonies and abuses, images, idols, and all that this may involve, to live in union and obedience of justice."[4] In addition, much of the struggle over images in the church, and the early episodes of iconoclasm in Germany and neighboring Zurich, were already past. There Ulrich Zwingli had determined that one showed proper reverence for God by carrying God in one's heart; images and all external mediations of the supernatural – even elaborate gravestones – were symbols of unbelief.[5] When Zwingli died (in battle) in 1531, the multiple altars that had lined the nave of the Zurich Munster were gone, the whitewashed walls bare of images.[6]

Calvin was well informed about these precedents; he had read his Luther and come, gradually it appears, to embrace the evangelical reforms. When he arrived in Geneva it is more accurate to say Calvin inherited a reform rather than sparked one. The medieval world with its novenas, processions, pilgrimages, and saint's plays was disappearing. The question that faced Calvin was not how to dismantle that way of life, but what kind of world would replace it. More to the point, what sort of images would shape that world? And what vision would allow one to see these new images? In this chapter I argue this emerging imaginary would grow from the careful attention Calvin paid to reforming the life and worship of the congregation, on the one hand, and the reformation of life in the larger world, on the other. Whatever Calvin's role in the development of democracy and

[2] Henri Naef, *Les Origines de la Réforme à Genève* (Genève: Librairie Droz, 1968), vol. I, pp. 135–218; Benedict, *Christ's Churches*, pp. 78–81.

[3] W. Fred Graham, *The Constructive Revolutionary: John Calvin and His Socio-Economic Impact* (Atlanta, GA: John Knox Press, 1978), pp. 98–100. Graham's argument is that Calvin provided explicit theological justification for Geneva's social experiment.

[4] Quoted in Fred Graham, *The Constructive Revolutionary*, p. 35.

[5] Garside, *Zwingli and the Arts* (New Haven, CT: Yale University Press, 1966), p. 175.

[6] Zurich was a particularly cogent example because the commissioning of ecclesiastical art had increased a hundredfold between 1500 and 1518. Garside, *Zwingli and the Arts*, p. 87. However, Mia Mochizuki has argued that even the practice of whitewashing the walls reflects an iconoclastic impulse that predated the Reformation. *The Netherlandish Image*, p. 1. And Naef has shown that the arts were already in decline in the early years of the sixteenth century, especially in Geneva. *Les Origines*, vol. I, p. 276.

capitalism, as Philip Benedict notes, his work in Geneva in proposing a different model of the Church and morals still resonates. As he argues: "The transformation of practice effected by every Reformed church created a new set of sensibilities over the long run … to those raised within it."[7]

In this chapter I argue these new sensibilities were made possible by the reconfiguration of the social world that Calvin's teachings made possible, and the way this opened up a shared and ordered public space. This was based on the structuring principles Calvin laid out in the *Institutes*, as these were set forth in the rhetoric of his preaching and teaching. The first edition of the *Institutes*, his guide to interpreting Scripture, had already appeared in 1536 before his arrival in Geneva. In this and the more complete 1539 edition (which was three times longer), organized around two poles – the work of God in creation and in recreation – he began to lay out the theological grounds for his work of reconstruction. How would this program be directed? Calvin was clear about this. Scripture, for Calvin, not only offered a clear image of creation and the application of Christ's redemption to the believer by the Spirit (I, ix, 2 and 3), but it also constituted a programmatic structure for life in the world.[8] As they heard the sermons week by week, and as the children learned their catechism, members of Calvin's Church were to imbibe the principles that were meant to order not only their religious lives but their lives in the larger world as well – plan and good order appear frequently in both the *Institutes* and Calvin's ecclesiastical writings. This plan laid out, I argue, a dramatic space in which the streets and markets of Geneva would take on fresh significance. Followers of Calvin were thrust out of the church to live – to enact – this divine drama in their everyday life. This space I am claiming took on both a new moral and aesthetic seriousness.

As we have done frequently, it might be useful to contrast this new space with the way meaning was inscribed on history in the medieval period. As I argued in Chapter 1, during that period, both theological and aesthetic meaning focused on a particular *historia* of the human journey to God. This journey is classically portrayed in Dante's *Commedia* where Virgil – the personification of classical wisdom, guides Dante-pilgrim through hell and up the mountain of Purgatory, where Beatrice – the symbol of God's love – leads him into the Empyrean and a final vision of God. Profiting from the early Renaissance's recovery of the classical heritage, Dante was able to

---

[7] Benedict, *Christ's Churches*, p. 532.
[8] Catherine Randall (Coats), "Structuring Protestant Scriptural Space in Sixteenth Century Catholic France," *Sixteenth Century Journal*, 25/2 (1994): 341–353.

broaden the potential of politics, and in this way anticipate developments that Calvin and other Reformers later encouraged. According to Justin Steinberg, Dante's vision included a more substantial role for the political authority than that represented by Augustine in *The City of God*.[9] For Dante, these structures are given not merely to suppress fallen human desire, as in Augustine, but, positively, to shape and direct it. The emperor in particular could serve as a kind of moral pilot to recover a just society directed by natural law when that had been lost. And the tradition of the arts could also serve to further these purposes. But note the poet's solution to having lost his way in the dark wood, Steinberg shows, "is not to insist upon the freedom of the individual or the autonomy of the artist," even if art objects can still function as guide and motivation. Especially in the *Purgatorio* art plays a significant role in the spiritual conditioning that is necessary to the pilgrim's reformation. And Dante-pilgrim's interactions with these forms are forms of bodily knowledge. But rather than offering a free space in which the individual artist could emerge, it represents a "collective tradition: a world of schoolroom exercises, sermons and church frescos."[10] These aesthetic and political powers promote for Dante a kind of enhanced political space, but it is not a free space. Rather, it is subordinated to the sacred purposes of the soul's journey to God. The narrative of the journey of the mind to God, Dante believes, is God's way of writing meaning into history. The political and natural world was playing an increasingly important role as the context for this journey, but, as Umberto Eco points out, medieval culture was based "not on a phenomenology of reality, but on a phenomenology of a cultural tradition."[11]

For Calvin, by contrast, there are contingencies that allow for real dramatic possibilities. The structure is laid out not in the liturgical provision for the human journey to God and the last judgment but in the public history of God's redemptive work in creation, Israel, and Christ. And within this story spaces are opening up for something new to appear – its orientation is ahead, not above. In the long discussions of Calvin's role in the development of modern economic and technological discussions, which we briefly consider, what has been consistently overlooked is the new historical situation that Calvin's theological impulses helped create. Whatever his direct or indirect

[9] *Dante and the Limits of the Law*, electronic edition (Chicago: University of Chicago Press, 2013), loc. 1545–1567. Quote at 1550.
[10] *Dante and the Limits of the Law*, loc. 1570.
[11] Eco, *Art and Beauty in the Middle Ages*, trans. Hugh Bredin (New Haven, CT: Yale University Press, 1986), p. 4. Eco goes on to qualify this judgment, noting the movement in that period toward renaissance ideas, something I have also noted.

influence on capitalism, his larger role was giving the created order – including its streets and workplaces – a new moral gravity. This led to a closer examination and evaluation of their visual textures, as these sparked the attention – and affections – of the participants of this drama. The real presence, so often debated in medieval discussions, was now Christ's presence in the believer and the responsibility this entails to participate with Him and with fellow believers in the ongoing work of re-creation.

Consider the end of Calvin's long discussion of the Eucharist, where he makes clear his own view of this long-standing discussion. The superstition of paying divine honor to the sign, and the presence of Christ in the bread, misses the central meaning of this practice, he argues. Rather, its presence was an exhortation to "purity and holiness of life, and also to charity, peace and concord" (*Institutes*, IV, xvii, 38). For the "real presence" has been transferred from the Eucharistic elements to the community, who all belong to one body. Calvin goes on to insist:

> we ought to take the same care of our brethren's bodies as we take of our own; for they are members of our body; and that as as no part of our body is touched by any feeling of pain which is not spread among all the rest, so we ought not to allow a brother to be affected by any evil, without being touched with compassion for him ... We cannot love Christ without loving him in the brethren. (*Institutes*, IV, xvii, 38)

The presence of Christ appears to believers now, not in the elements of the Mass but in the faces of their sisters and brothers. This connection among the community and the mutuality it entailed would have important influence on the developing modern world, and along the way, it would also open up new spaces for aesthetic attention and production.

A Theological Construction of the Public Sphere

What is encouraged in Calvin's plan is an increased awareness and interest in what we have come to call the public sphere, a connection that calls for closer scrutiny here. It is increasingly recognized that Calvin, in drawing attention to the larger public drama of creation that we have been tracing, played no small role in the eventual definition and contour of a new public space.[12] The roots of this are to be found in the *Institutes*, Book III, chapter 19, where Calvin treats Christian liberty as a necessary corollary of

---

[12] W. J. Torrance Kirby calls attention in particular to the culture of persuasion and Calvin's influence on this. This "contributed in no small part to the genesis of the early modern public

our justification. Though the believer is freed from the curse of the law and its ceremonies, Paul specifies in *Galatians* that this freedom is from bondage to the law and not to its claim on the believers' lives. Indeed Calvin insists (in III, xix, 2): "The whole life of Christians ought to be a sort of practice of godliness (*pietas*), for we have been called to sanctification." But the significance of this is to be seen especially in the freedom it offers from superstitious enslavement to external things (what Calvin calls *adiaphora*, things indifferent). The Christian whose conscience is freed from an overly scrupulous servitude to the law is at liberty to make use of the external goods of creation as she wishes. Calvin then proceeds to an explanation that holds great implications for the making and use of the goods of the world, including beautiful objects and artifacts. Some might think, he avers, that it is strange to raise questions "over the unrestricted eating of meat, use of holidays and of vestments, and such things, which seem to them vain frivolities. But these matters *are more important than is commonly believed*" (III, xix, 7, emphasis added). Though these external things may be indifferent as to one's justification before God, the Christian's liberty allows both their enjoyment and their use for the good of all. For it is there in the drama of creation that the good gifts of God may be freely enjoyed with thanksgiving to God as the source (Calvin references I Tim. 4:5). But there too, in the dramatic unfolding of creation, the struggle for righteousness is carried out, for Calvin typically goes on to warn against the abuse of such gifts and the danger of giving and taking offense toward our brother. For liberty, Calvin insists, is always subservient to charity (III, xix, 13).

Calvin then proceeds to delineate the distinction between the internal and external fora in section 15 of this chapter. For humans, Calvin explains, government is twofold. There is, on the one hand, the spiritual government (*forum conscientiae*) by which "the conscience is instructed in piety and reverencing God," and there is, on the other hand, the civil government (*forum externum*) "whereby man is educated for the duties of humanity and citizenship that must be maintained among men." The one concerns one's soul as this relates to God; the other "with the concerns of the present life – not only with food and clothing but with laying down laws whereby a man may live his life among other men holily, honorably and temperately." One's reconciliation with God then relates to *both* spheres, requiring, Calvin notes in another place, a double grace (*duplex gratia*, cf. III, 11, 11), that is, the necessity of receiving God's grace for both our justification and our

sphere." I am indebted to his discussion in what follows. *Persuasion and Conversion: Essays on Religion, Politics and the Public Sphere in Early Modern England* (Boston: Brill, 2013), p. 36.

sanctification, two distinct but inseparable gifts. As Torrance Kirby points out, this not only delineates what came to be called a "public sphere," but gives it a distinct moral ontology – that is, a human location where one is called to account before both God and one's fellow humans. And it is within this external space that the grace of God's gifts is to be explored and lived out. It follows that the government of that space is critical; as Torrance Kirby notes, "to deprive man of government is to deprive him of his very humanity."[13] And since this newly defined public space is the place where human life is played out – in its eating, dress, and holidays – it is unthinkable that this not open a free space and opportunities for artists to develop new cultural forms and distinctive visual cultures.[14]

Expansion of the conversation to include this larger arena represents a sea change, so I argue, in scholarship on the culture of the Reformation. Earlier attention to Reformation and the arts, or in our case, Calvinism and the arts, needed to give way to broader examination of the visual and material culture of the Reformation program of reconstruction.[15] At the same time, a focus on the – relatively rare – episodes of violent iconoclasm has been replaced by attempts to explore the broader iconoclastic impulse reflected in the incident in Zurich in 1525, and, more to the point, what came to fill the newly vacant spaces.[16] As Peter Matheson has argued: "the iconoclasm was not just a concern to remove superfluity and 'stubble,' but was complemented if not overshadowed by its iconopoesis, its vision of a human world which mirrored the divine in its banal, day to day reality."[17] John Calvin especially among the major Reformers was not simply concerned to remove

---

[13] *Persuasion and Conversion*, p. 49.

[14] Hence the question with which Mario Carpo begins his important book: Why did different regions of Europe produce such different visual environments? *Architecture in the Age of Printing: Orality, Writing, and Printed Images in the History of Architectural Theory*, trans. Sarah Benson (Cambridge, MA: MIT Press, 2001), p. 1.

[15] This is evident in the movement from classic treatments like Abraham Kuyper, "Calvinism and Art," in *Lectures on Calvinism* (Grand Rapids, MI: Eerdmans, 1931), and Léon Wencelius, *L'Esthétique de Calvin* (Paris: Société d'Edition "Les Belles Lettres," 1937), to broader explorations represented by Paul Corby Finney, ed., *Seeing beyond the Word: Visual Arts and the Calvinist Tradition* (Grand Rapids, MI: Eerdmans, 1999); William Dyrness, *Reformed Theology and Visual Culture* (Cambridge: Cambridge University Press, 2004); and Mia M. Mochizuki, *The Netherlandish Image after Iconoclasm* (Aldershot: Ashgate, 2008). For methodological reflections on this move, see Sally M. Promey and Shira Brisman, "Sensory Cultures: Material and Visual Religion," in Philip Goff, ed., *The Blackwell Companion to Religion in America* (Malden, MA: Wiley-Blackwell, 2010), pp. 177–205.

[16] Joseph Leo Koerner, *The Reformation of the Image* (Chicago: University of Chicago Press, 2004), p. 12.

[17] Matheson, *The Imaginative World of the Reformation* (Minneapolis, MN: Fortress Press, 2001), pp. 74–75.

superstitions but to develop a new – and in his mind a more biblical – way for Christians to live out their faith in the world. In this chapter I explore this new social imaginary of Calvin and his followers, and show briefly the impact of this on the visual and material culture of the sixteenth and seventeenth centuries.[18]

A Visual and Oral World

One of the dominant assumptions of earlier scholars of the Reformation has been that, with the rise of print culture, the visually mediated medieval world was replaced by an oral world – images were supplanted by words.[19] Throughout this book I have tried to nuance this oversimplified reading of the situation. For one thing, the medieval oral culture survived into the period of the Reformation. As we noted in earlier chapters, preaching continued the oral focus of the medieval period.[20] Magistrates competed with one another to attract the best preachers to their cathedrals; preaching had already become a primary form of mass media. Listening to a sermon, reciting the catechism, singing a psalm in church were oral performances, but they were also visual experiences. What was different for Calvin was the refusal to accept the medieval mediation of God's presence through sacramentals, and the insistence that God's presence was manifested primarily in particular worship performances – in preaching and teaching, singing praises and prayers.[21] And this was not because of any sacred quality inherent in these, but because the Spirit was present to enliven these practices. For Calvin the link assumed in medieval sacramentals was severed both

---

[18] I use social imaginaries in the sense developed by Charles Taylor, *A Secular Age* (Cambridge, MA: Harvard University Press, 2007), pp. 171–176. He describes a repertoire of practices a group uses to make sense of their world that is carried not only in ideas but in images, stories, and rituals, something that (unlike theory) was widely shared among the larger community. He specifically connects this new imaginary with the growing affirmation of everyday life resulting from the Reformation.

[19] See the classical discussion of this in Walter Ong, *Peter Ramus, Method and the Decay of Dialogue: From the Art of Discourse to the Art of Reason* (Cambridge, MA: Harvard University Press, 1958).

[20] Duffy, *Stripping of the Altars 1400–1580* (New Haven, CT: Yale University Press, 1992), p. 57.

[21] Carlos Eire argues, correctly in my view, that Calvin changed the metaphysics of this relationship by insisting the two spheres are connected only by worship – as long as one holds to Calvin's broadened understanding of worship. *War against Idols: The Reformation of Worship from Erasmus to Calvin* (Cambridge: Cambridge University Press, 1986), p. 213. On the Protestant refusal of sacramentals, see James F. White, *The Sacraments in Protestant Worship and Practice* (Nashville, TN: Abingdon, 1999), and Scribner, *Religion and Culture*, pp. 23, 24.

because of the finitude of the created order (*finitum non capax infiniti*),[22] and because of the human moral inability to imagine God aright. Only the Spirit working through the Word enables believers to participate in God. As Julie Canlis has argued, communion, for Calvin, involved a very real "participation" of the believer in God. But it is a "non-substantial participation in the person of Christ, made possible by . . . the Holy Spirit, who is a safeguard against substantial participation."[23]

Typically, scholars call attention to the rift this caused with the previous forms of piety,[24] and they are not wrong to do this. But here I want to further explore the emerging social imaginary this made possible. The oral and visual culture of the Reformation, fueled as it was by the regular preaching of the word, by learning the catechism, and by reading devotional literature, gradually developed an understanding of the world not as symbol but as reliable sign.[25] Images as disciplined by these performances were textualized; image and text formed a natural alliance that represented a new covenant between viewer and text (or image). As David Morgan describes this covenant in contemporary Protestantism, a modern form of this earlier poetics: "The imbrication of word, sound, thought and image encouraged the idea of an integrated aspect of a sign into a reliable representation of a stable world."[26]

Already in Calvin, when schooled by the sound investigation provided by Scripture, there was the assumption of a close fit between language and the world. As have seen, Calvin assumed the human mind, when its moral capacity had been restored, could grasp the world as it actually is.[27] The development of place logic and the ordering structures of the later Protestant scholastics are further developments of this assumption. This growing notion about how the world was arranged issued in a new imaginary, a new way of comprehending the created order, and it centrally involved a new way of seeing. As the century wore on, an entire repertoire

---

[22] *Institutes*, I, v, 1.

[23] Canlis, "Calvin, Osiander, and Participation in God," *International Journal of Systematic Theology*, 6/2 (April 2004): 184.

[24] See especially Eamon Duffy, *Saints, Sacrilege, and Sedition: Religion and Conflict in the Tudor Reformations* (London: Bloomsbury, 2012), pp. 101, 102, and passim.

[25] On this move, see Julia Kristeva, "From Symbol to Sign," in Toril Moi, ed., *The Kristeva Reader* (Oxford: Oxford University Press, 1986), pp. 62–73.

[26] Morgan, "Protestant Visual Piety and the Aesthetics of American Mass Culture," in Jolyon Mitchell and Sophia Marriage, eds., *Mediating Religion: Conversations in Media, Religion and Culture* (London: T&T Clark, 2003), p. 102.

[27] Cf. William J. Bouwsma, *John Calvin: A Sixteenth-Century Portrait* (New York: Oxford University Press, 1988), p. 98. On the development of this logic, see Dyrness, *Reformed Theology*, pp. 123–141.

of images began to appear that were congenial to this new way of seeing: broadsheets, book illustrations, and prints of all kinds. And these were often accompanied by texts with prayers or admonitions indicating the new role images would play as signs. As John King notes, for Protestants, images were meant to break down the barrier between the reader and text, or indeed to move the reader into the world of the text.[28] This is not a contemplative gaze that seeks to commune with the figures presented but a self-reflective gaze, which seeks to read the drama of creation aright and motivate an active participation in its unfolding display.

This led to development of a particular visual culture in which printed books gradually took over from more popular forms of prints and broadsides. Tessa Watt has described the rich oral and visual culture that resulted from this Protestant (and largely Calvinist) culture in England. She notes the first printed material consisted in songs – ballads – that were performed in the market, at home, and, initially at least, in church.[29] Changing Renaissance tastes played a role earlier, but by the end of the sixteenth century the Reformation aesthetic triumphed. As we noted in Chapter 6, while polyphony continued to develop in Cathedrals, psalm-singing in unison eventually became the norm in the parish churches. But this is not simply an aural parallel to the removal of images and whitewashing the walls; it offers a constructive, formational ritual for ordinary believers.

In part the development of multiple forms of print, generally embraced by the Reformers, was an expression of images' long-standing role as teaching mechanisms. Rebecca Zorach has proposed that prints were felt to be above the suspicion attending painted images and frescos, because they "possessed a special status as cognitive images" – something closer to a pure idea.[30] That is, prints, frequently accompanied with texts, could not be mistaken for holy images – the abstraction itself reminded viewers that they were not really in Christ's presence. Even better were the Ramist charts and diagrams (reflecting place logic) appearing toward the end of the century that allowed one to organize material in ways that reflected the world as God had created

---

[28] "Protestant religious images represent the inner experience of faith rather than autonomous devotional objects." John N. King, *English Reformation Literature* (Princeton, NJ: Princeton University Press, 1982), p. 154.

[29] She notes that earlier godly ballads, based on courtly music, were popular, but in 1550–1570 these were gradually replaced by psalm-singing both in church and at home. *Cheap Prints and Popular Piety* (Cambridge: Cambridge University Press, 1991), pp. 55, 56.

[30] Zorach, "Meditation, Idolatry, Math: The Printed Image in Europe around 1500," in Michael W. Cole and Rebecca Zorach, eds., *The Idol in the Age of Art: Objects, Devotions and the Early Modern World* (Farnham: Ashgate, 2009), p. 317.

it. Zorach argues that some, following Nicholas of Cusa, argued that mathematical symbols were the most appropriate reflection of divine realities. "Perhaps a diagrammatic rather than mimetic style of representation provides a structural counterpart . . . contrasting to Christ's presence."[31] This also contributed to moving the viewer beyond the sensible temptations – idolatry being after all a thing of the mind – toward an experience of insight, or intellection. But what these objects did, constructively, was to play a role in orienting viewers to the opportunities and challenges of the emerging conceptions of the public sphere.

The Drama of Reconstruction

The lingering debate over whether Calvin and Calvinism actually contributed to the emergence of capitalism and liberal democracy tends to obscure the obvious transformation of congregational life during the sixteenth century.[32] We tend to forget that the whole population of Geneva was expected to take part in the services provided, and in what amounted to a mass literacy program, all the children – rich or poor – were taught the catechism week by week at public expense – the Geneva congregations were coextensive with the larger community. Education was free to the poor and was compulsory.[33] In Geneva, as in many early modern cities, up to half the population would be considered poor in modern terms. During the 1540s and 1550s the population of Geneva of 10,000 swelled with the arrival of more than 5,000 refugees fleeing persecution in France. Calvin enhanced the biblical office of deacon, which was responsible for caring for the poor. Indeed the Church, that is, the community, as a body took responsibility for its members, even as leaders often struggled to raise the funds necessary to care for their confreres.[34] In this provision the council of the city and the ministers, representing as they did a single community, took equal responsibility.

---

[31] Zorach, "Meditation, Idolatry, Math," p. 340. Her article is a seminal discussion especially of the prints of humanist Charles de Borelles, who, following Geert Groote, proposed a theory of contemplation that was psychologically new.

[32] See the summary of the consensus that Calvinism's influence on modern institutions has frequently been overstated in Benedict, *Christ's Churches*, pp. 533–546.

[33] Graham, *The Constructive Revolutionary*, pp. 58–63. This pattern continued when the Geneva Academy was founded in 1558. For the population figures below, see p. 105.

[34] Wandel, *The Reformation*, p. 190. She notes congregations well into the seventeenth century offered lotteries and put on plays as fund-raising activities.

Calvin probably paid as much attention to the communal life of his city as any theologian of his time, and this included reflection on its economic and social character; he gave this a detailed attention that no previous theologian had given. Fred Graham could even claim that his "social and economic teachings were clearly just as important to Calvin himself [as his doctrinal teaching], and might just as well be used as the yardstick of Calvinist orthodoxy."[35] Though he did not develop any consistent or specific political teaching,[36] he was insistent that it was the special responsibility of the magistrates to care for the weak and the poor. As he wrote in his commentary on Psalm 82:3: "Determine the cause of the poor and the orphan. We are here briefly taught that a just and well-regulated government will be distinguished for maintaining the rights of the poor and afflicted."[37] To Paul's injunction to "steal no more" (Eph. 4:28), Calvin comments that Paul "does not simply bid us to abstain from unjust or unlawful seizure of goods, but also to assist our brethren as far as lies in our power . . . all must devote themselves to supplying each other's necessities." That is, not only does one work honestly to provide for our own needs, but we are responsible "to assist our brethren."[38]

Whatever the impact of his teaching and practice on modern institutions, it is clear that Calvin's economic and social teachings were for him deeply implicated in his theological vision. Again, we need to remind ourselves that Calvin's teachings were not in fact directed to the larger world where the institutions of modernity would be developed, but to the community of people that gathered week by week to listen to God's word. And for him it was clear that the liturgy of communion, as we have seen, entailed entering into communion with each other – with this worshipping body – in very tangible ways. As he wrote: "none of the brethren can be injured, despised, rejected, abused, or in any way offended by us, without at the same time, injuring, despising, and abusing Christ" (*Institutes*, IV, xvii, 38).

That this changed the way people thought about their community cannot be doubted, whatever its eventual impact would be as division between the religious and irreligious grew at the end of the century. By then, Tess Watt observes, religious reformers increasingly directed their energies within a closed circle of church and private household rather than to the larger

---

[35] *The Constructive Revolutionary*, p. 76.

[36] This is the conclusion of Harro Höpfl, *The Christian Polity of John Calvin* (Cambridge: Cambridge University Press, 1982). And Calvin consistently discouraged any efforts to overthrow existing government, however unjust.

[37] Ps. 82:3, trans. James Anderson, *Commentary* in loc.

[38] Eph. 4: 8, trans. T. H. L. Parker, *Commentary* in loc.

community, as they had done earlier. The replacement of the religious ballad with psalm-singing was an indication of the growing gap between the godly and the ungodly.[39] This gap was to grow wider in the next century until clashes between the various confessions of faith, and the competing images they had of themselves, would play a role in the religious wars.

These later developments betray the weakness of Calvin's communalism. While he could be eloquent in defending Christian liberty in what would become the public sphere, he was notoriously incapable of tolerating difference, or even lassitude, among believers in this new space. The struggle of Calvin and his supporters to ensure the council's role in the ongoing reformation of manners, something that was not fully accomplished until the 1550s, suggests an inability on the part of these leaders, and Calvin in particular, to reckon with human failings and the appropriate management of this new public space. Broader notions of tolerance would not emerge until the seventeenth century, and it is unfair to blame Calvin for not accepting the growing diversity evident in Geneva. Still, there is a certain irony in the fact that about the same time that Calvin was able to stamp out opposition to his social program, in the early 1550s, he was complicit in putting to death the famous heretic Michael Servetus. It was also during this time that he carried on a lengthy exchange with his former colleague and mentee, Sebastian Castellio, who had given up his evangelical faith because he had come to see that it entailed violent suppression of alternative views. Castellio famously argued that "to kill a man is not to defend a doctrine, but to kill a man."[40] Unfortunately, Castellio's voice went unheeded during his lifetime, and Calvin succumbed to the centuries-long practice of violent suppression of challenges to received orthodoxy.

Despite these weaknesses, the implications of Calvin's social program and its promotion of mutual care would become important to later Reformed impulses to restructure the world. The impact of this on public life and the economic order became especially evident by 1600, when Reformed churches had become established in Scotland, England, France, Hungary, the United Provinces of the Netherlands, and a dozen principalities in Germany.[41] One piece of evidence for this is visible in seventeenth-century Netherlands.

---

[39] *Cheap Prints and Popular Piety*, p. 70.

[40] An excellent recent discussion of this sad chapter of Reformation history, and its role in fostering the movement toward toleration, is to be found in Dominic Erdozain, *The Soul of Doubt: The Religious Roots of Unbelief from Luther to Marx* (New York: Oxford University Press, 2016), chapter 2.

[41] See Benedict, *Christ's Churches*, pp. 93–109. He notes that by 1560 Geneva had become a model for Reformed congregations throughout Europe, and its population had swollen to 21,000 (from about 10,000 when Calvin arrived).

After the upheavals of war with Spain and outbreaks of iconoclasm, churches throughout the United Provinces replaced the temporary market stalls that had filled the area around the cathedrals with permanents structures for these markets. This shows, Mia Mochizuki argues, the "increasing involvement of the Church masters in the economic welfare of the town."[42] And it was not incidental that these structures, and the activities they embodied, were arranged symbolically around the space where the Word was regularly preached. Such structures would not ordinarily be thought of in terms of religious visual culture, but they may be overlooked evidence of a religious life understood more broadly.

Seventeenth-Century Netherlands: Textualized Images

Accompanying the horizontal extension of attention to the larger world was the transformation of perception that has been a subtheme of my discussion. We have seen that the Renaissance humanists sought a more accurate and comprehensive investigation of the natural world, and Calvin gave theological warrant for this in his insistence that creation itself was a vast canvas on which God has given visual evidence of his glory. This carried deep implications for the extent and limits of human perception. Clearly, according to Calvin and the Reformers, the sacred images of the medieval period were mostly not to be trusted; indeed the Mass itself was a visual lie.[43] To be an appropriate sign, that could be read and understood, the bread and wine of the communion had to be what they appeared to be. True images were to be found primarily in what God had created and in his Word. The result was a world that was trustworthy; it was what it appeared to be.

Praying before an icon, celebrating a sacred liturgy in which icons are central, encouraged a fully embodied response of the worshiper – something that is often thought to have been lost in Reformed worship. But I have argued that the refusal to restrict the special presence of God to particular images (e.g., icons) or sacramental practices (e.g., the medieval Eucharist) may have expanded the possibilities of seeing and responding to that presence more broadly in the drama of redemption being played out in the world. And, it follows, this expanded landscape could become a grand staging area for aesthetic production. As Philip Sidney had insisted, echoing

---

[42] Mochizuki, *The Netherlandish Image*, p. 281.
[43] See Stuart Clark, *Vanities of the Eye: Vision in Early Modern Europe* (Oxford: Oxford University Press, 2007), pp. 3, 4. Clark's argument is that the growing challenges to Reformation certainties coalesced around whether sight was veridical.

Calvin, there is no "arte which does not take nature as its principle subject."[44] The presence worth noticing was everywhere one might look, and was possessed of a fresh solidity. The houses and streets of Delft, the coiffed hair and collars of Amsterdam merchants, and the woods around Haarlem become unexpected objects of admiration in the hands of Vermeer, Van Ruisdael, and Rembrandt. These painters are registering a new sense of presence that results from Calvin's theater of God's glory.

Scholarly attention on the naturalism of seventeenth-century Dutch painting has struggled to come to terms with the theological influence on what has been called the "art of describing."[45] Though the increasing realism of late medieval and Renaissance art has been widely recognized, only recently have scholars begun to explore possible theological sources. In laying out the various factors at work in this emerging realism, Thomas De Costa Kaufmann admitted a generation ago: "Perhaps most elusive, it also remained to be determined how ethical or religious beliefs ... could affect artistic production and scientific explanation."[46] While many factors were at work in Holland, it is clearly a mistake to see the turn toward landscape and portraits in purely secular terms.[47] In this period there is little doubt that a general Calvinist framework was widely influential, even on those artists who did not belong to Reformed churches.[48]

---

[44] *Defense of Poetry*, p. 7.

[45] Svetlana Alpers, *The Art of Describing: Dutch Art in the Seventeenth Century* (Chicago: University of Chicago Press, 1983). See the discussion in Dyrness, *Reformed Theology*, pp. 196–212.

[46] *The Mastery of Nature: Aspects of Art, Science and Humanism in the Renaissance* (Princeton, NJ: Princeton University Press, 1993), p. 5. He notes that such concerns have become evident only since the decline of the influence of Hans Burkhardt on Renaissance studies.

[47] A brief survey is found in Reindert L. Falkenberg, "Calvinism and the Emergence of Dutch Seventeenth-Century Landscape Art – A Critical Evaluation," in Finney, ed., *Seeing beyond the Word*, pp. 343–368. For a more comprehensive discussion, see Wayne Franits, ed., *Looking at Seventeenth-Century Dutch Art: Realism Reconsidered* (Cambridge: Cambridge University Press, 1997). And see the more recent survey of scholarly discussion in Boudewijn Bakker, *Landscape and Religion from Van Eyck to Rembrandt*, trans. Diane Webb (Burlington, VT: Ashgate, 2012), pp. 200–220.

[48] Christian Tümpel observes that the spirit of the age is often more powerful for artists than their own religious affiliation, and clearly the spirit of the age in Holland was Reformed. "Religious History Painting," in Albert Blankert et al., eds., *God's Saints and Heroes: Dutch Painting in the Age of Rembrandt.* (Washington, DC: National Gallery of Art, 1980), p. 48. Mia Mochizuki makes clear that despite the growing religious pluralism in the Netherlands, the Reformed churches still occupied the central place, both literally and figuratively, in Dutch cities. For example, she notes that though Catholics worshiped freely in their own spaces throughout the United Provinces, when they died they often sought burial within Reformed churches. *The Netherlandish Image*, pp. 276–277.

20 Johannes van Doetecum the Elder, after Pieter Bruegel, *Soldiers at Rest*, from the large landscape series, c. 1555–1556. Etching and engraving, 12 × 16 in.
Hieronymus Cock, Antwerp. Image courtesy of the Metropolitan Museum New York, 26.72.17. Harris Brisbane Dick Fund, 1926.

Beginning in the 1550s Pieter Bruegel, in prints and paintings, had rendered a series of large landscapes, with the natural world unfolding before the viewer. Influenced by the theological emphases of the Reformation and the dominant stoicism, he proposed a moral seeing that was especially taken by the aesthetics of the developing world view. As shown in Figure 20, two soldiers pause to enjoy the spectacle before them. The soldiers invite the viewer to gaze with them at the panorama, where, Boudewijn Bakker says, "all see – the first time in history – the landscape as a picture, as a painting waiting to be painted." Indeed, he claims, these images represent the "first instance of a modern purely aesthetic view of the landscape."[49]

Bakker thinks Breugel displays here all the major features that would come to characterize the classical Dutch landscapes in the coming century, its realism, simplicity, and restraint. Learning from the stoic view influential in Holland, Bruegel saw the world as a *fabrica*, both a work made and a

[49] *Landscape and Religion*, pp. 154–155.

self-revelation of God. In these large landscapes, often with small figures gazing into the distance, the viewer is invited to share this vision, so that, as Calvin stipulated, in contemplating the image they might be led to remember its maker. Bakker notes that among the humanists Erasmus contributed little to views of the world and creation; Calvin emphatically did.[50]

While reflecting multiple indigenous sources, it is important to take note of the transformation in attitudes toward the natural world Bruegel's landscape represents. As we have done frequently, consider the contrast between this emerging view of creation and medieval perspectives on the natural and man-made world: the one bound to the human journey to the last judgment, the other a spectacle open to the future. The medieval world thus tied the space of the city closely to this human spiritual journey. As Vincent Scully notes, a medieval town is not a grid with many paths, but a stage set for "monumental actions." He goes on: "The environment of the town was made not only to frame, but also to act with the actions of its citizens."[51] As we have stressed, with Calvin the city and streets of Geneva have been liberated from this stage set; they have become a frame with many paths.

In an illuminating essay, Jean-Marc Besse has highlighted these differences with respect to the work of Bruegel. For Bruegel, he notes, landscape is an object for a subject who is a spectator within the recital (*récit*) – both physical and theological – of the creation story. In the medieval world, by contrast, the earth "is the endpoint of the creation story, thus the beginning point of human history problematically oriented toward its final salvation" and the last judgment.[52] But in Dutch landscapes, and in Bruegel's work in particular, the natural world is no longer bound by the trajectory begun with Genesis; it has become the framework (*cadre*), the theater of its deployment, "the condition in which time and history develop their sense."[53] In biblical terms, Besse thinks, we have moved from Genesis 3 to Psalm 104. In presenting landscape as an object to be contemplated, Besse claims, Bruegel allows for a new moral geography, one that requires a moral as well as physical perception.

A major carrier transmitting this Calvinist imaginary to Holland was what is known as the Belgic Confession, which came to be widely used in

---

[50] *Landscape and Religion*, pp. 159–163. In his references to Erasmus he cites the work of Julius Müller-Hoofstede.
[51] Scully, *The Natural and the Manmade* (New York: St. Martins, 1991), p. 190.
[52] *Voir la terre: Six essais sure le paysage et la geographie* (Bruxelles: Actes Sud, 2000), pp. 47–48.
[53] *Voir la terre*, p. 48. For what follows, see pp. 58, 68.

Reformed churches.[54] The confession follows Calvin by portraying creation as a theater of God's goodness and splendor. Article 2 says: "[The creation] is before our eyes as a most elegant book, wherein all creatures, great and small are so many characters leading us to contemplate the invisible things of God, namely his eternal power and Godhead." This influence suggests one should be careful not to judge the seeming realism of Dutch painting as secular.[55] As Constantijn Huygens, the patron of Rembrandt, put it, "the goodness of God is to be seen in every dune's top."

The art that results appears completely natural, but this naturalness betrays an artifice that reflects the Calvinist imaginary. As Samuel van Hoogstraten, the pupil of Rembrandt, described this in his 1678 *Introduction to the Higher School of the Art of Painting*: "The art of painting is a science (*wetenschap*) representing all the ideas or images that the whole visible world contains, and it does so by deceiving the eye with line and color."[56] Calvin says nature is a mirror in which we can see God; art, Hoogstraten says, holds up a mirror to nature, which, observed carefully, will draw the viewer up to contemplate the creator. Note how this reflects the new way of looking at the world, a concentrated gaze that takes note and describes in detail what is there. But it also reflects the impulse to remake this world. Interestingly, the English word *landscape* itself comes from the Dutch (*landschap*), which was specifically used to describe land recovered from the North Sea.[57] In the terminology of the day, landscape was not simply natural, it was land made useful – literally creation recovered.

What is most striking in the developing landscape tradition is what most viewers call its realism. In the memorable words of Ann Jensen Adams, at first glance it looks "as if the scales had suddenly and collectively fallen from the seventeenth-century Dutch artists' eyes." But as she goes on to note, theirs is a constructed naturalism, one having, she argues, the specific goals of shoring up their new communal and religious identities. In this

---

[54] *Belijdenis des Geloofs der Gereformeerde Kerken in Nederland*, published in 1561, was deeply influenced by the French Reformed Confession of 1559, written by John Calvin. The churches also accepted the similarly Reformed Heidelberg Catechism published in 1563. These were taught in church and school, thus penetrating the entire society. See the discussion in E. John Walford, *Jacob van Ruisdael and the Perception of Landscape* (New Haven, CT: Yale University Press, 1991), p. 20.

[55] Eddy de Jongh, "Realism and Seeming Realism," in Franits, ed., *Looking at Seventeenth-Century Dutch Art*, pp. 21–56. Quote that follows is at p. 26.

[56] Samuel van Hoogstraten, *Inleyding tot de Hooge Schoole der Schilderkonst: Anders de zichbaere Werelt verdeelt in regen Leerwinkels, uder bestiert eene der Zanggodinnen* (Rotterdam: Francois van Hoogstraeten, 1678), p. 24. My translation. The reference to being led up to the creator is at p. 292.

[57] Gina Crandell, *Nature Pictorialized: "The View" in Landscape History* (Baltimore, MD: Johns Hopkins University Press, 1993), pp. 101, 103. On this, see Dyrness, *Reformed Theology*, pp. 198–200.

21 Jacob van Ruisdael, *Three Great Trees in a Mountainous Landscape*, 1667.
Norton Simon Museum, Pasadena, California, courtesy Norton Simon Foundation. F.1971.2.P.

respect landscape represents one of the most important registers of the developing Dutch identity.[58] Thus while appearing natural, Dutch landscape represents a composed image; Dutch artists freely moved recognizable objects and put motifs together to project their intended vision.

One could not find a better example of this staged naturalism than the landscapes of Jacob van Ruisdael, a contemporary of Rembrandt. Consider the painting *Three Great Trees in a Mountainous Landscape* from 1667 (Figure 21). What first appears as a natural beauty, when examined more closely, is shown to reflect a selected naturalness, one that reflects a Calvinist social imaginary. If we look carefully, we can see a spiritual drama being played out: there is a broken-down house by the river, and three stricken beech trees in the foreground. As John Walford argues in his study of this painter, the best reading

<hr>

[58] Adams, "Competing Communities in the 'Great Bog of Europe': Identity and Seventeenth-Century Dutch Landscape Paintings," in W. J. T. Mitchell, ed., *Landscape and Power* (Chicago: University of Chicago Press, 1994), pp. 35–40, quote at p. 35. She notes that landscape was the most popular genre of the century.

of the *vanitas* theme so common to the preaching of this period is "broken-ness."[59] The dramatic presence of sin and the fragility of life have given the beauty of Ruisdael a depth that is absent, for example, in his contemporary Claude Lorraine. Creation is both a theater for the glory of God and the dramatic site of sin and brokenness. Still, there is hope, light breaks through the clouds, and the men are going out to their labor until the evening as in Psalm 104:23 – a familiar text for preachers during that time.[60]

Van Ruisdael offers an image that may be enjoyed on many levels. Dutch burghers could bring this picture into their homes and visit these pleasant places via their imagination from the comfort and safety of their homes. It played multiple social, aesthetic, and religious roles. But in order for it to be seen and properly appropriated, it must be placed into a larger frame; it must be "textualized" by the Reformed narrative of creation and redemption. So the delights of rural life are typically mixed with signs of darkness and struggle. The light in the sky could signal hope, but the darkness reminded them of the fragility of life – a threat that Dutch people viscerally understood living in a land threatened by the sea. These images call for a reflective gaze, one in which the viewer is led to ask: "what kind of spiritual life does consideration of the theater of the world lead us?"[61]

The engagement of Dutch artists with their environment, and what they ask of the viewer, gives the lie to the charge that the Calvinist imaginary is responsible for a disinterested gaze. The investment of these artists in their surroundings involved a fully embodied posture. This impulse is evident in the training that artists received during this period. In Holland in 1618 artist Hendrick Goltzius and Cornelius Corneliszoon van Haarlem established an influential drawing school where they taught students to work *nae t'leven* (near to life).[62] This recalls the goal of Renaissance portraits that were done *ad vivum*, but it takes that impulse further. Apprentice artists in this school were encouraged to consider their own bodily experience "translating the individual sensorium into knowledge applicable to the variety of nature" (p. 156). *Nae t'leven* was meant to spark in the viewer "the qualities of

---

[59] On this theme, see *Jacob van Ruisdael*, pp. 33–38. Walford's research included an intensive study of themes of Reformed preaching of the time which often focused on *vanitas*.

[60] Light breaking in often conveyed divine providence and redemption in Van Ruisdael. *Jacob van Ruisdael*, p. 99.

[61] Besse, *Voir la terre*, p. 68.

[62] Caroline D. Fowler, "Presence in Seventeenth-Century Practice and Theory," *Word and Image: A Journal of Verbal/Visual Enquiry*, 30/2 (2014): 155–167. Pages cited in the text are to this work.

another present body to the viewer" (p. 160).[63] Note what is claimed here is that *nae t'leven* went beyond sense of sight to include the multisensory experience of being present, of sharing space with another extended body (p. 164). One can see how developments in optics could contribute to this, but one also sees the enlarged dramatic possibilities of language and images. Critics have suggested that this expansion of the possibilities inherent in descriptive language simply hides a deeper fear of images. Rather, as I would argue, does this not allow language to trigger experiences that elaborate and extend what images can do? Equally important, does this not reflect the broader conception of "presence" that we have been tracing?

Perhaps there is no better support for this claim than the late portraits of Rembrandt van Rijn (1606–1669). While the majority of Rembrandt's portraits date from the 1630s, a decade later they began to take on a more deeply psychological and spiritual dimension. In this respect Rembrandt has often been thought unrepresentative of Dutch art in this period. Svetlana Alpers, for example, notes that Vermeer's paintings offer the viewer a "flood of observed, unmediated details drawn from nature."[64] Rembrandt, by contrast, Alpers notes, does not fit this model, but rather displays an estrangement from his own context, "offering a rare entry into invisible human depths."

Now it is important that we carefully understand what Rembrandt's achievement – his estrangement from his context, if that is what it was – amounts to. It does not mean reading our post-Romantic notions of the person back into these portraits. Rembrandt's self-portraits, for example (there were probably around forty of them), should not be read as exercises in self-examination.[65] The person in Rembrandt's portraits recalls Montaigne's comment that the "'I' is what connects me to all mankind, not that which distinguishes me" from this. It is also important to recognize that the outpouring of portraits in this period often celebrated more broadly the status of the sitter and the skill of the artist. For the latter, artists often sought *voncken* (sparkle), skin that appears to be real flesh, that is, simply true naturalness in Alpers's sense of the word. Rembrandt's later work

---

[63] She notes that later Descartes was struck by how marks on a page could summon the particularity of extension, even evoking other qualities of taste, touch, and smell (p. 164).

[64] This is supportive of her general thesis that Dutch art of this period displays a frame of the world as seen, what she calls the art of describing. *The Art of Describing*, p. 222. Quote that follows is at p. 225.

[65] Christopher White and Quentin Buvelot, eds., *Rembrandt by Himself* (London and New Haven, CT: National Gallery and Yale University Press, 1999), pp. 10–35 for this whole paragraph. Rembrandt quote at p. 35.

22 Rembrandt van Rijn, *Bathsheba at Her Toilet*, 1643, oil on wood, 22½ × 30 in.
Courtesy of the Metropolitan Museum, New York. Bequest of Benjamin Altman, 1913.

rejected these qualities, and for that reason they were often considered "unfinished." His response to this charge was to say it was finished if it "achieved [the artist's] intention in it."

But what was his intention? As many commentators have pointed out, from the 1640s this involved, especially for his biblical subjects, capturing a specific moment of recognition, a coming to awareness. And this psychological insight displayed a special connection to the artist's purposes. During the 1630s one can trace Rembrandt's work from the commissions and patrons, but from 1641 to 1654 there were few commissions, and the artist seems to have chosen subjects he was drawn to.[66] This is seen, for example, in his 1643 *Bathsheba at Her Toilet* (Figure 22). Here typically the figure is highlighted, thrust forward as Simon Schama puts it, "a summation of character through body language and the illumination of face and hands."[67] In this work, Rembrandt exhibits the *nae t'leven* that glows, Schama thinks, with "the robust warmth of full blooded life."

[66] See Gary Schwartz, *Rembrandt: His Life, His Painting* (New York: Viking, 1985), p. 226.
[67] *Rembrandt's Eyes* (New York: Knopf, 1999), p. 338.

These cannot be described as icons in any traditional sense, but neither do they fit with the developing realism of the fifteenth century – what Alistair MacIntyre calls the antithesis of iconography; they represent, rather, a new kind of icon.[68] As Simon Schama notes, the frame of these pictures is not a window, surely not a "window to heaven" as in the Orthodox icon, but more a self-dissolving threshold "through which both beholder and beheld may unnervingly pass."[69] The drama of Bathsheba is a drama that the viewer also shares – it is the drama of sin and salvation that Calvin had announced in his preaching. Because, as Hans Jantzen argues, Rembrandt succeeds in showing "the spiritual form of such a figure ... [t]his form encompasses a human fate ensnared in guilt ... In it the gathering and denouement of the whole Bathsheba tragedy is condensed."[70]

Rembrandt's figures combine a timelessness and truthfulness that is fully embodied. His portraits convey not only the material effects of the passing of years but also the complexity of brokenness and healing. Michael Taylor believes the painter's skill is about a "quality of mind, or perhaps simply an awareness – an aliveness to the world."[71] This aliveness encompassed an engagement with the narrative of sin and redemption that we have highlighted. It may not be accidental that the model for Bathsheba is Hendrickje, Rembrandt's common law wife, who would later be called before the Reformed Church Council to answer charges that she was sleeping with Rembrandt. Taylor suggests the council's harsh decision may have been influenced by this painting.

Nae t'leven leaves us with a paradox. We are drawn closer to the living person, but like Calvin, our painter guide clearly mistrusts the evidence of sight – consider how Rembrandt was frequently drawn to paint the blind. Alpers suggests this is because Rembrandt's images show us that "it is the word (or the Word) rather than the world that conveys the truth."[72] This is because in the figure of Bathsheba, Rembrandt captures the depths of the human drama that viewers are meant to live out as external icons. On one level Rembrandt's meditation on the biblical event recalls the Franciscan invitation for the viewer to imagine these events as though present. Van Hoogstraeten is said to have adopted Rembrandt's practice of assigning biblical subjects to his students so they would learn to visualize

---

[68] MacIntyre's claim is that Rembrandt achieves a synthesis: "The naturalistic portrait is now rendered as an icon, but an icon of a new and hitherto inconceivable kind." *After Virtue*, p. 90.

[69] *Rembrandt's Eyes*, p. 473.

[70] Quoted in Christian Tümpel and Astrid Tümpel, *Rembrandt: Images and Metaphors* (London: Haus Publishing, 2006), p. 233.

[71] Taylor, *Rembrandt's Nose* (New York: Art Publishers, 2007), p. 107. For what follows, see p. 113.

[72] *The Art of Describing*, p. 227.

them effectively.[73] But the direction of the imaginative construction is decidedly different. The story is to be properly visualized not so viewers could place themselves in that story but so that they could see their own lives in a new light – as an extension of that story. The Old Testament events, as Olivier Millet argued, are not shadows but tableaux vivants; not symbols to decipher, but experiences to discover.[74]

Above all in Dutch art, unlike medieval imagery, the material world, creation, is not diminished, but its dramatic dimension, "the tragic content of human entanglement," is laid bare.[75] Rembrandt has given us, in the image of a human figure, a theological likeness of the redemptive drama – everyday life, awaiting redemption.

Texts as Images

One can discern this theological likeness, that is, if these images are read properly. That is, they needed an interpreter. And for the Dutch believer of this period this interpretation was found in the preaching and the Scripture that guided that preaching. The images of landscape and everyday life that characterized seventeenth-century Dutch art needed to be textualized. But the reverse was true as well: texts themselves could become images. Mia Mochizuki has described the impact of this alliance between text and image on the material and visual culture of the Netherlands. Her study focuses on what she calls "text images" or "text panels" that emerged after the outbreak of iconoclasm in 1566.[76] Throughout churches in Holland, often in the very decorated frames of the old altarpieces, there appeared elaborate texts of historical events, or of Scripture texts, as shown in Figure 23.

What is striking about this image is its location behind the altar, in the very spot occupied by the altarpiece of the medieval church – often using the same support system.[77] The ornamental frame that could have held an image of Mary or a saint now holds an oil painting of the passage from I Corinthians 11 where Paul recounts Jesus' institution of the Last Supper. The medieval images that mixed the natural and the supernatural and invited a contemplative gaze that led believers astray are gone. But this void is now filled with

---

[73] Walter Liedtke, "Style in Dutch Art," in Franits, ed., *Looking at Seventeenth-Century Dutch Art*, p. 125.

[74] *Calvin et la dynamique de la Parole*, pp. 375, 423.

[75] Quoted in Tümpel and Tümpel, *Rembrandt: Images and Metaphors*, p. 233.

[76] *The Netherlandish Image*, pp. 10–14. She notes that this date roughly marks the end of Catholic control over the Dutch imagination. See p. 108.

[77] Mochizuki, *The Netherlandish Image*, pp. 127–152.

23 Anonymous, *Last Supper Scripture*, c. 1581, Haarlem, Great or St. Bavo Church.
Courtesy of Mia Mochizuki; photograph by Tjeerd Frederikse.

the words of institution – what Mochizuki calls a rehabilitated religious image.[78] The word has now become an image, a kind of perpetual sermon for the congregation, now admitted into the sacred precinct around the altar, which has become a table of fellowship with the living Lord. Previously, Mochizuki notes, words were in the service of images. Now matters have been reversed: images are in the service of the word – indeed, they have become words. These images are not meant to be contemplated as previously, but neither were they simple ciphers; they must now be read, memorized, understood, and then practiced. Like the Renaissance texts we encountered in Chapter 4, they have been liberated from the closed circle of medieval interpretation and have become subject to extended gloss and commentary. And the textual character of the image, like the prints we examined earlier, reminds viewers of the physical absence of Christ. For

[78] This reflects, she argues, the creativity of iconoclasm. *The Netherlandish Image*, p. 7.

Calvin, Christ had ascended into heaven and so could not be present in the sacrament. Rather, in the event of preaching and communion, believers were joined with Christ in heaven spiritually – that is, by the Spirit.[79] The very absence of traditional imagery made available space for a creative elaboration of the event of communion and the encounter with their neighbors, as defined by this biblical text.

So, both in the images that were hidden texts and in texts that had become visible images, a covenant was represented of the natural alliance between word and world that was assumed in this new imaginary; the natural landscape betrays a hidden artifice and the text appropriates (and subverts) a received artfulness. This new way of seeing the world, which encouraged and supported the impulse to change it, has become so much a part of the modern imagination that we no longer see it as new. But it is already evident, hidden in the visual culture of seventeenth-century Holland.

Architecture as Restoration: Huguenot Aspirational Architecture in Seventeenth-Century France

The visual and material culture of the Netherlands in the seventeenth century reflects a traditional Northern Renaissance insistence on simplicity and naturalness, but also a new dramatic reading of the created order that suggests the influence of Calvinism.[80] Further south in France other Renaissance streams reflect the recovery of classical sources, which Huguenot architects were able to integrate with their Calvinist sensitivities in projecting a new creation.

The Protestant influence on the developing empiricism and experimentalism in England has been widely acknowledged. Puritans reflected the Calvinist imagination and the call to restore human dominion over the created order and thus reverse the effects of the fall, and they were dominant figures in the forming of the Royal Academy.[81] The Reformation, they

---

[79] Cf. Calvin's comments on Ps. 138: "Believers in drawing near to God are withdrawn from the world, and rise to heaven in the enjoyment of fellowship with angels," which constitute a "heavenly theater." Ps. 138:1, trans. James Anderson, *Commentary* in loc.

[80] Mochizuki argues, as I have, that the changes were more a bending of than a breaking with the past. *The Netherlandish Image*, p. 5.

[81] Charles Webster, *The Great Instauration: Science, Medicine and Reform: 1626–1660* (New York: Holmes and Meier, 1975). "Committed Puritans and parliamentarians were ... the dominant element in the scientific community, and they were responsible for the great bulk of the scientific publications" (p. 491). See also Peter Harrison, *The Bible, Protestantism and the Rise of Natural Science* (Cambridge: Cambridge University Press, 1998).

believed, was the beginning of the new era, reflected in Francis Bacon's *Novum Organum* (1620), which sought to do away with Aristotelian logic reflected in the syllogism and replace it with an inductive method, a careful examination of creation that properly orders things and turns them to appropriate use.[82] A utopian imagination fed by millenarian interpretations of Daniel and Revelation fueled belief they were entering a new era. And this involved reordering a broken creation as well. Bacon opined that since God planted a garden, gardening "is the purest of Human Pleasures." This desire to remake creation, reverse the curse, and recover the beauty of Eden had a lasting imprint on the Huguenot architects in France.

From the 1520s followers of Luther and then Calvin in France, called Huguenots, grew especially among the merchant classes, though they were always a small and embattled community, never comprising more than 5–10 percent of the population. After experiencing some openness under Francis I, the reign of Henry II (1543–1559) brought increasing persecution, highlighted by his creation of the *chambre ardente* in 1547 charged with suppressing the Reformed faith. Because of their very different political situations, these Calvinists developed in ways that diverged from their English counterparts. Less doctrinally and devotionally focused, the central drama for them involved, as Philip Benedict put it, "the demonstration of genuine conviction by remaining firm to the true faith in the face of pressure to abjure."[83] Their corporate life was determined less by psychology than the socio-historical situation in which they found themselves, and "the pastoral strategies developed in response to these situations."

Perhaps for these reasons the most characteristic aesthetic profile of this community was created by its architects. Always struggling to stake out a public space in this increasingly hostile Catholic context, their places of worship stood at the center of Huguenot life, even as their buildings, and their inscriptions, offered "a visceral challenge and affront to the Catholic hierarchy."[84] While it has been widely acknowledged that Huguenot

---

[82] Interestingly, the subtitle of Bacon's work is *Instauratio Magna*, that is, the great restoration that would return the fallen order to its intended divine purposes. Webster notes that the Puritans believed that the spiritual renewal of the Reformation would be accompanied – and in their view perfected – by a renewal of dominion over nature. *The Great Instauration*, p. 325.

[83] Benedict, *The Faith and Fortunes of France's Huguenots 1600–1685* (Aldershot: Ashgate, 2001), p. 228. Quote that follows is at this page.

[84] Andrew Spicer, "'Qui est de Dieu oit la Parole de Dieu': The Huguenots and Their Temples," in Raymond Mentzer and Andrew Spicer, eds., *Society and Culture in the Huguenot World* (Cambridge: Cambridge University Press, 2002), p. 180. Spicer notes that even as Louis XIII boasted about the defeat of heresy in France, he permitted construction of temples, even granting them funds, perhaps reflecting the respect he owed Huguenot architects (p. 188).

architects were significant players in the development of sixteenth-century French architecture, only recently have scholars begun to explore the possible role of their religious beliefs.[85]

In their sheer numbers and influence, the impact of Huguenot architects is impressive. Catherine Randall goes so far as to claim that "Calvinist architects designed and constructed the vast majority of architectural structures built from mid-sixteenth to early seventeenth centuries in France."[86] Randall's argument is that though these architects worked in an environment frequently hostile their Protestant faith, they found ways, often by indirection and code, to express their desire to restore a fallen order to the beauty of God's original creation.

The story begins with the Italian architect and writer Sebastiano Serlio (1475–1554), who converted to the Evangelical faith early on and is widely credited with bringing classical forms to France. It was Serlio, more than any other author, who revived interest in the classical Orders of Vitruvius. After studies in Rome, he moved to Venice in 1527 where he began work on his monumental five-volume *Five Books of Architecture* (1537 and later years), translating Vitruvius' ideas into common language so that even the most mediocre builder could compose lovely buildings *all'antica* (after the style of the ancients).[87] The third of his five books, dedicated to Francis I, brought him to the attention of the French royalty, and in 1541 he moved to France as the "premier peintre et architecte" at Fontainebleau. In his "Grand Ferrare" at Fontainebleau and the Château d'Ancy-le-Franc (c. 1546), he is credited for providing "the French with exemplary exercises in the classicizing of the traditional forms."[88] Like all the Reformed architects Serlio frequently quoted Scripture, making special reference to the parable of casting pearls before swine – perhaps to rationalize his Nicodemism (secret faith) that had been necessary in Italy, and which Calvin had denounced. His architectural emphasis on utility and simplicity

[85] See Catherine Randall (Coats), *Building Codes: The Aesthetics of Calvinism in Early Modern Europe* (Philadelphia: University of Pennsylvania Press, 1999); Randal Carter Working, *Visual Theology: Towards an Architectural Iconology of Early Modern French Protestantism 1535–1623* (Eugene, OR: Pickwick Publications, 2016).

[86] *Building Codes*, p. 2. She goes on to claim that is difficult to find architectural manuals or buildings erected by Catholic architects during this period.

[87] Mario Carpo locates Serlio's project of presenting Vitruvius within the impulse toward producing vernacular texts of Scripture: "The entire project of the diffusion of Renaissance classicism in France was also part of a translational phenomenon." *Architecture in the Age of Printing*, pp. 51–71, at 71.

[88] Christopher Tadgell, *Reformations: From High Renaissance to Mannerism in the New West of Religious Contention and Colonial Expansion* (New York: Routledge, 2012), p. 316. Interestingly, though Tadgell begins his book with a summary of the religious situation, the aesthetic implications of these differences make no appearance in the rest of his otherwise rich and helpful discussion.

reflects his Calvinist leanings, as he wrote in his *Seventh Book* "of how to distinguish, with [his] small intellect, a sober, simple . . . architecture from one that is weak, facile, affected, obscure and confused."[89] Selio dedicated his *Fifth Book*, the one on churches, to Marguerite de Navarre, where he paraphrased II Corinthians 6:16: "True temples are in the hearts of pious Christians."

Serlio's work not only brought classical ideas to France but was especially influential on Huguenot architects such as Philiberte de l'Orme, Salomon de Bray, and Bernard Palissy. The recovery of classical orders allowed these Reformed architects to go back behind the corruption of medieval faith (which they saw reflected in Gothic architecture) to what they regarded as a purer style that reflected biblical values. Their focus on the goodness of creation resonated with the classical elements: *firmitas* (steadfastness), *utilitas* (the structure's usefulness), and *venustas* (loveliness). In their architectural treatises, they go even further back, to seek in the Old Testament the fundamental proportions that were displayed in the Temple.[90]

Philibert de L'Orme (or Delorme, 1514–1570), one of the most influential and also controversial architects of his time, followed Serlio closely, working on significant commissions in the 1540s – including St. Maur and the Chateau at Anet. He also wrote treatises that were widely read, including *Nouvelles Inventions* (1561) and *Le Premier tome de l'Architecture* (1567). Like Serlio he wrote in as simple – even popular – style as possible, in the first person. In his theory he always preferred *utilitas* to *venustas*, rejecting the "richness of houses made only to please the eye and not for any benefit to the health of men." For Delorme ornament was always disciplined by rationality; the parts subordinated to the whole with horizontals and verticals coordinated.[91]

Delorme's most famous work was his design for the Tuileries Palace and garden commissioned by Catherine de Medici in the 1560s. This monumental project, which developed over succeeding centuries, was initiated by Catherine in 1561 when she acquired the land, with construction beginning in 1564. Hampered by financial constraints and religious unrest, it is hard to know how much was actually built, since much of the early parts were subsequently destroyed. On Delorme's death in 1570, direction of the project passed to Jean Bullant, another Huguenot, who finished the two structural wings that Delorme

[89] Quoted in *Building Codes*, p. 80. She also describes here his use of Scripture.
[90] L'Orme, *Le Premier tome de l'Architecture* (1567); de Bray, *Architectura Moderna* (1631). They sought a "construction based upon a mathematical regularity which in turn could ultimately be traced back to divine origins." Mochizuki, *The Netherlandish Image*, p. 222.
[91] Tadgell, *Reformations*, p. 344. And see Vaughan Hart with Peter Hicks, ed., *Paper Palaces: The Rise of the Renaissance Architectural Treatises* (New Haven, CT: Yale University Press, 1998), p. 230.

had begun.[92] Whatever his exact contribution, Delorme's work for the Queen mother, Christopher Tadgell believes, provided "an essential ingredient of the architectonic repertory of decorative detail with which French Classical architecture was to be reformed in the age of the Enlightenment." Delorme thus developed a sumptuous new style "which foreshadowed the decorative 'mannerism' of the later sixteenth-century French practice and pattern books."[93]

If preaching and singing constituted the default sixteenth-century Protestant engagement with what we today call media, the architecture of the sixteenth and seventeenth centuries constituted what passed then for mass media, having the ability to convey a message to those outside the church walls, something particularly important to Huguenots, as we have observed.[94] And the message these architects sought to convey was the need to restore the fallen and disordered creation to its original splendor. In their work for the French royalty they opposed the emerging Baroque excesses, opting rather for the modest, strong classical style.[95] And this constructive impulse consciously reflected interaction with Calvin's *Institutes*. Randall Working argues that "all French Calvinist architecture was built upon an 'intertext,' a conceptual interplay between the words of Scripture and Calvin's *Institutes*."[96] In this they were motivated by Calvin's vision for the restoration of creation. Working concludes: "Protestant architects and designers working in France and Switzerland believed themselves to be participating in a recovery of nature as a part of the larger work in which God was restoring creation and making a new Eden."

This vision was particularly evident in the work of Bernard Palissy (1510–1589), best known for his work on the grottos for the Tuileries gardens. While widely admired, scholars have only recently seen the connection of his work with Calvin's theology of creation. In his *La Recept véritable* (1563) he lays out his intention to work with nature, by meditating on Psalm 104, in order to develop his plans for a "delectable garden," a striking image of salvation and a place of rest and refuge from the

---

[92] Guillaume Fonkenell, *Le Palais des Tuileries* (Paris: Honore Clair, 2010), pp. 12–18. See also Laura D. Corey et al., *The Art of the Louvre's Tuileries Garden*, catalogue of exhibits at the High Museum of Atlanta and the Toledo Museum (New Haven, CT: Yale University Press, 2013).

[93] *Reformations*, p. 344.   [94] *Building Codes*, p. 225n4.

[95] Randall notes the irony of these Calvinists dialectically playing a major role "in the construction of an official idiom for the French absolutist nation-state." *Building Codes*, p. 7.

[96] *Visual Theology*, p. 126. This was especially true of the work of Bernard Palissy. Quote that follows is at p. 187.

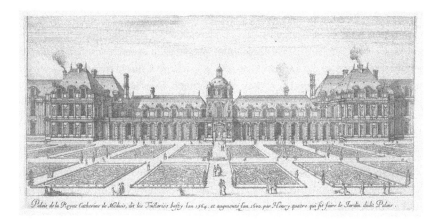

Palais de la Reyne Catherine de Médicis, dit les Tuilleries basty l'an 1564. et augmenté l'an 1600. par Henry quatre qui fit faire le Jardin. dudit Palais .

24 Tuileries gardens and palace, 1567, designed by Philiberto Delorme, grotto by Bernard Palissy.

persecution that Huguenots were experiencing.[97] Catherine Randall goes so far as to argue that Palissy's description of the "delectable garden" explicitly follows the structure implied in Calvin's *Institutes*. The world, though fallen, can be restored. "Palissy's garden renders literal Calvin's conception of believers as a new garden of Eden."[98] Palissy believed that when one finds refuge in God one can see the world in terms of the wisdom God has placed there, as a kind of visual wisdom. Catherine de Médici, though a patron and protector of Palissy,[99] could not save him from eventual martyrdom in 1590, but his influence on the design of gardens lived on (see Figure 24).

Research on the specific Reformed influence on these architects is still in its infancy, but we have learned enough to see the general impact of the Calvinist imaginary. And it is possible to claim that the impulse to restore and renew the world shared by these Huguenot architects lives on in the modern world. It was this urge to useful repristinization, the call to reorder a fallen creation, that the Puritan settlers brought with them to North America

---

[97] Palissy, *Les Oeuvres de Maistre Bernard Palissy*, ed. P. Fillon (Niort: Clouzot Librairie, 1888), vol. 1, pp. 1–129.

[98] *Building Codes*, p. 55. Leonard N. Amico avers that Palissy seemed to nurture ambiguity as to whether his garden plan was a work of art or a call for social upheaval. *Bernard Palissy: In Search of Earthly Paradise* (Paris: Flammarion, 1996), p. 160.

[99] The exact nature of his commissions remains unclear. See Amico's discussion of the Grotto for the Tuileries and his relationship with Catherine in *Bernard Palissy*, pp. 69f. See also Corey et al., *The Art of the Louvre's Tuileries Gardens*. Palissy is also considered by some to have played a role along with Bacon in the rise of a scientific method. See Thomas Clifford, *Bacon, Palissy and the Revival of Natural Science* (Oxford: Oxford University Press, 1914).

and that has become such a persistent theme of American aesthetics, something that can be seen, for example, in the Hudson River School and Frederick Olmsted's public parks. What Charles Taylor calls the disciplinary society may well have its roots here. He describes this impulse as "Human beings forming societies under the normative provisions of the Modern Moral Order, and fulfilling their purposes by using what nature provides, through the accurate knowledge of this nature, and the contrivances which we will later call technology."[100] Indeed scholars of technology have noted this connection. Friedrich Klemm has argued that one factor in the intensification of research into nature in the second half of the seventeenth century, to gain control of its resources, "is to be found in the practical ethics of Calvinism with its clear concern with the world around us."[101]

Conclusion

One cannot claim the Calvinist imaginary issued in specific artistic and cultural programs. Robert Scribner's summation of the popular imagery of the Reformation could characterize Calvinist sensitivities more broadly: "It did not produce the powerful new symbols of allegiance which might have created a new 'symbolic universe' distinctly different from the old faith."[102] Still, in its promotion of a new way of seeing the world and its activist impulse, it may have anticipated much that we associate with modern attitudes, even if in its indirection and subtlety this is often overlooked. As in the case of realistic theater it was in part Protestant suspicions that opened up new ways of approaching the drama of the world. In the same way here, Protestant desacralization opened the way to new ways of seeing the natural world, even to a delineation of the particular art genres that express this. The skepticism about God's attachment to matter, Jacob Wamberg has argued, was "a crucial condition enabling the new and more sensory image genres of the late Middle Ages – portrait, genre, landscape, still life – to be emancipated from their previous status as mere backgrounds, to sacred or mythological figure based painting and instead to become genres

---

[100] Taylor, *A Secular Age* (Cambridge, MA: Harvard University Press, 2007), p. 294.
[101] Klemm, *A History of Western Technology*, trans. Dorthea W. Singer (London: Allen and Unwin, 1959), p. 171. He notes that places where this influence was present – England and Holland – "were all the scenes of important scientific and technological development."
[102] Scribner, *For the Sake of the Simple Folk* (Cambridge: Cambridge University Press, 1981), p. 248.

in their right."[103] So that over the course of the sixteenth century there was emerging a system of the arts – literature, drama, architecture, painting – that we would recognize as modern.[104] Surely the broadened attention given to the moral drama of the world attendant on Reformation attitudes had something do to with this categorical expansion.

One has to keep in mind, however, that the major Reformers were facing comprehensive social and religious challenges, so that their impact on what we call the arts was mostly indirect. One recalls in this connection the observation in William Perkins's influential instructions that when they mount the pulpit to preach, they "ought in public to conceal all these [sources] from the people and not to make the least ostentation."[105] Perhaps nothing better describes the "plain style" and hidden impact of the Calvinist imagination in its many forms since that day.

---

[103] Wamberg, *Landscape as World Picture: Tracing Cultural Evolution in Images*, trans. Gaye Kynoch (Aarhus: Aarhus University Press, 2009), vol. II, p. 14. He notes that this freed these genres to be explored without religious constraint. He connects this desacralization specifically with Calvin's influence.

[104] Clark Hulse, "Tudor Aesthetics," in Arthur F. Kinney, ed., *Cambridge Companion to English Literature: 1500–1600* (Cambridge: Cambridge University Press, 2000), p. 29.

[105] Perkins, "The Art of Prophesying," in *Workes of the Famous and Worthy Minister William Perkins* (London: John Legatt, 1631), vol. II, p. 670. The expression can be traced to Ovid, Artis Amatoriae, Book ii, l, 313, (c. 1 BC), "If art is concealed it succeeds."

8

EPILOGUE
The Cultural Afterlife of Protestant Aesthetics

THOUGH WE HAVE SUGGESTED SOME INFLUENCE OF THE Calvinist aesthetic in Holland and France, it would be a mistake to overestimate the influence of this contested and diverse tradition during the seventeenth century. During that century England in fact experienced its own counter-reformation in which the arts returned to the service of the Church and its worship and, in the process, served to resanctify space, objects, and priests.[1] On the continent Luther's more positive attitude toward the arts had a profound influence on music, though it did little to nurture a creative tradition in the visual arts. Erwin Panofsky has noted a general decline in North German art in the late sixteenth century and throughout the seventeenth century.[2] And the later development of a vital landscape tradition in Northern Europe has been attributed to the influence of Calvin rather than Luther.[3]

While specific influences are difficult to trace, however, this book has argued that the real significance of this period for aesthetics lies in a more

---

[1] Graham Parry, *The Arts of the Anglican Counter-Reformation: Glory, Laud and Honour* (Woodridge: Boydell Press, 2006). Parry frames this movement as a reaction to many decades of austerity and iconophobia. But Panofsky belittles the art made in this period. In England: "Music and poetry reached their zenith when English painting reached their nadir." "Comments on Art and Reformation," in *Symbols in Transformation*, ed. Craig Harbison, p. 12.

[2] The only exception to this may be Albrecht Dürer, though his work did not contribute to developing a Protestant tradition in the arts; and visual art in Holland went into decline in the seventeenth century from which it never recovered. Panofsky, "Comments," pp. 9–14. See also Carl C. Christensen, "Religious reform was achieved at the expense of cultural loss." *Art and the Reformation in Germany* (Athens: University of Ohio Press, 1979), p. 179; Michalski, *The Reformation and the Visual Arts* (New York: Routledge, 1993), p. 40.

[3] Robert Rosenblum, *Modern Painting and the Northern Romantic Tradition: Friedrich to Rothko* (London: Thames and Hudson, 1975). See the discussion of the religious influences on this tradition in Jonathan Anderson and William Dyrness, *Modern Art and the Life of a Culture: The Religious Impulses of Modernism* (Downers Grove, IL: InterVarsity Press, 2017), pp. 142–196.

general transformation of perception. As a part of the developing world picture influenced by late medieval piety, Renaissance humanism, and the expanding global consciousness represented by the voyages of discovery, the Calvinist focus on the created order as the locus of God's creative and re-creative activity, as this was laid out in Scripture and embodied in the rhetoric of Calvin's preaching and teaching, was intended to awaken believers to play their part in the theater of the world. While it enlarged and encouraged developments already at play, Calvin's theology of creation added its unique accent to changing aesthetic sensitivities that, over time, helped shape modern attitudes toward the arts. Just as the expanding devotion to late medieval sacramentals increased the aesthetic possibilities during that period, so, to a greater extent, the Reformation conviction of God's presence in the details of creation, and the dramatic potential of that presence, opened up a wider array of experiences and objects considered worthy of aesthetic attention.

The American Aesthetic Imaginary: Taking the World Seriously

In North America in particular where Calvin's followers came to escape religious persecution in Europe, this general impulse, I would argue, continues to shape the way the arts are defined and experienced. While this claim cannot be defended in any detail here, some general lines of evidence may – suggestively and tentatively – be adduced.[4] The first and most obvious of these would clearly be the persistent focus on the beauty and preservation of the natural world that has been a consistent part of the American imagination. Even a brief summary of the history of ecological movements in America shows the clear influence of this Reformed heritage. Mountaineer John Muir; Louis Agassiz, the Harvard naturalist; transcendentalist writer Ralph Waldo Emerson; Gifford Pinchot, founder of the US Forest Service; Frederick Olmsted, designer of Central Park; botanist Asa Gray; even Rachel Carson, all to a greater or lesser extent, traced their love of nature to their Presbyterian or Scots Calvinist heritage. However, even here the paradoxes of this tradition, which we have noted, are also evident: for many of these at various points, even as they were formed by it, intentionally rejected this heritage. This leads Belden Lane to comment wryly that the Calvinist tradition "has the dubious distinction of being the most prevalent

---

[4] I have outlined the Calvinist influence on Puritan culture in *Reformed Theology and Visual Culture*, chapters 6 and 7.

ex-religious commitment of all American nature writers and activists."[5] Lane attributes this to the subsequent focus of Calvin's followers on predestination, which eclipsed his focus on creation as a theater for God's glory, a development I have also noted. Lane says of this later evolution: "If one understands Reformed theology ... as primarily absorbed with predestination and God's overwhelming work of redemption, viewing original sin as distorting every aspect of the created order, there is little reason to seek God in the natural world. If, on the other hand, one perceives Reformed theology (after Calvin) as *beginning* with creation, discerning God's glory in all its wonders despite the ravages of sin, there is every reason to take the world seriously."

The tensions evident in this tradition may account for the charge that this tradition, while influential in American literary culture, has as often served to constrict its imagination as to encourage it. Tracy Fessenden, for example, has argued that a particular form of Protestantism, rooted in Puritan's New World narrative, emerged as an "unmarked category" in American religious and literary history. This tradition tended to portray Americans as bearers of a divine mandate to possess the land, displace its inhabitants, and by their Scriptural common schools promote Anglo-Saxon supremacy.[6] By aligning itself with an emerging middle class, this Protestant Christianity "was able to render itself unspoken, to become a kind of silent, natural looking power," pervasive if elusive. Like Protestant-influenced ecological writers, Fessenden notes that American writers often promoted their journey of freedom and discovery by reacting against the "absolute certainty" of their Calvinist heritage.

Still, taking the world seriously, and celebrating its aesthetic potential, may arguably be considered the major contribution of this tradition to aesthetics in North America. This is true not only of movements like the nineteenth-century Hudson River School but even of more recent developments in contemporary art that draw on this aspect of the American imaginary. Consider one prominent example. In 1958, two years after Jackson Pollock's tragic death, artist Allan Kaprow wrote an influential assessment of that painter's accomplishment.[7] Pollock, while creating great

---

[5] Lane, *Ravished by Beauty: The Surprising Legacy of Reformed Spirituality* (New York: Oxford University Press, 2011), pp. 43, 44. Quotes at pp. 43 and 44, respectively. Emphasis in original. I have made use of his list of nature writers showing this influence. He notes that Perry Miller was among the first to point out this connection.

[6] Fessenden, *Culture and Redemption: Religion, the Secular and American Literature* (Princeton, NJ: Princeton University Press, 2007), pp. 6–9. Quote that follows at p. 88, and cf. p. 143.

[7] Kaprow, "The Legacy of Jackson Pollock," in Jeff Kelley, ed., *Essays on the Blurring of Art and Life* (Berkeley: University of California Press, 1993). Pages cited in the text are to this work. For what

work, Kaprow argued, actually "destroyed painting" (p. 2). This was because the boundaries of Pollock's paintings were artificial; they merely indicated places where he stopped working, where his activity in the painting stopped. The significance of this, Kaprow thinks, lay in proposing that artistic activity should extend outside; indeed, it should simply ignore any such boundary. Here is how he described this possibility:

> Pollock, as I see him, left us at the point where we must become preoccupied with and even dazzled by the space and objects of our everyday life, either our bodies, clothes, rooms, or, if need be, the vastness of Forty-Second Street. Not satisfied with the suggestion through paint of our senses, we shall utilize [as artistic media] the specific substances of sight, sound, movements, people, people odors, touch. Objects of every sort are materials for the new art: paint, chairs, food, electric and neon lights, smoke, water, old socks, a dog, movies, a thousand other things that will be discovered by the present generation of artists. (pp. 7, 9)

Kaprow's suggestions were prophetic, anticipating not only his own "happenings," but the whole trajectory of contemporary art to the present, which has consistently directed attention outward to the world of everyday life. All that lies around us, "to which we are more than normally attentive" (pp. 16–17), has the potential to become aesthetically interesting. Clearly, Kaprow and those following in his wake were protesting the narrowing of the aesthetic focus to objects in the sacred spaces of museums or galleries. Rather, they were intent on redirecting aesthetic expectations to the theater of the world. Surely, Kaprow's Jewish heritage and his experience with Buddhism played a role in this expanded focus, but he was also well acquainted with Christian theology – even if he was critical of the mid-century American church.[8]

Kaprow was also influenced by John Cage, whose classes he attended at the New School for Social Research, after Kaprow became an art teacher at Rutgers University in 1957. Cage was similarly determined to blur the boundary between art and life or, in his case, between "music" and "noise."[9] Cage's background included significant experiences in Christian churches as well as a passage through Eastern philosophy. In the early 1950s he had

---

follows, see the discussion in Anderson and Dyrness, *Modern Art and the Life of a Culture*, pp. 285–298. For Calvin's influence on the Hudson River School, see Gene Veith, *Painters of Faith: The Spiritual Landscape in Nineteenth-Century America* (Washington, DC: Regnery, 2001).

[8] See the discussion in *Modern Art and the Life of a Culture*, pp. 290, 291. Earlier quote is from Kaprow, "A Spring Happening," in Kelley, ed., *Essays on the Blurring of Art and Life*.

[9] For what follows, see *Modern Art and the Life of a Culture*, pp. 293–298.

begun a series of experiments with sound and, more importantly, with silence, when at Harvard he visited an anechoic chamber to experience true silence. He became convinced that one needed to silence oneself in order to truly hear the sounds constantly produced by the world around, a conviction that led to his famous piano composition, "4′33″" (1952) – three movements of total silence, first "performed" by pianist David Tudor in Woodstock, New York, on August 29, 1952. The dismayed audience was understandably frustrated by the experience, but as critics soon pointed out, the "silence" was in fact full of sounds – bird calls, sounds of traffic or creaking wood, even the shuffling and coughing of the audience. Cage believed that paying attention to the sounds of one's life was an "art" that the modern world had lost. Surely his discovery of Buddhist "mindfulness" played a role in this discovery, but Cage himself – who as a young man was devoted to his Protestant church and considered going into ministry – linked his love for the sounds of his environment to Jesus' admonition to "consider the lilies." In his *Sermon on the Mount* Jesus asks his disciples: "Is not life more than food and the body more than clothing? . . . Consider the lilies of the field, how they grow; they neither toil nor spin; and yet I say to you, even Solomon and all his glory was not clothed like one of these" (Matt. 6:25, 26, 28–30, NRSV).[10] The significance of this attitude toward life was signaled by Kaprow in a later article on Cage. As Cage brought the noisy world into the concert hall, Kaprow proposes, the next step was to simply forget all the "framing devices" – the boundaries – of the art world. Kaprow goes on to suggest the significance of this: "But here . . . is the most valuable part of John Cage's innovations in music: experimental music, or any experimental art of our time, can be an introduction to right living; and after that introduction art can be bypassed for the main course."[11] Paying attention to life, then, is tied to right living; it is a moral quality that sees the theater of the world holding us accountable. It may not be a stretch to see this attitude not only resonating with the tradition I have described, but as owing something to the influence of that heritage as an "unmarked category" in American culture.

---

[10] *Modern Art and the Life of a Culture*, p. 296. Calvin in his commentary on this passage encourages similar attention to this display of beauty: "The meaning is, that the blessing of God, which glows upon the plants and flowers excels all that men may achieve by their wealth or influence or by any other means. Believers ought to be convinced that they will want nothing that is necessary for their full satisfaction, provided they continue to enjoy the blessing of God alone." *Commentary on the Harmony of the Gospels*, trans. A. W. Morrison, in loc.

[11] Kaprow, "Right Living," in *Essays on the Blurring of Art and Life*, p. 225.

Art as a Vehicle to Something Higher

Though often unstated, the question accompanying all discussions of art and art objects is this: Why do we need to pay attention to what is there? What drives us to pursue all that has come to be included as aesthetic experience? Here the answer provided by the tradition of Western art is consistent: we pay attention to these objects and encounters because they are a means of finding some higher and deeper meaning for life in the world. And such a broad consensus, I argue, may also be a residue of the Reformation heritage we have explored. As we saw in our brief discussion of the medieval period, attention to the art object was understood as the first step in linking the physical to something higher, eventually to spiritual truth. Recall Herbert Kessler's claim that engaging physical sight begins the process of attracting attention away from mundane things and focusing one's perception on more elevated things; that is, it facilitates the process of displacement and reorientation, replacing one thing, the physical, with something better, the spiritual.[12]

My claim in this book is that Calvin resituated the aesthetic potential attendant on that spiritual journey by framing the created order as a dramatic theater where God's work of recreation is performed and where believers are enlisted in the chorus of praise. In the period since the Reformation this process of taking the world as a symbol of "something higher" has come under increasing attack, or to put the matter more accurately, it has been transformed from a vertical journey toward a higher spiritual reality to an interior search for something "beyond" – some deeper or more satisfying way of knowing and living life. Charles Taylor has provided the most influential description of this post-Romantic development, which he frames as a response to the secular arc of the Enlightenment. During the Romantic period, he has argued, artists expanded the territory in which the creative imagination could work and shaped the post-Romantic lens in which modern people live and experience the world.[13] Taylor acknowledges these developments occurred against the background of "fading … metaphysical beliefs about the Great Chain of Being, the order of things and the like" (p. 354), that is, the weakening of traditional views of a world created and governed by God or the divine. Still, these artists moved beyond a mere mimetic representation of reality to re-create the *response* to the depths

---

[12] Kessler, "Turning a Blind Eye," in Hamburger and Bouché, eds., *The Mind's Eye*, pp. 415, 417.

[13] Taylor, *A Secular Age* (Cambridge, MA: Belknap/Harvard University Press, 2007), pp. 354–359. Pages cited in the text are to this work.

previously represented by this religious description of things – a creative response to the experience, Taylor says, without the story. But, whatever their religious convictions, these moves staked out a new aesthetic territory that would soon be filled by the verbal symbolism of Stéphane Mallarmé, or the non-representational art of Wassily Kandinsky, and, more recently, by experiences like Kaprow's happenings and Cage's music of silence. While the ontic commitment of these artists maybe uncertain, Taylor argues, they are not closed (p. 356). As a result, these artists and their contemporary heirs "serve to disclose very deep truths which in the nature of things can never be obvious, nor available to everyone, regardless of spiritual condition" (p. 356).[14]

Nicholas Wolterstorff, while not referring to Taylor directly, has recently disputed this reading of what he calls the grand narrative of modern art: that the past centuries represent an irresistible development of art and aesthetics toward the view that art makes the transcendent – or the higher reality of life, however this is understood – present to the viewer when engaged "disinterestedly."[15] The result of this narrative, Wolterstorff believes, is to leave out of account practices that do not fit into this narrative: memorial art, social protest art, art for veneration, and art that simply enhances life – like work songs.

Wolterstorff's extension of the sites of art practice fits well with the changed aesthetic situation that, I propose, resulted from Calvin's changing dramatic focus. But it leaves unanswered the larger question: What is it that makes these practices special? Why do they attract our attention at all, and what funds this attraction? Modern people refer to this enhanced quality variously as "inspiration" or "genius," that is, an attribute that goes beyond mere skill or technique, even if these are present. Now Calvin was able to recognize excellence when he saw it, and he regularly attributed such specialized ability to the Holy Spirit. This "gifting" allowed him to express admiration even for pagan artists and craftsmen. As he writes in his

---

[14] Taylor in his earlier work, *Sources of the Self* (Cambridge, MA: Harvard University Press, 1989), had argued that one of the grounds of the development of the modern self and, by extension, the aesthetic possibilities outlined in *A Secular Age,* lay in the Reformation's affirmation of everyday life.

[15] Wolterstorff, "Beyond Beauty and the Aesthetic in the Engagement of Religion and Art," in Oleg V. Bychkov and James Fodor, eds., *Theological Aesthetics after von Balthasar* (Canterbury: Aldershot, 2008), pp. 119–134. He has described the practices this narrative excludes, and that I list briefly, in more detail in *Art Rethought: The Social Practices of Art* (New York: Oxford University Press, 2017). Wolterstorff's protest about the reduction of contemporary art to disinterested contemplation is fueled by his own Reformed convictions. See his earlier book, *Art in Action: Toward a Christian Aesthetic* (Grand Rapids, MI: Eerdmans, 1980).

commentary on *Genesis*: "For the invention of the arts, and of other things which serve to the common use and convenience of life, is a gift of God and by no means to be despised, and a faculty worthy of commendation ... And we see, at the present time, that the excellent gifts of the Spirit are diffused through the whole human race."[16] The particular "grace" that attended these gifts, then, was the result of the Spirit, even if Calvin nowhere specifically addressed what was "aesthetic" about them – that is why we are attracted to them. But given the medieval heritage that we have elicited, and the theological grounding intentionally referenced during the Reformation and post-Reformation era, is it not possible to suggest that these prevailing theological assumptions lie behind and provide warrant, however unconsciously, for this secular vocabulary of fullness and depth? The critic George Steiner offers some general support for this hypothesis. Though not referring to Calvinism in particular, Steiner characterizes the weight that attends works of art – what he terms "saturated phenomena" – as dependent on something he calls, suggestively, *logos*, an axiomatic leap toward meaning. Indeed, he thinks the agnostic and atheist artist discovers it "immensely difficult ... to find words for his making, for the 'vibrations of the primal' which quicken his work. Pervasively, however, major art in our vexed modernity has been like all great shaping before it, touched by the fire and the ice of God." Steiner claims this hermeneutical tradition of seeking a presence in a work of art and its prevalence in modern critical discussions, however this is defined, owes a deep and unpaid debt to the Judeo-Christian scriptural and exegetical traditions.[17] Whatever its sources, Steiner's claim resonates with the changing notion of "presence" that follows from Calvin's theology of creation. Presence is shared with the facts of the created order and the humanly produced artifacts made from this, but only as these are properly evaluated and celebrated through praise.

However it is understood, what Walter Benjamin called almost a century ago the "aura" that accompanies works of art has become an inescapable dimension of the discourse of art. How can one account for its power? Taylor insists this vocabulary of excess cannot be avoided for our generation and indeed points to something essential to our humanity. In an afterward to

---

[16] Gen. 4:20, *Commentary on the First Book of Moses, Genesis*, trans. John King, in loc.

[17] Steiner, *Real Presences: Is There Anything in What We Say?* (Chicago: University of Chicago Press, 1989), p. 223. The argument of the unpaid debt is made in *Real Presences: The Leslie Stephen Memorial Lecture at the University of Cambridge, 1 November 1985* (Cambridge: Cambridge University Press, 1986). Literary explication and symbolism, he thinks, are "the immediate heirs to the textualities of Judeo-Christian theology and biblical Patristic exegetics" (p. 20). See also p. 19.

a volume discussing his work, and in which his use of "fullness" was subject
to criticism, Taylor argued that too often we miss what drives other people:

> So I think it was a very, very useful idea to try to introduce this notion of a
> general facet or dimension of the human condition where people strive
> for – have sense of – what really, fully, authentically, living would be, and
> to feel either they aren't there or they are there ... and so on. This is
> something that plays a role in peoples' lives.[18]

Taylor's response recalls Kaprow's description of Cage. Experiences of this
kind finally relate to the possibility of right, pleasing, and satisfying living,
suggesting that aesthetics is, in large part, peoples' awakening to the world
that Calvin described in which something or someone has called them to
account.

Iconoclasm and the Prophetic Tradition

Iconoclasm represents one of the most fraught aspects of the Protestant
Reformation, and even if it is not the central category it is often made out
to be, it calls for comment in the context of Calvin's contribution. I have
noted that though both Luther and Calvin were opposed to iconoclasm in
the narrow sense of physical destruction of images in churches; they both
espoused a broader sense of the need to reconstruct the medieval journey to
God. And for Calvin this surely involved eliminating many of the received
practices and images that facilitated that journey. But this needs to be
understood, I have argued, within the constructive project that Calvin
undertook. In other words it is possible to understand what I have called
the iconoclastic impulse as the need to challenge, even to deconstruct what
that Reformer believed was an appropriate way to access God's favor. This
made possible the defects that became evident in this tradition, but it also
allowed for a continuing (and generally positive) influence of the more
ancient biblical and prophetic tradition that ultimately fueled Calvin's
insights. The defects had their source in the movement from the destruction
of images and artifacts to the elimination of people deemed promoters of

---

[18] "Afterward," in Michael Warner et al., eds., *Varieties of Secularism in a Secular Age* (Cambridge,
MA: Harvard University Press, 2010), p. 317. And see Walter Benjamin, "The Work of Art in the
Age of Technical Reproducibility" (1936), in *The Work of Art in the Age of Its Technological
Reproducibility and Other Writings on Media*, ed. Michael W. Jennings et al., trans. Edmund Jephcott
et al. (Cambridge, MA: Harvard University Press/Belknap, 2008), pp. 19–55.

these superstitions, a move we observed already in Calvin's lifetime and one with a dismal subsequent presence in Western colonial history.[19]

Rather than exploring that history in any detail, I want here simply to reflect on two aspects of this impulse that might suggest something of the continuing impact of the constructive vision of Calvin. First, consider the well-known characteristic of Calvinist churches as barren of any religious imagery and structured to focus attention on the preaching and hearing of the word of God. Now there has been a great deal of rethinking of the details of this influence and it has become obvious that the issues that troubled Calvin are no longer issues with which contemporary Christians wrestle.[20] Wondering why Calvin paid so little attention to beauty in art, John de Gruchy's reflection is apt: "The reason is to be found in the polemical situation in which Calvin found himself in opposing both the proliferation of religious images in the church that seemed to aid and abet superstition, and the extravagant opulence of the wealthy that showed little respect for the poor."[21] In addressing the former concern, Calvin not only kept images out of the church space, but insisted that outside of hours of worship the church is to be locked, so that no one "may enter for super-stitious reasons." As he detailed this: "If anyone be found making any particular devotion inside or nearby, he is to be admonished; if it appears to be a superstition which he will not amend he is to be chastised."[22] Calvin's instructions, as has become clear, do not follow simply from an iconoclastic logic – that would be to seriously misrepresent his intentions. The church is locked because the drama in which Calvin sought to enlist his congregants unfolded not in that space, but out in the creation where God was working to restore the order of things. And out on the streets of Geneva, the disorder of that creation – among which was surely the preening of the wealthy who disregarded the poor – was on full display.

---

[19] For the description of this history, which brought with its achievement the dispensability of human life, see Walter D. Mignolo, *The Darker Side of Western Modernity: Global Futures, Decolonial Options* (Durham, NC: Duke University Press, 2011), p. 6 and passim. And for the complex history of Iconoclasm, see Alain Besançon, *The Forbidden Image: An Intellectual History of Iconoclasm* (Chicago: University of Chicago Press, 2000).

[20] Even Calvin recognized that his restrictions might be a kind of temporary measure. After a scathing indictment of images and ceremonies in the *Institutes*, Calvin surprisingly allows that "this present age offers proof of the fact that it may be a fitting thing to lay aside, as may be necessary in the circumstances, certain rites that in other circumstances are not impious or indecorous" (IV, x, 32). Five hundred years later, we are clearly presented with "other circumstances."

[21] De Gruchy, *John Calvin: Christian Humanist and Evangelical Reformer* (Eugene, OR: Cascade Books, 2013), p. 200.

[22] Calvin, *Theological Treatises*, ed. J. K. S. Reid (London: SCM Press, 1954), p. 79.

These comments suggest what might be a reasonable and constructive way forward for churches that seek to follow in the path opened up by Calvin. Since the superstitions that Calvin abhorred are not a primary temptation of modern Western people, many Protestant churches are now realizing there is no reason why the church space cannot also be an aesthetic site – a poetic space. But its poetics, if it truly understands Calvin's reading of the biblical account, will be a poetics of creation. That is, the space of worship will seek to create not a heavenly intrusion into our mundane world, as Orthodox worship has proposed, but a vision of a renewed earth; the beauty reflected will be the visible new creation, not some distant heaven. This is the thrust of David O. Taylor's argument in *The Theater of God's Glory*. He finds Calvin's separation of public worship from material creation unpersuasive. And he proposes, following Calvin, that if creation embodies and celebrates the glory of God in all its splendor, there is no reason that this praise cannot be "work that creation continues to perform in the life of the Church," and indeed within its physical space.[23]

But there is one final way the impulse of iconoclasm may continue to play a mostly unnoticed but constructive role, both in the life of the Church and beyond. In characteristic ways, the impulse of iconoclasm represented by this tradition, Jérôme Cottin points out, resonates with the recovery in the last century of what he terms the semantics of iconoclasm, in all it multiple forms, in which a constructive role for iconoclasm has emerged. This was first represented ethically, in opposition to injustice and poverty, but it also has appeared in twentieth-century aesthetics, for example, in the work of Kandinsky and Mondrian. This new abstract painting, Cottin argues, "is not Christian painting. But its remains strongly marked by Christianity," especially that of Calvin.[24] Thus the iconoclastic heritage of this tradition, Cottin thinks, may offer a distinct hermeneutical advantage – the capacity to protest and to invent. That is, understood in the broad sense, the impulse to critically challenge received notions, whether religious or aesthetic, may

---

[23] *The Theater of God's Glory: Calvin, Creation and the Liturgical Arts* (Grand Rapids, MI: Eerdmans, 2011), pp. 84, 86. Quote at p. 86. Though Taylor does argue that in its worship the Church does anticipate the life of heaven, the New Testament does not see these as opposed realities. See also Dyrness, *Poetic Theology: God and the Poetics of Everyday Life* (Grand Rapids, MI: Eerdmans, 2011), chapter 8, "Aesthetics of Church," where the idea of church as a poetic space is developed.

[24] Jérôme Cottin, in "Iconoclasme: Du geste destructeur au geste créateur," *Foi et Vie: Revue de culture protestante*, 1 (March 2015): 6–19. Quote at p. 17. He acknowledges multiple sources for these developments. As to the hermeneutical advantage, he suggests, because there is no tradition of what an image ought to be, "therefore a total openness to the creativity and to the inventive approach to materials, forms and themes" (p. 3).

reflect a broader Judeo-Christian heritage that draws its inspiration from the
biblical prophets and from Jesus and Paul.[25] But this also resonates with
Calvin's idea that the dramatic stage includes the whole of life in God's
creation, in all of its glorious and disordered splendor. The impulse to
challenge the excesses of the medieval period, in Calvin's mind, surely
represented a further iteration of that biblical tradition, but it may also have
laid the groundwork for modern critical projects that seek to challenge
and deconstruct ideologies that disrupt natural and wholesome relations
among people and with the created order. Though the theological warrant
has frequently been lost, the impulse to challenge, deconstruct, oppose what
is seen as unjust and oppressive continues to flourish. The Reformed
tradition offers one important source for this angle of vision and its attendant
cultural projects.

The modern semantics of iconoclasm and the movement of art objects
away from imitation (*mimesis*) toward a non-figurative autonomy has also
called attention to the broader impact of aesthetic experience. Our affective
relationship with our environment can never be adequately captured by
literal description and photographic likeness. Strikingly, Paul Ricoeur has
claimed that non-figurative art can provide an "iconic augmentation," a
dynamic transgressive space.[26] Such possibilities follow from Calvin's special
call to "follow nature," not simply in prosaic description but in the expansive
celebration so characteristic of his praise of creation.

Such an aesthetic imagination might offer, then, not only a challenge to
despair but an antidote to this. Health activist Ophelia Dahl has famously
suggested that broad-based health challenges call not simply for intervention
and treatment, but for holistic projects that address larger systemic problems,
involving expanded attention to the broader natural (and cultural) context.
But this leads her to describe the seething splendor of the created context,
and its possibilities, not simply in utilitarian but also in aesthetic terms.
She proposes we think of such systems in poetic terms: "I loved thinking
about life cycles, or mosquitoes and how they're connected to these tropical
diseases and how a parasite goes through the liver of a sheep before its
recirculated. I mean, that stuff – that's literature. That's the poetry of systems."[27]

---

[25] The argument of Merold Westphal in *Suspicion and Faith: The Religious Uses of Modern Atheism*
(Grand Rapids, MI: Eerdmans, 1993) is that the critical theories of Marx, Nietzsche, and Freud
developing in the modern period have their origin and borrow their moral leverage from this
Judeo-Christian prophetic tradition.

[26] Cf. Cottin, "Iconoclasme," p. 15.

[27] Quoted in Ariel Levy, "The Poetry of Systems: Curbing Maternal Mortality in Sierra Leone,"
The New Yorker, December 18, 25, 2017, Vol. 93, no. 41, p. 64.

Disenchantment and the Secular Age

This last comment leads naturally to a final point that may be the most salient aspect of Calvin's heritage. Here we need to remember that Calvin made it possible, indeed he insisted, that we perceive the *theatrum mundi* in aesthetic terms. And recall that our argument was premised on a broadened under-standing of aesthetics that includes all those objects, practices, and experi-ences, employing various media, in which the affective and felt qualities, that is, the look and feel, become essential to what sparks our love.[28] This broader aesthetic conception implies that human health and wholeness, "right living," has to do, in part, with appropriate affective relationships among people, and even between people and objects in their physical environment – the moral and aesthetic are connected. This goes well beyond considering our relations with art objects, Stephen Pattison thinks, even if it feeds off those experiences; it also includes interactions with all the artifacts of our daily lives. Satisfying relations with these objects is critical, he argues, and has deep-seated aesthetic implications. Pattison writes: "It can be argued that in many ways our lives depend upon appropriate affective relationships with common, everyday visual artefacts."[29] This follows from the admonition to pay attention to the world in which we are placed – heeding its call to celebration. As Susan Stewart argues, there is a built-in invocatory drive in people arising out of sense experience that projects them into fields of significance (pp. ix, 63). She goes on – referencing Genesis I and John I – to describe the way making sense experience intelligible to others draws figures out of the darkness, making aesthetic forms essential to encounter between people (p. 3). The rhythm of the world, its sounds and colors, she thinks, are to be received in the "expectation of meaning" (p. 79). Her overriding thesis is a fitting summary of the thrust of my argument: the sensual forms that these impulses take – the pitches, patterns, and colors – are meant for both social and aesthetic ends. In discussing why we love the voices of our loved ones, Stewart claims that "sound is *formed* for pleasurable, beautiful and ultimately social ends" (p. 109, emphasis in original). This notion of aesthetics, though not developed by Calvin, was surely implicit in his insistence that creation, in part and the whole, displayed glory that reflected God. If this is so, it was intended in the first instance to *show* itself, not merely to contribute to some practical end, or to symbolize some higher

[28] Cf. Brown, *Religious Aesthetics*, p. 22.
[29] See here *Seeing Things: Deepening Relations with Visual Artifacts* (London: SCM Press, 2007), p. 145. And for what follows, see Susan Stewart, *Poetry and the Fate of the Senses* (Chicago: University of Chicago Press, 2002). Pages cited in the text are to this work.

and more "substantial" reality – as in Plato's forms.[30] We recall that Calvin gave to both creation and the public sphere enabled by this extended worldly drama a moral ontology that allowed it to present itself with fullness of meaning and beauty, apart from all use and exploitation. As Torrance-Kirby points out in his discussion of the developing public sphere, these reflections remind us that "modern secularity is at root a profoundly theological orientation, whether or not it knows itself to be so."[31] And this orientation also suggests that any move toward disenchantment – of peoples' cultures and their created locations – is bound ultimately to fail.

The expanded canvas that celebrates all creation and all people calls to mind the influence of Calvin on the American ecology movement and on nature writers. Though sadly Calvin's followers did not always follow up the implications of his theology of creation, the resources are there to connect the land with spirituality and not with commodity,[32] and to see the aesthetics of life as a summons to pleasurable and appropriate affective relations with God, one's neighbor, and the earth.

---

[30] I have been stimulated toward these reflections by Jeffrey Kosky's wonderful discussion of Walter de Maria's "Lightning Fields." See *Arts of Wonder: Enchanting Secularity* (Chicago: University of Chicago Press, 2013), p. 21. Going to witness the lightning fields, Kosky says, "is where one goes to see the world flash into light."

[31] W. J. Torrance-Kirby, *Persuasion and Conversion* (Boston: Brill, 2013), p. 41.

[32] This is one of the possibilities Walter Mignolo sees for overcoming the darker side of modernity: "decolonizing religion to liberate spirituality" in the contemporary period, even, we might add, for decolonizing the tradition that was founded by John Calvin. See *The Darker Side of Western Modernity*, p. 63.

BIBLIOGRAPHY

Primary Sources

Allan Kaprow, "The legacy of Jackson Pollock, in Jeff Kelley, ed., *Essays on the Blurring of Art and Life*, Berkeley: University of California Press, 1993.

Ames, William, *Conscience with Power and Cases*, London: W. Christiaens et al., 1639.

Anon., *Meditations on the Life of Christ: An Illustrated Manuscript of the Fourteenth Century*, trans. and eds. Isa Ragusa and Rosalie B. Green, Princeton, NJ: Princeton University Press, 1961.

Aquinas, Thomas, *Summa Theologiae*, vol. 2: *Existence and Nature of God* (Ia. 2–11), trans. Timothy McDermott, London: Blackfriars, 1964.

Aristotle, *Poetics*, trans. S. H. Butcher, Mineola, NY: Dover, 1997.

Augustine of Hippo, *On Christian Teaching (De Doctrina Christiana)*, trans. R. P. H. Green, New York: Oxford University Press, 1999.

Becon, Thomas, *The Worckes of Thomas Becon*, London: John Day, 1564.

Bèze, Theodore de, *A Tragedie of Abraham's Sacrifice*, English trans. Arthur Golding, 1575, ed. Malcolm Wallace, Toronto: University Library, 1906.

   Icones id ests varae Imagines Virorum Doctrina simul et pietate illustrium, Menston: Scolar Press, 1971 [1580].

Bilson, Thomas, *The True Difference betweene Christian Subiection and UnChristian Rebellion*, Oxford: Joseph Barnes, 1585.

Bonaventure, *Journey of the Soul to God, Itinerarium mentis in Deum*, http://faculty.uml.edu/rinnis/45.304%20God%20and%20Philosophy/ITINERARIUM.pdf.

   De Reductione Artium ad Theologiam, ed. and trans. Sister Emma Healy, St. Bonaventure, New York: St. Bonaventure College, 1939.

Calvin, John, *Inventory of Relics*, trans. H. Beveridge, Edinburgh: Calvin Translation Society, 1844.

   Commentaries on Timothy, Titus, Philemon, trans. John King (1844–1856), Eerdmans, 1948.

   Complete Old Testament Commentaries, trans. John King, James Anderson, C. W. Bingham, and William Pringle (1844–1856), Grand Rapids, MI: Eerdmans, 1948.

   Theological Treatises, ed. J. K. S. Reid, London: SCM Press, 1954.

   New Testament Commentaries, ed. D. W. Torrance and T. F. Torrance, trans. T. H. L. Parker, Ross MacKenzie, and A. W. Morrison, Grand Rapids, MI: Eerdmans, 1959–1972.

Institutes of the Christian Religion, ed. John T. McNeil, Philadelphia: Westminster Press, 1960.

Camden, William, *The Historie of the Most Renowned and Victorious Princesse Elizabeth, the Late Queen of England*, London: Thomas Harper for Benjamin Fisher, 1630.

Coleridge, Samuel Taylor, *The Collected Works of Samuel Taylor Coleridge; Lectures 1808–1819 on Literature*, ed. Kathleen Coburn, Princeton, NJ: Princeton University Press, 1987.

Dante Alighieri, *The Paradiso*, trans. John Ciardi, New York: Signet/New American Library, 1961.

Donne, John, *The Divine Poems*, ed. Helen Gardner, Oxford: Clarendon Press, 1978.

Gosson, Stephen, *The School of Abuse*, ed. Edward Arber, London: Alex Murray, 1869 [1579].

Gregory the Great, *Dialogues IV*, 60, trans. Odo John Zimmerman, New York: Fathers of the Church, 1959.

Greville, Fulke, "A Dedication to Sir Philip Sidney," in John Gouws, ed., *The Prose Works of Fulke Greville: Lord Brooke*, Oxford: Clarendon, 1986 [1552].

Guigo II, *The Ladder of Monks: A Letter on the Contemplative Life*, trans. Edmond Colledge and James Walsh, Kalamazoo, MI: Cistercian Publications, 1981.

Herbert, George, *The Works of George Herbert in Prose and Verse*, London: Frederick Warne, n.d.

Heywood, Thomas, *An Apology for Actors*, London: Nicholas Okes, 1612.

Homes, Nathanael, *Gospel Musick or the Singing of David's Psalms in the Publick Congregations or Private Families Asserted and Vindicated*, London: Henry Overton, 1644.

Jewell, John, Controversy with M. Harding "Of Adoration of Images," in *The Works of John Jewell*, ed. John Ayre, Cambridge: The Parker Society/Cambridge University Press, 1847 [1564].

John of Damascus, *On the Divine Images*, trans. David Anderson, New York: St. Vladimir's Press, 2002.

Lodge, Thomas, *A Reply to Stephen Gosson's "School of Abuse" in Defence of Poetry, Musick and Stage Plays*, in *The Complete Works of Thomas Lodge*, London: Hunterian Club, 1883.

Luther, Martin, *Lectures on Galatians*, in *Luther's Works*, ed. J. Pelikan, St. Louis, MO: Concordia, 1963 [1535], vol. 26.

Milton, John, *The Poetical Works of John Milton*, ed. H. C. Beeching, London: Henry Frowde, 1904.

Nowell, A., *Catechisme, or First Instruction and Learning of Christian Religion*, London: John Daye, 1571.

Palissy, Bernard, *Les Oeuvres de Maistre Bernard Palissy*, ed. P. Fillon, Niort: Clouzot Librairie, 1888, vol 1.

Perkins, William, *The Arte of Prophesying: The Works of that Famous and Worthy William Perkins*, London: John Legatt, 1631 [1592], vol. II.

Serenus of Marseilles, *Nicene and Post-Nicene Fathers*, series 2, New York: Scribners, 1900.

Sidney, Philip, *An Apologie for Poetrie*, ed. Evelyn S. Shuckburgh, Cambridge University Press, 1891 [1595].

Spenser, Edmund, *The Faerie Queene*, ed. Thomas P. Roche, Jr., New Haven, CT: Yale University Press, 1978.

Sternholde, Thomas, *The First Parte of the Psalms Collected into English Meter*, London: John Day, 1564.

Stubbes, Philip, *The Anatomie of Abuses*, ed. Margaret Jane Kidnie, Tempe: Arizona Center for Medieval and Renaissance Studies, 2002 [1583].

van Hoogstraten, Samuel, *Inleyding tot de Hooge Schoole der Schilderkonst: Anders de zichbaere Werelt verdeelt in regen Leerwinkels, uder bestiert eene der Zanggodinnen*, Rotterdam: Francois van Hoogstraeten, 1678.

Secondary Sources

Adams, Ann Jensen, "Competing Communities in the 'Great Bog of Europe': Identity and Seventeenth-Century Dutch Landscape Paintings," in W. J. T. Mitchell, ed., *Landscape and Power*, Chicago: University of Chicago Press, 1994.

Adams, Marilyn McCord, *Some Later Theories of the Eucharist: Thomas Aquinas, Giles of Rome, Duns Scotus and William of Occam*, New York: Oxford University Press, 2010.

Aers, David, "Reflections on the Current Histories of the Subject," *Literature and History*, Second Series, 2.2 (1991).

Alpers, Svetlana, *The Art of Describing: Dutch Art in the Seventeenth Century*, Chicago: University of Chicago Press, 1983.

Amico, Leonard M., *Bernard Palissy: In Search of Earthly Paradise*, Paris: Flammarion, 1996.

Anderson, Jonathan, and William Dyrness, *Modern Art and the Life of a Culture: The Religious Impulses of Modernism*, Downers Grove, IL: InterVarsity Press, 2017.

Asad, Talal, *Formations of the Secular*, Stanford, CA: Stanford University Press, 2003.

Aston, Margaret, *Faith and Fire: Popular and Unpopular Religion 1350–1600*, London: Hambledon Press, 1993.

Auerbach, Erich, *Mimesis: The Representation of Reality in Western Literature*, trans. W. R. Trask, Princeton, NJ: Princeton University Press, 1953.

Bakker, Boudewijn, *Landscape and Religion from Van Eyck to Rembrandt*, trans. Diane Webb, Burlington, VT: Ashgate, 2012.

Bätschmann, Oskar, and Pascal Griener, *Hans Holbein*, Princeton, NJ: Princeton University Press, 1997.

Baxandall, Michael, *Painting and Experience in Fifteenth-Century Italy*, 2nd edition, Oxford: Oxford University Press, 1988.

Bayer, Oswald, "Hermeneutical Theology," trans. Gwen Griffith-Dickson, *Scottish Journal of Theology*, 56/2 (2003).

Belting, Hans, *Likeness and Presence: A History of the Image before the Era of Art*, trans. Edmund Jephcott, Chicago: University of Chicago Press, 1994.

Benedict, Philip, *The Faith and Fortunes of France's Huguenots 1600–1685*, Aldershot: Ashgate, 2001.

   Christ's Churches Purely Reformed: A Social History of Calvinism, New Haven, CT: Yale University Press, 2002.

Benjamin, Walter, "The Work of Art in the Age of Its Technological Reproducibility" (1935), in Michael W. Jennings et al., eds., *The Work of Art in the Age of Its Technological Reproducibility and Other Writings on Media*, trans. Edmund Jephcott, Cambridge, MA: Harvard University Press/Belknap, 2008.

Besançon, Alain, *The Forbidden Image: An Intellectual History of Iconoclasm*, University of Chicago Press, 2000.

Besse, Jean-Marc, *Voir la terre: six essais sur le paysage et la geographie*, Bruxelles: Actes Sud, 2000.

Bevinton, David, *Medieval Drama*, Boston: Houghton-Mifflin, 1975.

"Literature and Theater," in David Loewenstein and Janel Mueller, eds., *The Cambridge History of Early Modern English Literature*, Cambridge University Press, 2002.

Blackburn, Ruth, *Biblical Drama under the Tudors*, The Hague: Mouton, 1971.

Bossy, John, *Christianity in the West 1400–1700*, Oxford: Oxford University Press, 1985.

Boulton, Wayne, "'Ever more deeply moved': Calvin on the Rhetorical, Formational Function of Scripture," in Karen Spierling, ed., *Calvin and the Book*, Gottingen: Vandenhoeck and Ruprecht, 2015.

Bouwsma, William, *John Calvin: A Sixteenth-Century Portrait*, New York: Oxford University Press, 1988.

Britton, Dennis, "Popular Worship and Visual Paradigms in 'Love's Labor Lost,'" in J. H Degenhardt and Elizabeth Williamson, eds., *Religion and Drama in Early Modern England*, Burlington, VT: Ashgate, 2011.

Brown, Christopher Boyd, *Singing the Gospel: Lutheran Hymns and the Success of the Reformation*, Cambridge, MA: Harvard University Press, 2005.

Brown, Frank Burch, *Religious Aesthetics: A Theological Study of Making and Meaning*, Princeton, NJ: Princeton University Press, 1989.

Brown, Susan Tara, *Singing and the Imagination of Devotion: Vocal Aesthetics in Early Protestant Culture*, Colorado Springs, CO: Paternoster Press, 2008.

Brotton, Jerry, *The Sultan and the Queen: The Untold Story of Elizabeth and Islam*, New York: Viking, 2016.

Bynum, Caroline, *Christian Materiality*, New York: Zone Books, 2011.

Candler, Peter M. Jr., *Theology, Rhetoric, Manduction, or Reading Scripture Together on the Path to God*, Grand Rapids, MI: Eerdmans, 2006.

Canlis, Julie, "Calvin, Osiander and Participation in God," *International Journal of Systematic Theology*, 6/2 (April 2004).

Calvin's Ladder: A Spiritual Theology of Ascent and Ascension, Grand Rapids, MI: Eerdmans, 2010.

Carpo, Mario, *Architecture in the Age of Printing: Orality, Writing, and Printed Images in the History of Architectural Theory*, trans. Sarah Benson, Cambridge, MA: MIT Press, 2001.

Carruthers, Mary, *The Craft of Thought 400–1200*, New York: Cambridge University Press, 1998.

Cartwright, Kent, *Theatre and Humanism: English Drama in the Sixteenth Century*, Cambridge: Cambridge University Press, 1999.

Christensen, Carl, *Art and the Reformation in Germany*, Athens: Ohio University Press, 1979.

Clark, Ira, *Christ Revealed: The History of the Neo-Typological Lyric in the English Renaissance*, Gainesville: University Presses of Florida, 1982.

Clark, Stuart, *Vanities of the Eye: Vision in Early Modern European Culture*, Oxford University Press, 2007.

Clifford, Thomas, *Bacon, Palissy and the Revival of Natural Science*, Oxford: Oxford University Press, 1914.

Coliva, Anna, and Bernard Aikema, eds., *Cranach: A Different Renaissance*, Rome: 24 ore Cultura, 2010.

Collins, Gregory, *The Glenstal Book of Icons*, New York: Liturgical Press, 2002.

Collinson, Patrick, *The Elizabethan Puritan Movement*, Berkeley: University of California Press, 1967.

The Birthpangs of Protestant England: Religious and Cultural Change in the Sixteenth Century, Basingstoke: Macmillan, 1988.

Elizabethans, New York: Hambledon and London, 2003.

Comensoli, Viviana, et al., "Subjectivity, Theory and Early Modern Drama," *Early Theatre*, 7/2 (2004).

Corey, Laura D., et al., *The Art of the Louvre's Tuileries Garden*, catalogue of exhibits at the High Museum of Atlanta and the Toledo Museum, New Haven, CT: Yale University Press, 2013.

Cottin, Jérôme, *Le regard et la Parole: une théologie protestante de l'image*, Geneva: Labor et Fides, 1994.

"Loi et Evangile chez Luther et Cranach," *Revue d'Histoire et de Philosophie Religieuses*, 76/3 (1996).

"Iconoclasme: du geste destructeur au geste créateur," *Foi et Vie: Revue de culture protestante*, 1 (March 2015).

Crandell, Gina, *Nature Pictorialized: "The View" in Landscape History*, Baltimore, MD: Johns Hopkins University Press, 1993.

Crouzet, Denis, *Jean Calvin: Vies Parallèls*, Paris: Foyard, 2000.

Cummings, Brian, *The Literary Culture of the Reformation: Grammar and Grace*, Oxford University Press, 2007.

Dawson, Anthony B., and Paul Yachnia, *The Culture of Playmaking in Shakespeare's England: A Collaborative Debate*, Cambridge: Cambridge University Press, 2001.

de Gruchy, John, *Christianity, Art and Transformation*, Cambridge: Cambridge University Press, 2001.

John Calvin: Christian Humanist and Evangelical Reformer, Eugene, OR: Cascade Books, 2013.

de Jongh, Eddy, "Realism and Seeming Realism," in Franits, ed., *Looking at Seventeenth-Century Dutch Art*.

Diehl, Huston, *Staging Reform, Reforming the Stage: Protestantism and Popular Theatre in Early Modern England*, Ithaca, NY: Cornell University Press, 1997.

Dimmick, Jeremy, et al., eds., *Images, Idolatry and Iconoclasm in Late Medieval England*, Oxford: Oxford University Press, 2002.

Doran, Susan, *Queen Elizabeth I*, New York: New York University Press, 2003.

Duffy, Eamon, *Stripping of the Altars: Traditional Religion in England, c. 1400–1580*, New Haven, CT: Yale University Press, 1992.

Saints, Sacrilege and Sedition: Religion and Conflict in the Tudor Reformations, London: Bloomsbury, 2012.

Dyrness, William, *Reformed Theology and Visual Culture: The Protestant Imagination from Calvin to Edwards*, Cambridge: Cambridge University Press, 2004.

Poetic Theology: God and the Poetics of Everyday Life, Grand Rapids, MI: Eerdmans, 2011.

Senses of Devotion: Interfaith Aesthetics in Buddhist and Muslim Communities, Eugene, OR: Cascade Books, 2013.

Eco, Umberto, *Art and Beauty in the Middle Ages*, trans. Hugh Bredin, New Haven, CT: Yale University Press, 1986.

Eire, Carlos, *War against Idols: The Reformation Worship from Erasmus to Calvin*, Cambridge: Cambridge University Press, 1986.

Elliot, John, *History in the Making*, New Haven, CT: Yale University Press, 2012.

Erdozain, Dominic, *The Soul of Doubt: The Religious Roots of Unbelief from Luther to Marx*, Oxford University Press, 2016.

Evdokimov, Paul, *The Art of the Icon: A Theology of Beauty*, trans. Steven Bigham, Redondo Beach, CA: Oakwood Publications, 1990.

Falco, Raphael, "Medieval and Reformation Roots," in Arthur Kinney, ed., *A Companion to Renaissance Drama*, Oxford: Blackwell, 2002.

Fairfield, Leslie P., *John Bale: Mythmaker of the English Reformation*, West Lafayette, IN: Purdue University Press, 1976.

Falkenberg, Reindert L., "Calvinism and the Emergence of Dutch Seventeenth-Century Landscape Art – A Critical Evaluation," in Paul Corby Finney, ed., *Seeing beyond the Word: Visual Arts and the Calvinist Tradition*, Grand Rapids, MI: Eerdmans, 1999.

Febvre, Lucien, and Henri-Jean Martin, *The Coming of the Book: The Impact of Printing 1450–1800*, trans. David Gerard, London: NLB, 1976.

Fessenden, Tracy, *Culture and Redemption: Religion and the Secular in American Literature*, Princeton, NJ: Princeton University Press, 2007.

Finney, Paul Corby, ed., *Seeing beyond the Word: Visual Arts and the Calvinist Tradition*, Grand Rapids, MI: Eerdmans, 1999.

Foister, Susan, Ashok Roy, and Martin Wyld, *Making and Meaning: Holbein's Ambassadors*, Washington, DC, and New Haven, CT: National Gallery and Yale University Press, 1997.

Fonkenell, Guillaume, *Le Palais des Tuileries*, Paris: Honore Clair, 2010.

Forse, James H., "Religious Drama and Ecclesiastical Reform in the Tenth Century," *Early Theatre*, 5/2 (2002).

Fowler, Caroline D., "Presence in Seventeenth-Century Practice and Theory," *Word and Image: A Journal of Verbal/Visual Enquiry*, 30/2 (2014).

Franits, Wayne, ed., *Looking at Seventeenth-Century Dutch Art: Realism Reconsidered*, Cambridge: Cambridge University Press, 1997.

Freedberg, David, *The Power of Images: Studies in the History and Theory of Response*, Chicago: University of Chicago Press, 1989.

Friedlander, Max, and Jakob Rosenberg, *The Paintings of Lucas Cranach*, rev. ed., Ithaca, NY: Cornell University Press, 1978.

Gant, Andrew, *O Sing unto the Lord: A History of English Church Music*, Chicago: University of Chicago Press, 2017.

Garside, Charles, *Zwingli and the Arts*, New Haven, CT: Yale University Press, 1966.

George, Charles H., *The Protestant Mind of the English Reformation: 1570–1640*, Princeton, NJ: Princeton University Press, 1961.

Gilman, Ernest B., *Iconoclasm and Poetry in the English Reformation*, Chicago: University of Chicago Press, 1986.

Gilmont, Jean-François, "Protestant Reformations and Reading," in Guglielmo Cavallo and Roger Chartier, eds., *A History of Reading in the West*, Amherst: University of Massachusetts Press, 1995.

Gitelman, Lisa, *Always Already New: Media, History and the Data of Culture*, Cambridge, MA: MIT Press, 2008.

Gordon, Bruce, *John Calvin's "Institutes of the Christian Religion": A Biography*, Princeton, NJ: Princeton University Press, 2016.

Grafton, Anthony, "The Humanist as Reader," in Guglielmo Cavallo and Roger Chartier, eds., *A History of Reading in the West*, Amherst: University of Massachusetts Press, 1995.

Graham, W. Fred, *The Constructive Revolutionary: John Calvin and His Socio-Economic Impact*, Atlanta, GA: John Knox Press, 1978.

Green, Jonathan, *Printing and Prophecy: Prognostication and Media Change 1450–1550*, Ann Arbor: University of Michigan Press, 2012.

Greenblatt, Stephen, *Will in the World: How Shakespeare Became Shakespeare*, New York: Norton, 2004.

Gregory, Brad, *The Unintended Reformation: How a Religious Revolution Secularized Society*, Cambridge, MA: Belknap/Harvard University Press, 2012.

Groves, Beatrice, *Texts and Traditions: Religion in Shakespeare 1592–1604*, Oxford: Clarendon Press, 2007.

Guite, Malcolm, *Mariner: A Theological Voyage with Samuel Taylor Coleridge*, Downers Grove, IL: InterVarsity Press, 2018.

Hackett, Helen, *Virgin Mother, Maiden Queen: Elizabeth I and the Cult of the Virgin Mary*, New York: St. Martins, 1995.

Haight, Roger, *Christian Communities in History: Comparative Ecclesiologies*, New York: Continuum, 2005.

Hamburger, Jeffrey, "The Place of Theology in Medieval Art History," in Hamburger and Bouché, eds., *The Mind's Eye: Art as Theological Argument in the Middle Ages*.

Hamburger, J., and Anne Marie Bouché, eds., *The Mind's Eye: Art as Theological Argument in the Middle Ages*, Princeton, NJ: Princeton University Press, 2006.

Hamilton, Donna, and Richard Strier, eds., *Religion and Politics in Post-Reformation England: 1540–1688*, New York: Cambridge University Press, 1996.

Happé, Peter, *John Bale*, London: Prentice Hall, 1996.

Hardison, O. B., *Christian Rite and Christian Drama: Essays in the Origin and Early History of Modern Drama*, Baltimore, MD: Johns Hopkins University Press, 1965.

Harris, Jesse W., *John Bale: A Study of the Minor Literature of the Reformation*, Urbana: University of Illinois Press, 1940.

Harrison, Peter, *The Bible, Protestantism and the Rise of Natural Science*, Cambridge: Cambridge University Press, 1998.

Harrison, Robert Pogue, "The Book from Which Our Literature Springs," *New York Review of Books*, February 9, 2012, pp. 40–45.

Hart, Vaughan, with Peter Hicks, ed., *Paper Palaces: The Rise of the Renaissance Architectural Treatises*, New Haven, CT: Yale University Press, 1998.

Hawkins, Peter, *Dante's Testaments: Essays in Scriptural Imagination*, Stanford, CA: Stanford University Press, 1999.

Hervey, Mary F. S.. *Holbein's "Ambassadors": The Picture and the Men*, London: George Bell and Sons, 1900.

Hill, Basil, "Calvin against the Calvinists," in G. E. Duffield, ed., *John Calvin*, Appleford: Sutton Courtenay Press, 1966.

Hill, Christopher, *Society and Puritanism in Pre-Revolutionary England*, London: Secker and Warburg, 1964.

Höpfl, Harro, *The Christian Polity of John Calvin*, Cambridge: Cambridge University Press, 1982.

Horton, Michael, *Covenant and Eschatology: The Divine Drama*, Louisville, KY: Westminster John Knox Press, 2002.

Huizinga, Johann, *The Waning of the Middle Ages: A Study of the Forms of Life, Thought and Art in France and the Netherlands in the Fourteenth and Fifteenth Centuries*, London: Edward Arnold, 1927.

Hulse, Clark, "Tudor Aesthetics," in *Cambridge Companion to English Literature: 1500–1600*, Cambridge University Press, 2000.

Hunter, G. K., "Shakespeare and the Church," in John. M. Mucciolo, ed., *Shakespeare's Universe: Renaissance Ideas and Conventions: Essays in Honor of W. R. Elton*, Aldershot: Scolar Press, 1996.

Jeffrey, David, "English Saints Plays," in Neville Denny, ed., *Medieval Drama*, London: Edward Arnold, 1973.

Johnston, Alexandra, "Tudor Drama, Theatre and Society," in Robert Tittler and Norman Jones, eds., *A Companion to Tudor Britain*, Oxford: Blackwell, 2004.

Kaufmann, Thomas De Costa, *The Mastery of Nature: Aspects of Art, Science and Humanism in the Renaissance*, Princeton, NJ: Princeton University Press, 1993.

Kessler, Herbert, "Turning a Blind Eye," in Hamburger and Bouché, eds., The Mind's Eye.

King, John N., *English Reformation Literature: The Tudor Origin of the Protestant Tradition*, Princeton, NJ: Princeton University Press, 1982.

   Tudor Royal Iconography: Literature and Art in an Age of Religious Crisis, Princeton, NJ: Princeton University Press, 1989.

Kleinig, John, "*Oratio, Meditatio, Tentatio*: What Makes a Theologian?," *Concordia Theological Quarterly*, 66 (2002).

Klemm, Friedrich, *A History of Western Technology*, trans. Dorthea W. Singer, London: Allen and Unwin, 1959.

Koepplin, Dieter, "Cranach's Paintings of Charity in the Theological and Humanist Spirit of Luther and Melanchthon," in Bodo Brinkmann, ed., *Cranach*, London: Royal Academy of Arts, 2008.

Koerner, Joseph Leo, *The Moment of Self-Portraiture in German Renaissance Art*, Chicago: University of Chicago Press, 1993.

   "Confessional Portraits," in Mark Roskill and John Oliver Hand, eds., *Hans Holbein: Paintings, Prints and Reception*, London and New Haven, CT: National Gallery and Yale University Press, 2001.

   The Reformation of the Image, Chicago: University of Chicago Press, 2004.

Kosky, Jeffrey, *Arts of Wonder: Enchanting Secularity*, Chicago: University of Chicago Press, 2013.

Kristeva, Julia, "From Symbol to Sign," in Toril Moi, ed., *The Kristeva Reader*, Oxford University Press, 1986.

Kuyper, Abraham, *Lectures on Calvinism*, Grand Rapids, MI: Eerdmans, 1931.

Lane, Belden, *Ravished by Beauty: The Surprising Legacy of Reformed Spirituality*, New York: Oxford University Press, 2011.

Lazareff, Victor, "Studies in the Iconography of the Virgin," *Art Bulletin*, 20 (1938).

Levy, Ariel, "The Poetry of Systems: Curbing Maternal Mortality in Sierra Leone," *The New Yorker*, December 18 and 25, 2017.

Lewalski, Barbara K., *Protestant Poetics and the Seventeenth-Century Lyric*, Princeton, NJ: Princeton University Press, 1979.

Liedtke, Walter, "Style in Dutch Art," in Franits, ed. *Looking at Seventeenth-Century Dutch Art*.

Lin, Erika T., "'It is requir'd you do awake your faith': belief in Shakespeare's theater." in J. H. Degenhardt and Elizabeth Williamson, eds., *Religion and Drama in Early Modern England*, Burlington, VT: Ashgate, 2011.

MacCulloch, Diarmaid, *Thomas Cranmer: A Life*, New Haven, CT: Yale University Press, 1997.

MacGregor, Neil, with Erika Langmuir, *Seeing Salvation: Images of Christ in Art*, London: National Gallery, 2000.

MacIntyre, Alistair, *After Virtue: A Study in Moral Theory*, Notre Dame, IN: Notre Dame University Press, 1981.

Marsden, Peter V., "Religious Americans and the Arts in the 1990s," in Alberta Arthurs and Clenn Wallach, eds., *Crossroads: Art and Religion in American Life*, New York: New Press, 2001.

Marshall, Peter, *Heretics and Believers: A History of the English Reformation*, New Haven, CT: Yale University Press, 2017.

Matheson, Peter, *The Imaginative World of the Reformation*, Minneapolis, MN: Fortress Press, 2001.

Mattes, Mark C., *Martin Luther's Theology of Beauty: A Reappraisal*, Grand Rapids, MI: Baker Academic, 2017.

McKee, Elsie, ed., *John Calvin: Writings on Pastoral Piety*, Mahway, NJ: Paulist Press, 2001.
"Spirituality," in Selderhuis, ed., The Calvin Handbook.

Michalski, Sergiusz, *The Reformation and the Visual Arts: The Protestant Image Question in Western and Eastern Europe*, New York: Routledge, 1993.

Mignolo, Walter D., *The Darker Side of Western Modernity: Global Futures, Decolonial Options*, Durham, NC: Duke University Press, 2011.

Millet, Olivier, *Calvin et la dynamique de la Parole: Étude de rhétorque Réformé*, Geneva: Editions Slatkine, 1992.
"Art and Literature," in Selderhuis, ed., The Calvin Handbook.

Mitchell, W. J. T., *What Do Pictures Want? The Lives and Loves of Images*, Chicago: University of Chicago Press, 2005.

Mochizuki, Mia M., *The Netherlandish Image after Iconoclasm: 1566–1672: Material Religion in the Dutch Golden Age*. Aldershot: Ashgate, 2008.

Monta, Susannah Brietz, "'It is requir'd you do awkae your faith': Belief in Shakespeare's Theater," in J. H. Degenhardt and Elizabeth Williamson, eds., *Religion and Drama in Early Modern England*, Burlington, VT: Ashgate, 2011.

Morgan, David, "Protestant Visual Piety and the Aesthetics of American Mass Culture," in Jolyon Mitchell and Sophia Marriage, eds., *Mediating Religion: Conversations in Media, Religion and Culture*, London: T&T Clark, 2003.

Moxey, Keith, "Mimesis and Iconoclasm," *Art History*, 32/1 (2009).

Muir, Edward, *Ritual in Early Modern England*, Cambridge: Cambridge University Press, 1997.

Muller, Richard, *The Unaccommodated Calvin*, New York: Oxford University Press, 2000.

Naef, Henri, *Les Origines de la Réforme à Genève*, Genève: Librairie Droz, 1968, vol. I.

Noble, Bonnie, *Lucas Cranach the Elder: Art and Devotion of the German Reformation*, Lanham, MD: University Press of America, 2009.

"'Wittenberg Altarpiece' an Image of Identity," *Reformation*, 11 (2006).

Norland, Howard B., *Drama in Early Tudor Britain: 1485–1558*, Lincoln: University of Nebraska Press, 1995.

Ong, Walter, *The Presence of the Word: Some Prolegomena for Cultural and Religious History*, New Haven, CT: Yale University Press, 1967.

Ong, Walter, and Peter Ramus, *Method and the Decay of Dialogue: From the Art of Discourse to the Art of Reason*, Cambridge, MA: Harvard University Press, 1958.

Ouspensky, Leonid, and Vladimir Lossky. *The Meaning of Icons*, ed. Urs Graf-Verlag, trans. G. E. H. Palmer and E. Kabloubovsky, Crestwood, NY: St. Vladimir's Press, 1982.

Ozment, Stephen, *The Serpent and the Lamb: Cranach, Luther, and the Making of the Reformation*, New Haven, CT: Yale University Press, 2011.

Panofsky, Erwin, "Comments on Art and Reformation," in *Symbols in Transformation: Iconographic Themes at the Time of the Reformation. An Exhibition in Memory of Erwin Panofsky*, The Art Museum, Princeton University, March 15–April 13, 1969.

Parry, Graham, *The Arts of the Anglican Counter-Reformation: Glory, Laud and Honour*, Woodridge: Boydell Press, 2006.

Pettegree, Andrew, *Reformation and the Culture of Persuasion*, New York: Cambridge University Press, 2005.

"Calvin and Luther as Men of the Book," in K. Spierling, ed., *Calvin and the Book*, Gottingen: Vandenhoeck and Ruprecht, 2015.

Piper, John, David Mathis, and Julius Kim, eds., *With Calvin in the Theatre of God: The Glory of Christ and Everyday Life*, Wheaton: Crossways, 2010.

Promey, Sally M., and Shira Brisman, "Sensory Cultures: Material and Visual Religion," in Philip Goff, ed., *The Blackwell Companion to Religion in America*, Malden, MA: Wiley-Blackwell, 2010.

Randall, Catherine, *Building Codes: The Aesthetics of Calvinism in Early Modern Europe*, Philadelphia: University of Pennsylvania Press, 1999.

"Structuring Protestant Scriptural Space in Sixteenth-Century Catholic France," *Sixteenth Century Journal*, 25/2 (1994).

Reid, W. Stanford, "The Battle Hymn of the Lord," in *Sixteenth-Century Essays and Studies*, St. Louis, MO: Foundation for Reformation Research, 1971, vol. II, pp. 36–54.

Ringbom, Sixten, *Icon to Narrative: The Rise of the Dramatic Close-Up in Fifteenth-Century Devotional Painting*, Åbo: Akademi ABO, 1965.

Rosebrock, Matthew, "The Highest Art: Martin Luther's Visual Theology in Oratio, Meditatio, and Tentatio," PhD dissertation, Fuller Theological Seminary, 2017.

Rosenberg, Harold, *The Anxious Object: Art Today and Its Audience*, New York: Horizon Press, 1964.

Rosenblum, Robert, *Modern Painting and the Northern Romantic Tradition: Friedrich to Rothko*, London: Thames and Hudson, 1975.

Roskill, Mark, and John Oliver Hand, *Hans Holbein: Painting, Prints and Reception*, Washington, DC/New Haven, CT: National Gallery and Yale University Press, 2001.

Sanchez, Michelle C., "Ritualized Doctrine? Rethinking Protestant Bodily Practice through Attention to Genre in Calvin's Institutio," *Journal of the American Academy of Religion*, 85 (2017).

Schama, Simon, *Rembrandt's Eyes*, New York: Knopf, 1999.

Schottenloher, Karl, *Books and the Western World: A Cultural History*, trans. W. D. Boyd and I. H. Wolfe, London: McFarland, 1968.

Schreiner, Susan, *Theater of His Glory: Nature and the Natural Order in the Thought of John Calvin*, Grand Rapids, MI: Baker, 1995.

Schwartz, Gary, *Rembrandt: His Life, His Painting*, New York: Viking, 1985.

Schwartz, Regina, *Sacramental Poetics at the Dawn of Secularism: When God Left the World*, Stanford, CA: Stanford University Press, 2008.

Scribner, Robert, *For the Sake of the Simple Folk*, Cambridge: Cambridge University Press, 1981.
   "Popular Piety and Modes of Visual Perception," in *Religion and Culture in Germany 1400–1800*, Leiden: Brill, 2001.

Scully, Vincent, *The Natural and the Manmade*, New York: St. Martins, 1991.

Selderhuis, H. J., ed., *The Calvin Handbook*, Grand Rapids, MI: Eerdmans, 2009.

Shuger, Deborah, *Habits of Thought in the English Renaissance: Religion, Politics and the Dominant Culture*, Berkeley: University of California Press, 1990.
   "Subversive Fathers and Suffering Subjects," in Donna Hamilton and Richard Strier, eds., *Religion and Politics in Post-Reformation England: 1540–1688*, Cambridge University Press, 1996.
   "Literature and the Church," in David Loewenstein and Janel Mueller, eds., *Cambridge History of Early Modern English Literature*, Cambridge University Press, 2002.

Spicer, Andrew, "'Qui est de Dieu oit la Parole de Dieu': The Huguenots and Their Temples," in Raymond Mentzer and Andrew Spicer, eds., *Society and Culture in the Huguenot World*, Cambridge: Cambridge University Press, 2002.

Steinberg, Justin, *Dante and the Limits of the Law*, Chicago: University of Chicago Press, 2013.

Steiner, George, *Real Presences*, Chicago: University of Chicago Press, 1989.

Stewart, Susan, *Poetry and the Fate of the Senses*, Chicago: University of Chicago Press, 200

Streete, Adrian, *Protestantism and Drama in Early Modern England*, Cambridge: Cambridge University Press, 2009.

Strong, Roy, *The Portraits of Queen Elizabeth*, Oxford: Clarendon Press, 1963.
   The English Icon: Elizabethan and Jacobean Portraiture, New York: Pantheon, 1969.
   The Cult of Elizabeth: Elizabethan Portraits and Pageantry, Berkeley: University of California Press, 1977.
   The English Renaissance Miniature, New York; Thames and Hudson, 1983.
   Gloriana: The Portraits of Queen Elizabeth, New York: Thames and Hudson, 1987.

Tachau, Katherine H., "Seeing as Action and Passion in the Thirteenth and Fourteenth Centuries," in Hamburger and Bouche, eds., The Mind's Eye.

Tadgell, Christopher, *Reformations: From High Renaissance to Mannerism in the New West of Religious Contention and Colonial Expansion*, New York: Routledge, 2012.

Taylor, Charles, *Sources of the Self: The Making of the Modern Identity*, Cambridge, MA: Harvard University Press, 1989.
   A Secular Age, Cambridge, MA: Harvard University Press, 2007.
   "Afterward," in Michael Warner et al., eds., *Varieties of Secularism in a Secular Age*, Cambridge, MA: Harvard University Press, 2010.

The Language Animal: The Full Shape of Human Linguistic Capacity, Cambridge, MA: Harvard University Press, 2016.

Taylor, David O., *The Theater of God's Glory: Calvin, Creation and the Liturgical Arts*, Grand Rapids, MI: Eerdmans, 2017.

Taylor, Michael, *Rembrandt's Nose*, New York: Art Publishers, 2007.

Thiessen, Gesa Elsbeth, ed., *Theological Aesthetics: A Reader*, Grand Rapids, MI: Eerdmans, 2004.

Torrance-Kirby, W. J., *Persuasion and Conversion: Essays on Religion, Politics and the Public Sphere in Early Modern England*, Boston: Brill, 2013.

Trigg, Stephanie, "Medievalism and Theories of Temporality," in Louise D'Arcens, ed., *Cambridge Companion to Medievalism*, Cambridge: Cambridge University Press, 2016.

Trueman, Carl, "Calvin and Calvinism," in Donald McKim, ed., *The Cambridge Companion to John Calvin*, Cambridge: Cambridge University Press, 2004.

Tümpel, Christian, "Religious History Painting," in Albert Blankert et al., eds., *God's Saints and Heroes: Dutch Painting in the Age of Rembrandt*, Washington, DC: National Gallery of Art, 1980.

Tümpel, Christian, and Astrid Tümpel, *Rembrandt: Images and Metaphors*, London: Haus Publishing, 2006.

Turner, Victor, *Dramas, Fields, and Metaphors: Symbolic Action in Human Society*, Ithaca, NY: Cornell University Press, 1974.

"Are There Universals of Performance in Myth, Ritual and Drama?," in Richard Schechner and Willa Apel, eds., *By Means of Performance: Intercultural Studies of Theatre and Ritual*, New York: Cambridge University Press, 1990.

Tyacke, Nicholas, *Anti-Calvinists: The Rise of English Arminianism c. 1590–1640*, Oxford: Oxford University Press, 1990.

ed., *England's Long Reformation: 1500–1800*, New York: Routledge, 1998.

Van der Kooi, Cornelius, *As in a Mirror: John Calvin and Karl Barth on Knowing God*, trans. Donald Mader, Leiden: Brill, 2005.

Vanhoozer, Kevin, *The Drama of Doctrine: A Canonical-Linquistic Approach to Christian Theology*, Louisville, KY: Westminster John Knox Press, 2005.

Veith, Gene Edward Jr., *Reformation Spirituality: The Religion of George Herbert*, Lewisburg, PA: Bucknell University Press, 1985.

Painters of Faith: The Spiritual Landscape in Nineteenth-Century America, Washington, DC: Regnery, 2001.

Von Balthasar, Hans Urs, *The Glory of the Lord: A Theological Aesthetics*, trans. Erasmo Leiva Merikakis, San Francisco, CA: Ignatius Press, 1982.

Walford, E. John, *Jacob van Ruisdael and the Perception of Landscape*, New Haven, CT: Yale University Press, 1991.

Wamberg, Jacob, *Landscape as World Picture: Tracing Cultural Evolution in Images*, trans. Gaye Kynoch, Aarhus: Aarhus University Press, 2009, vol. II.

Wandel, Lee Palmer, *The Reformation: Towards a New History*, Cambridge: Cambridge University Press, 2012.

Warner, Malcomb, "Anglophilia into Art," in M. Warner and Robyn Aselson, eds., *Great British Paintings from American Collections: Holbein to Hockney*, New Haven, CT: Yale University Press, 2001.

Watt, Tessa, *Cheap Prints and Popular Piety: 1550–1640*, Cambridge: Cambridge University Press, 1991.

Weber, Max, *The Protestant Ethic and the Spirit of Capitalism*, New York: Scribner, 1930.

Webster, Charles, *The Great Instauration: Science, Medicine and Reform: 1626–1660*, New York: Holmes and Meier, 1975.

Wencelius, Léon, *L'Esthétique de Calvin*, Paris: Société d'Edition "Les Belles Lettres," n.d. [1937].

Wendel, François, *Calvin: The Origins and Development of His Religious Thought*, London: Collins, 1965.

Westphal, Merold, *Suspicion and Faith: The Religious Uses of Modern Atheism*, Grand Rapids, MI: Eerdmans, 1993.

White, Christopher, and Quentin Buvelot, eds., *Rembrandt by Himself*, London and New Haven, CT: National Gallery and Yale University Press, 1999.

White, James F., *The Sacrament in Protestant Practice and Faith*, Nashville, TN: Abingdon, 1999.

White, Paul W.. *Theatre and Reformation: Protestantism, Patronage and Playing in Tudor England*, Cambridge: Cambridge University Press, 1993.

Williams, Rowan, *The Edge of Words: God and the Habits of Language*, London: Bloomsbury, 2013.

Willis, Jonathan P., *Church Music and Protestantism in Early Modern England*, London: Routledge, 2010.

Wilson, Derek, *Hans Holbein: Portrait of an Unknown Man*, London: Weidenfeld and Nicolson, 1996.

Wilson, Peter H., *The Heart of Europe: A History of the Holy Roman Empire*, Cambridge, MA: Belknap/Harvard University Press, 2016.

Witvliet, John, and Nathan Bierma, "Liturgy," in Selderhuis, ed., The Calvin Handbook.

Wolterstorff, Nicholas, *Art in Action: Toward a Christian Aesthetic*, Grand Rapids, MI: Eerdmans, 1980.

   Works and Worlds of Art, New York: Oxford University Press, 1980.

   "Beyond Beauty and the Aesthetic in the Engagement of Religion and Art," in Oleg V. Bychkov and James Fodor, eds., *Theological Aesthetics after von Balthasar*, Aldershot: Ashgate, 2008.

   Art Rethought, New York: Oxford University Press, 2016.

Working, Randal Carter, *Visual Theology: Towards an Architectural Iconology of Early Modern French Protestantism 1535–1623*, Eugene, OR: Pickwick Publications, 2016.

Wuthnow, Robert, *Communities of Discourse: Ideology and Social Structure in the Reformation: The Enlightenment and European Socialism*, Cambridge, MA: Harvard University Press, 1989.

   All N' Sync: How Music and Art Are Revitalizing American Religion, Berkeley: University of California Press, 2003.

Yang, Edward, "Sanctifying Space: A Reformed Theology of Places for Corporate Worship," PhD dissertation, Fuller Theological Seminary, 2016.

Yates, Frances, *Astraea: The Imperial Theme in the Sixteenth Century*, London: Routledge, Kegan and Paul, 1975.

Zachman, Randall, *Image and Word in the Theology of John Calvin*, Notre Dame, IN: Notre Dame University Press, 2007.

Zorach, Rebecca, "Meditation, Idolatry, and Mathematics: The Printed Image in Europe around 1500," in Michael W. Cole and Rebecca Zorach, eds., *The Idol in the Age of Art: Objects, Devotions and the Early Modern World*, Farnham: Ashgate, 2009.

INDEX

Abraham's Sacrifice (Theodore Beza, 1550), 146
Accommodation in Calvin, 102
Acts and Monuments (John Foxe), 116, 120
Adams, Ann Jensen, 183
Adams, Marilyn McCord, 55–57
Aesthetic judgment, 111
Aesthetics
  definition of, 3
  emerging in the Reformation, 54
  Medieval, 12–13
  modern, 54
Anatomie of Abuses (Philip Stubbes, 1583), 143
Anechoic chamber, 203
Aniconic religion, 134
Apology for Actors (Thomas Heywood, 1612), 152
Aquinas, Thomas, 55–56
Aristotle
  and drama, 74
  Poetics, 60
Art
  aura of, 52, 206
  history of, traditional, 4
  modern, grand narrative of, 205
  objects, in modern period, 54
Arte of Prophesying, The (William Perkins, 1592), 158
Aston, Margaret, 16
Auerbach, Erich, 60
Augustine, 73
Augustine of Hippo, 169

Bacon, Sir Francis, 192
Baillods, Jules, 29
Bakker, Boudewijn, 181
Bale, John, 113, 117, 129, 139

Basel, 20, 22
Batschmann, Oscar, 27
Beauty, classical ideas, 55
Becon, Thomas, 130
Belgic Confession, 182
Belting, Hans, 2, 3
Benedict, Philip, 168, 192
Benjamin, Walter, 52, 206
Besse, Jean-Marc, 182
Beza, Theodore, 136, 146
Bible
  Calvin's horizontal reading of, 96
  King James Version (1611), 86
  in the Reformation, 85
  rhetoric of, 95
  in the vernacular, 89
Biblical drama, 159
Biblical typology, 160–161
Boleyn, Anne, 24
Bonaventure, 13
  The Mind's Journey to God (1259), 11
  Retracing the Arts to Theology (De Reductione Artium ad Theologiam), 11
Book(s), in the sixteenth century, 84; *see also* Printing and literacy; Prints
Bossy, John, 88
Boulton, Wayne, 102
Bouwsma, William, 59
Brethren of the Common Life., 17
Brian Cummings, 88
Brisma, Shira, 110
Brown, Christopher Boyd, 48
Brown, Frank Burch, 3
Brown, Susan Tara, 164
Bruegel, Pieter, 181

Cage, John, 202
   "4'33''" (1952), 203
   influence of "Sermon on the Mount," 203
Calvin, John, 6, 19, 52, 183, 205, 208; *see also*
   names of specific works
   as an actor in God's drama, 85
   arrival in Geneva, 53
   on Christian life, 74
   on congregational singing, 105
   on conscience, 171
   on creation, 72
   on Cross of Christ, 73–74
   on drama, 150
   on drama of creation, 143
   on drama and time, 80–81
   dramatic movement in, 109
   on everyday life, 85
   on God and beauty of creation, 66
   on godliness (pietas), 171
   on grace, double (duplex gratia), 171
   humanism of, 93
   and images, 78
   influence in England, 118
   Inventory of Relics, 69
   and language, 85
   on language and images, 104
   on liturgy and sacraments, 77
   on living images, 58, 135
   on the limitation of language, 96
   on locked church, 208
   and music, 107
   on painting and sculpture, 70
   on Psalms, 106
   on the real presence of Christ, 59
   on rhetoric, 94–95
   on seeing and hearing, 69
   on the space of the church, 58
   on Spirit, 94, 97, 174, 206
   on the use of theater, 59
   on visual beauty, 71
Calvinism, 77
   in England, 114
   influence on English poetry, 154
Calvinist imaginary, 185
   in Holland, 185
Calvinist imagination, 198
Candler, Peter, 100
Canlis, Julie, 67
Carruthers, Mary, 28
Cartwright, Kent, 63
Case, J., 123

Castellio, Sebastian, 178
Catechisme (Alexander Nowell, 1571), 130
Catholic Church in France, 192
Charles V, Emperor in Germany, 119
Churchyard, Thomas, 123
Cicero, Marcus Tullius, 94
City of God, The (Augustine), 169
Clark, Ira, 160
Clark, Stuart, 54
Classical architecture, French, 195
Classical orders, 194
Coleridge, Samuel, 153
Collinson, Patrick, 118, 128, 133
Commedia Divina (Dante), 168
Communalism, weakness of Calvin's, 178
Congregation, 89
Conscience, Calvin on, 171
Corpus Christi play, 118
Cottin, Jérôme, 42, 44, 49, 103, 209
Counter-reformation in England, 199
Cranach, Lucas the Elder
   Adam and Eve (painting) (1530), 35
   development of his work, 40–41
   Law and Gospel (painting), Prague type (1529),
      43
   relation with Luther, 38
   Wittenberg Altarpiece (painting), 45–47
Cranmer, Thomas, 133
Creation
   Calvin on, 72
   drama of, 109
Cromwell, Thomas, 140
Cross of Christ
   Calvin on, 73–74
Crouzet, Denis, 85
Cummings, Brian, 89, 101, 145, 157–158

da Carcano, Fra Michele, 27
Dahl, Ophelia, 210
Dante Alighieri, 56; *see also names of specific works*
   and the limitation of language, 95
Davies, Sir John, 123
De Doctrina Christiana (Augustine), 73
de Gruchy, John, 208
de L'Orme, Philibert, 194
de Selve, George, Bishop, 24
Diehl, Huston, 50, 148–150
Dinterville, Jean of, 22
Disenchantment, modern, 212
Donne, John, 156, 159
Dostoyevsky, Fyodor, 29

Drama
  Medieval and Renaissance, 80–81
  and time, in Calvin, 80–81
Dramatic movement in Calvin, 109
Duffy, Eamon, 53, 88, 134
Dürer, Albrecht, 21
Dutch art, 189

Eastern Orthodoxy, 74
Ecological movements, in America, 200
Eire, Carlos, 16
Elizabeth I, 123
  "Cult" of, 128
  and music, 163
  as new Constantine, 120
  portraits of, 137
  Processions of Accession Day, 125
  and visual imagery, 117
Elliot, John, 114
Empiricism, in England, 191
Erasmus, 21
Eucharist, 55, 111, 149
  in Calvin, 170
  medieval, 56
Evdokimov, Paul, 10, 17
Eworth, Hans, 119

Faerie Queene (Spenser, 1590), 124, 127
Febvre, Lucien, 84
Fessenden, Tracy, 201
Ficino, Marsilio, 64
Figure, Protestant suspicion of, 144
Five Books of Architecture (Sebastiano Serlio, 1537), 193
Foxe, John, 116, 150; see also names of specific works
  drama of martyrdom in, 151
Francis I, 24
Francis of Assisi, 75
Franciscan movement, 13, 62
Frederick, Elector of Saxony, 31
Freedberg, David, 51, 134
Friedlander, Max, 31

Geneva, 63, 81, 89
  artists in, 82
  Calvin's arrival in 1536, 166
Gheeraerts, Marcus the Younger
  Ditchley portrait (1592), 127
Giotto di Bordone, 13, 76
Gitelman, Lisa, 115, 128

Glory of God, in creation, 65
Godliness (pietas), in Calvin, 171
Goltzius, Hendrick, 185
Gosson, Stephen, 142
Gower, George, 119, 126, 129
  Armada portrait (1588), 126
Grace, double (duplex gratia), in Calvin, 171
Grafton, Anthony, 97
Graham, Fred, 177
Greenblatt, Stephen, 138–139
Gregory the Great, 61
  Letter to Serenus, 8–9
Grenier, Pascal, 27
Greville, Fulke, 145–146
Grindel, Edmund, 132
Groves, Beatrice, 139
Guigo II, 35, 56
Guite, Malcolm, 153

Hackett, Helen, 129, 132
Hamburger, Jeffrey, 4
Hamlet, 150
Happé, Peter, 140
Hardison, O. B., 62, 148
Harris, Jesse, 140
Hawkins, Peter, 96
Henry VIII, 24
Herbert, George, 156, 159
  "A True Hymn," 159
Herman, Nicolas, 49
Hervey, Mary, 23
Heywood, Thoms, 152
Hilliard, Nicholas, 116, 119, 129
  Art of Limning (1598), 129
  Pelican portrait (1572), 121
Historia, medieval, 57
Hoefnagel, Joris, 120
  Queen Elizabeth and the Three Goddesses (painting, 1569), 120
Holbein, Hans the Younger
  Allegory of Old and New Testament (painting, 1535), 50
  The Dead Christ in the Tomb (painting, 1521), 22
Homes, Nathanael, 164
Hudson River School, 197, 201
Huguenot architects, 193
Huizinga, Johann, 16
Humanism, Renaissance, 21, 179
Hunter, G. K., 148

Icon(s), Eastern Orthodox, 10, 188
*Icones id est verae Imagines Virorum Doctrina simul
    et pietate illustrium*
    (Theodore Beza, 1580), 136
Iconoclasm, 6, 53, 172, 207, 209
Imagery, Protestant suspicion of, 141
Images, 5
    in Calvin, 78
    as hidden texts, 191
    living images, in Calvin, 58, 135
    in Luther, 42
    in Luther and Cranach, 14–16
    medieval, 14–16, 109
    Protestant, 175
    in Spanish life, 114
Images of Both Churches (John Foxe), 117
Imaginative vacuum, in sixteenth-century
    England, 134
Imitatio Christi, 17
In Praise of Folly, 20
Institutes of the Christian Religion, 19, 64, 106
    in France, 195
    as structuring device, 100–102
Interlude, 140
Introduction to the Higher School of the Art of Painting
    (Samuel van Hoogstraten, 1678), 183
Inventory of Relics, 69

Jesuits in England, 133
Jewell, John, 131
    Apology (1562), 131
John of Damascus, 9
John, Gospel of, 74
Johnston, Alexandra, 113
Jud, Leo, 136

Kaprow, Allan, 201
    "happenings," 202
Kaufmann, Thomas de Costa, 180
Kessler, Herbert, 204
King John (John Bale, c. 1533–1538), 140
Klemm, Friedrich, 197
Koerner, Joseph Leo, 19, 28, 35, 42, 44, 47, 103

Ladder of Monks (Guigo I), 35
Landscape tradition, Dutch, 183–186
Lane, Belden, 64, 66, 200
Language
    in Calvin, 85
    as constitutive and designative, 90–92
    in the Reformation, 88, 90

Language Animal, The (Charles Taylor, 2016), 90
Lewalski, Barbara, 157
Lin, Erika, 151
Literacy program, in Geneva, 176
Liturgy and sacraments, in Calvin, 77
Lodge, Thomas, 142
Logos, 206
London, theater in, 142
Luther, Martin, 6
    "Against the Heavenly Prophets" (1525), 44
    Commentary on Galatians, 39
    and devotional images, 103
    drama of Christian life, 38
    interpretation of images, 41
    interpretation of Scripture, 38
    and music, 43–46
    and the Reformation, 53
    theological method, 37
    view of images, 43–47

MacCulloch, Diarmaid, 133
MacGregor, Neil, 31
MacIntyre, Alistair, 188
Marot, Clément, 107
Martin, Henri-Jean, 84
Mary Magdalene (Lewis Wagner, 1564), 141
Mass. *See* Eucharist
Material culture, Protestant, 118, 157
Matheson, Peter, 172
Mattes, Mark, 39, 42
McKee, Elsie, 81
Media studies, 114
Meditations on the Life of Christ, 14
Melanchthon, Philip, 22
Michael, Erika, 26
Millet, Olivier, 93–94, 96, 105, 147, 160, 189
Mitchell, W. J. T., 52
Mochizuki, Mia, 179, 189
Modern art, grand narrative of, 205
More, Thomas, 22, 89
Mortality, 26
Moxey, Keith, 26
Music
    in the Lutheran Reformation, 48
    Luther's influence on, 199
Music in Protestant England, 162–164
Mystery plays, 14, 56, 62

Nae t'leven (near to life), in Dutch art, 185, 188
Nicodemism, 193
Noble, Bonnie, 42, 44, 46–47

North German art, 199
Novum Organum (Francis Bacon, 1620), 192
Nowell, Alexander, 130

Oecolampadius, Johannus, 20, 22
Old Testament, in Calvin, 147
Olmsted, Frederick, 197
Oral culture
early modern, 99
in the Reformation, 173
Ozment, Stephen, 30–31, 47

Palissy, Bernard, 195
Panofsky, Erwin, 80, 199
Pattison, Stephen, 211
Paul the Apostle, 96
Perkins, William, 137, 158–159, 198
Pettegree, Andrew, 84
Place logic, 174
Plan and good order, in Calvin's *Institutes*, 168
Play-making
in England, 139
Protestant, 139–141
Play of God in Calvin, 64
Poetry
English, 154
of systems (Ophelia Dahl), 210
Pollock, Jackson, 201
Prayer book, Protestant, 138
preaching
dominant mass communication in
Reformation, 89
and interpretation of Scripture in Holland, 189
Medieval and Reformation, 87–89
Presence, 55, 62, 206
Printing and literacy in Calvin and Luther, 87
Prints as cognitive images, 175
Promey, Sally, 110
Prophesyings, 142
Protestant aesthetic, 158
Psalm-singing, in England, 162; *see also* Singing, congregational
Public sphere
Calvin's influence on, 168–170

Randall, Catherine, 193, 196
Reading and writing, Protestant, 154
Recusants, Catholic, in England, 133
Reformation, 5, 53, 191
origin of, 84
Reformed faith, in France, 192

Rembrandt van Rijn, 186
Bathsheba at Her Toilet (painting, 1643),
187
Renaissance drama, 78
Renaissance portraits, 20
Representation, 26, 83, 144
in media, 115
Rhetoric
in Calvin, 93–94
Classical and Renaissance, 93
Ricoeur, Paul, 210
Romanticism, influence on modern aesthetics,
204
Rosebrock, Matthew, 35, 38–40
Rosenberg, Harold, 1

Sacra conversione, 17
Saints, Sacrilege and Sedition (Eamon Duffy, 2012)
134
Sanchez, Michelle C., 101
Sanders, Nichols, 137
Schama, Simon, 188
School of Abuse, The (Stephen Gosson, 1579),
142
Schottenloher, Karl, 85
Schwartz, Regina, 78, 149, 151
Scribner, Robert, 5, 92, 197
Scriptures. *See* Bible
Scully, Vincent, 182
Serlio, Sebastiano, 193
"Grand Ferrare" at Fontainbleau, 194
Sermon on Indulgence and Grace, 84
Servetus, Michael, 178
Shakespeare, Hamnet, 138
Shakespeare, William, 138
critical evaluation of, 153
Hamlet (1600), 138
Othello (1603), 151
psychological creativity, 148
Shuger, Debora, 149, 151, 156
Sidney, Philip, 129, 144–145, 179
Apology for Poetry (1582), 144
Sight and seeing
medieval, 14
Medieval and Reformation, 27
Protestant, 8, 150
in Rembrandt, 188
in the Reformation, 69
Singing, congregational; *see also* Psalm-singing
Calvin on, 105
in Geneva, 107

Space of the Church, in the Reformation, 58
Spanish Armada, defeat of 1588, 126
Spenser, Edmund, 124
Sphaera civitatis (J. Case, 1588), 123
Spirit, in Calvin, 94, 97, 174, 206
Spirituality, medieval, 72, 87
Steinberg, Justin, 169
Steiner, George, 206
Sternholde, Thomas, 162
Stewart, Susan, 211
Strasbourg, 107
Streete, Adrian, 144
Strong, Roy, 116, 129
Stubbes, Philip, 143
Symbol, 10, 135
System of the arts, modern, 198

Tadgell, Christopher, 195
Taylor, Charles, 90, 110, 197, 204, 207
Taylor, David O., 209
Taylor, Michael, 188
Temptation of our Lord (John Bale, c. 1536–1538),
   140
Text images, in Holland, 189
Theater
   Calvin on, 59
   changing views in the Reformation,
      60–62
   humanist, 63
   in the Renaissance, 60
   of the world, Calvinist, 200
Theater of God's Glory, The (David Taylor, 2011),
   209
Theatrum mundi, 2, 27, 152, 211
   change in during Reformation, 64
Thomas à Kempis, 17
Time, Reformers' view of, 81
Torrance-Kirby, W. J., 172, 212
Tudor, David, 203
Tuileries Palace, 194
Turner, Victor, 57
Tyndale, William, 86, 89

van Doetecum the elder, Johannes, 181
van Hoogstraten, Samuel, 183
van Ruisdael, Jacob
   Three Great Trees in a Mountainous Landscape
      (painting, 1667), 184
Vanhoozer, Kevin, 64, 97
Visible words, sacraments in Calvin, 104
Visio Dei (vision of God), in Calvin, 72
Vitruvius, 193
von Balthasar, Hans Urs, 86
von Haarlem, Cornelis Cornelisz, 185
Vulgate, Latin, 90

Wagner, Lewis, 141
Wamberg, Jacob, 197
Wandel, Lee Palmer, 53
Waning of the Middle Ages, The, 16
Watt, Tessa, 118, 175, 177
Watts, Isaac, 108
Weber, Max, 77
Wencilius, Léon, 71
Wendel, François, 77
White, Paul, 117
Williams, Rowan, 111
Wolterstorff, Nicholas, 205
Word, preached in Calvin, 174
Word and image, in the Reformation, 86
Working, Randall, 195
Worship
   corporate, 3
   Medieval and Lutheran, 53
   Protestant, in Geneva, 107–109
Wuthnow, Robert, 89

Yates, Frances, 119, 123, 128

Zachman, Randall, 72
Zorach, Rebecca, 175
Zuccaro, Frederigo, 121
   Darnley portrait (1575), 121
Zurich, 166–167
Zwingli, Ulrich, 19, 167